Business Law Made Simple

Stephen G. Christianson, Esq.

Edited and prepared for publication by New England Publishing Associates, Inc.

MADE SIMPLE BOOKS

A Made Simple Book
DOUBLEDAY   New York London Toronto Sydney Auckland

WITHDRAWN

Brentwood Public Library
Brentwood, Tenn. 37027

This book is not intended to be a substitute for the services, legal or otherwise, of a qualified professional, when such services are required. This book will *not* answer all of the questions that the reader may have regarding a particular legal matter. The publisher and the author therefore strongly advise that the reader seek professional advice for any such questions.

The publisher and the author are not rendering any professional advice, legal or otherwise, in this book. The publisher and the author will not be responsible for any proximate or consequential damages to the reader relating in any way to any or all of the material contained herein. Due to the changing nature of the laws and legal principles discussed in this book, some material may become outdated. The reader must consult original sources and ensure that his or her information is current and accurate with respect to any specific matter or legal problem.

Edited and prepared for publication by New England Publishing Associates, Inc.
Copy Editor: Joanne Wlodarczyk
Page Composition: Teri Prestash
Administration: Susan Brainard Matterazzo

A MADE SIMPLE BOOK
PUBLISHED BY DOUBLEDAY
a division of Bantam Doubleday Dell Publishing Group, Inc.
1540 Broadway, New York, New York 10036

MADE SIMPLE and DOUBLEDAY are trademarks of Doubleday,
a division of Bantam Doubleday Dell Publishing Group, Inc.

Appendix Three, Tax Guide for Small Businesses, is reprinted from IRS Publication 334.

Library of Congress Cataloging-in-Publication Data
Christianson, Stephen G., Esq.
    Business law made simple/Stephen G. Christianson, Esq.; edited and
    prepared for publication by New England Publishing Associates, Inc.
    p.   cm.
    "A Made Simple Book."
    Includes bibliographical references (p.) and index.
    ISBN 0-385-47557-8
    1. Business law—United States. I. Title.
    KF889.6.C48 1995
    346.73'07—dc20   94-41819
    [347.3067]   CIP

Copyright © 1995 by Doubleday, a division of
Bantam Doubleday Dell Publishing Group, Inc.
ALL RIGHTS RESERVED
NO CLAIM TO U.S. GOVERNMENT WORKS
PRINTED IN THE UNITED STATES OF AMERICA
OCTOBER 1995
10 9 8 7 6 5 4 3 2 1

CONTENTS

INTRODUCTION 7

PART ONE: BUSINESS ENTITIES

Chapter 1: **Corporations** *11*
The Different Roles of Officers, Directors, and Shareholders *12*
Is a Corporation Right for You?
  The Advantages and Disadvantages of Corporations *15*
How to Incorporate *16*

Chapter 2: **Partnerships** *23*
General Partnerships *23*
Is a Partnership Right for You?
  The Advantages and Disadvantages of Partnerships *26*
Limited Partnerships *27*

Chapter 3: **Subchapter S Corporations and Limited Liability Companies** *31*
What Is a Subchapter S Corporation? *32*
Subchapter S Forms *37*
What Is a Limited Liability Company? *37*

Chapter 4: **Basic Principles of Business Entity Liability** *39*
Liability for the Acts of Employees *39*
Personal Liability of Individuals in Business Entities *40*

PART TWO: BUSINESS TRANSACTIONS AND ACTIVITIES

Chapter 5: **Contracts** *45*
The Elements of a Contract: Offer, Acceptance,
  and Consideration *46*
Liability for Breach of Contract *48*
Enforcing a Contract *49*

Chapter 6: **The Uniform Commercial Code and Business Transactions** *53*
Sale of Goods *54*
Secured Transactions *56*

CONTENTS

Chapter 7: **Intellectual Property** *59*
Patents *59*
Trademarks and Servicemarks *60*
Copyrights *62*
A Final Comment *63*

PART THREE: **EMPLOYMENT LAWS AND REGULATIONS**

Chapter 8: **Hiring and Firing** *67*
Proper Hiring Procedures: Antidiscrimination Laws and Regulations *67*
Americans with Disabilities Act *69*
Employment Agreements *70*
Limitations on the Employment at Will Doctrine *70*

Chapter 9: **Obligations of Employers** *77*
Federal and State Withholdings *77*
Workers' Compensation *78*
Unemployment Compensation *78*
The Difference Between an Employee and an Independent Contractor *79*
Federal Labor Laws *80*

PART FOUR: **OTHER LAWS AND REGULATIONS AFFECTING BUSINESSES**

Chapter 10: **Zoning and Environmental Law** *93*
Zoning *93*
Nonconforming Uses *94*
Variance *95*
Environmental Law *95*
State and Local Environmental Laws and Regulations *96*

Chapter 11: **Federal and State Securities Laws** *103*
What Is a Security? *104*
Effect of the Federal Securities Laws *105*
State Blue Sky Laws *106*
A Final Note *107*

Chapter 12:	Bankruptcy Law *113*	
	Alternatives to Bankruptcy *114*	
	Chapter 7 Bankruptcy *115*	
	Chapter 11 Bankruptcy *117*	
	Chapter 13 Bankruptcy *118*	
APPENDIX ONE:	EEOC FACT SHEETS *119*	
APPENDIX TWO:	THE AMERICANS WITH DISABILITIES ACT: QUESTIONS AND ANSWERS *137*	
APPENDIX THREE:	TAX GUIDE FOR SMALL BUSINESSES *159*	
GLOSSARY:	BUSINESS LAW TERMS *197*	
RESOURCES:	FOR FURTHER INFORMATION *205*	
INDEX *207*		

INTRODUCTION

In 1992, the most recent year for which statistics are available, there were 8,805,000 business concerns in the United States. In 1991 alone, 629,000 new businesses were incorporated. Each and every one of these businesses, whether it is a long-standing blue-chip company such as IBM or a newly incorporated small business, must meet the various legal requirements imposed by federal, state, and local authorities on conducting business. These legal requirements are generically termed *business law*. This book's 12 chapters explain the fundamental principles of business law and cover the following topics:

- Corporations
- Partnerships
- Subchapter S corporations and limited liability companies
- Basic principles of business entity liability
- Contracts
- The Uniform Commercial Code and business transactions
- Intellectual property
- Hiring and firing
- Obligations of employers
- Zoning and environmental law
- Federal and state securities laws
- Bankruptcy law

At the end of this book there is a glossary, which contains definitions of the most commonly used words and phrases in business law, and a bibliography, containing a list of helpful reference sources.

PART ONE

BUSINESS ENTITIES

CHAPTER ONE

Corporations

KEY TERMS

articles of incorporation
corporation
directors
dissolution
incorporation
limited liability
liquidation
minutes
officers
partnership
perpetual existence
registered agent
shareholders
sole proprietorship
stock
stockholders

Hundreds of years ago, when trade and industry first began to dominate the economy of England and Europe, there was no such thing as a corporation. If a person made money in business, that person pocketed the profits. If a person lost money in business, that person suffered the loss. If the person involved was acting alone, he or she was what we today call a **sole proprietor.** When several people made or lost money in business and shared the profits or losses that resulted, they were acting as what we today call a **partnership.** But the problem with both sole proprietors and partnerships was that the risk of loss to the individuals concerned was potentially unlimited, as is illustrated in the following example:

> Chelsea wants to ship goods from Northport to Southport. Chelsea rents Hillary's boat and promises to compensate Hillary if the boat is damaged. The boat is hit by a storm and sinks. The value of the boat is more than Chelsea is worth. Not only has Chelsea lost all of the goods on the boat, but Chelsea will be penniless if Hillary sues to collect the promised compensation for damage to the boat.

To solve this problem, a new form of business was created: the **corporation.**

The corporation would be a "thing" that existed, and it could own property, have money, enter into contracts, and conduct business just like an individual. But if there were losses, only what the corporation held in its own name was at risk. Let's take the previous example, but this time add a corporation to the mix:

> Chelsea wants to ship goods from Northport to Southport. Her company, Corporation X, rents Hillary's boat. When the boat sinks, Hillary sues, cleaning out everything Corporation X owns, which still isn't enough to repay Hillary for the boat. Nevertheless, Chelsea's personal assets cannot be touched, because it was the corporation that rented the boat.

The principle that the risks and potential losses of business are limited to the corporation's assets and do not extend to the persons who own or operate the corporation is called **limited liability.**

Corporations have become a fundamental part of the American legal system. Corporations can only exist, however, if there are laws that say they can exist. With some exceptions, such as those for large banks, Congress leaves these laws to the states. Every state and the District of Columbia has its own corporate laws. These govern everything relevant to setting up a corporation—a process called **incorporation**—such as how the corporation functions and what its legal obligations are. Since each state has its own corporate laws, a state can change its laws at will or enact statutes that are different from those in other states. In some states, such as Delaware, the corporate laws are very pro-business; in other states, the laws are restrictive. Although corporate laws vary from state to state, in every jurisdiction they provide for

- Limited liability for the stockholders, who own the corporation, and the officers and directors, who run the corporation.
- Evidence of ownership of the corporation, called **stock** or shares of stock, which can be bought and sold.
- The possibility of **perpetual existence,** which means that the corporation has no fixed or preset end to its existence. The person or persons who set up the corporation may die or sell their stock, but the corporation can live on.
- Four ways in which people can be legally connected with the corporation. As **stockholders,** or **shareholders:** They own the stock and, thus, own the corporation. As **officers:** The president, vice president, treasurer, secretary, and others run the company's day-to-day business operations. As **directors:** They don't own the company or run it from day-to-day, but they control certain vital functions. As the **registered agent:** The registered agent has a strictly limited but important legal role; he or she receives legal papers on the corporation's behalf if the corporation is sued.

The Different Roles of Officers, Directors, and Shareholders

A corporation's shareholders are its owners. Normally, they are like the American voter. Just as the "owners of the country" don't run the country but elect the people who do, shareholders normally don't run the corporation. Instead, shareholders vote at the annual shareholders' meeting for or against candidates to the board of directors. At the annual meeting, which is required by law, shareholders must decide whether or not to keep the directors they elected at the previous year's meeting. The shareholders can also vote on other matters. In the 1980s, for example, you may have read about shareholders in big multinational corporations voting to have their companies stop doing business in South Africa. Usually, however, the only matter that is required to be accomplished at the annual meeting is the election of the board of directors.

In addition to the annual meeting, there may be other special shareholders' meetings. Sometimes special meetings are called because the law requires that the shareholders approve certain actions, such as mergers or amendments to the corporate **articles of incorporation,** the legal document filed and recorded with the state that creates the corporation. Other times, special meetings are called to add or remove directors or to take care of other business that can't wait until the annual meeting. Both annual meetings and special meetings are usually recorded in documents called **minutes,** in which the matters voted on and the number of votes for and against are recorded.

Unlike the vote in a true democracy, a shareholder's vote is not based on "one person, one vote." For every share owned, the shareholder gets one vote. So, if you own one share of IBM stock, you get one vote at IBM's shareholders' meeting. But a millionaire who owns 10,000 shares gets 10,000 votes. However, there is such a thing as nonvoting stock, which gives the person who owns it no right to vote. There can also be different classes of stock, which give different voting rights, dividend rights, and so forth, depending on whether you own an "A" share, a "B" share, or whatever.

The directors elected by the shareholders control and manage the corporation. Just as shareholders must have an annual meeting to choose directors, the directors must have an annual meeting to elect officers. The directors may, and usually do, meet more than once a year to change the officers or to discuss other matters. These meetings are also recorded in minutes.

Normally, shareholders can also be directors, and directors can also be shareholders of the corporation. The directors and the shareholders, however, do not typically hold their meetings together. Even in small corporations, where the directors and the shareholders may be one and the same, the meetings are usually separate. Is this a big inconvenience for small corporations? Not really. I have seen annual meetings that have lasted a total of two minutes. The shareholders have their annual meeting on the last business day of the year, say at noon, and vote themselves as directors. Then at 12:01 P.M., they simply call the meeting their annual board of directors' meeting, elect the officers (again, typically themselves), and adjourn at 12:02 P.M. Why does the law require this rigmarole? Because corporate statutes are generally based on a one-size-fits-all approach: What works for big corporations like IBM, Exxon, and so forth is what small corporations must adapt to.

State law specifies how many directors the corporation is required to have. This is usually a minimum of one to three directors. Each director has one vote, regardless of the amount of stock he or she may own. When the board of directors acts, it must act together: Individual directors normally don't have any power to act for the corporation. The directors are required to approve most major acts by the corporation's officers if these acts are not part of the ordinary course of business, such as mergers, liquidating the corporation, acquiring debt, and purchasing real estate. Directors have the power to set salaries for themselves and the corporation's officers and employees. The directors also decide what dividends, if any, will be paid to the shareholders and whether or not new stock will be sold.

Finally, there are the officers. They run the day-to-day operations of the corporation. Unlike the shareholders and directors, the officers are not required by law to have any sort of formal annual meeting. They meet whenever they want and keep track of their decisions by whatever means that they see fit. They do, however, have a certain role in the shareholders' and the directors' meetings. Typically, the secretary records the minutes for both the shareholders' and the directors' meetings, and the president presides over the shareholders', but not the directors', meetings.

There are four principal types of corporate officers. First, there is the president. The president is the principal executive officer of the corporation and, subject to the board of directors' control, supervises and controls corporate affairs. He or she may hire and fire employees; sign documents on the corporation's behalf, if these are in the ordinary course of business; and take such further actions as the board of directors authorizes.

The second type of officer is the vice president. The vice president takes over the president's powers if the president dies, is absent, or is unable or unwilling to perform his or her duties. Otherwise, the vice president performs whatever job duties are assigned to him or her by the president or the board of directors.

The third officer is the secretary. The secretary keeps the minutes of the shareholders' and the board of directors' meetings; sees that notices of meetings and other matters are given; and keeps the corporate records and the corporate seal, a stamp sometimes used on corporate documents. The secretary also keeps a record of the shareholders' addresses, keeps a record of transfers of stock, witnesses the president's or the vice president's signature, and takes care of other administrative tasks.

The fourth, and final, type of corporate officer is the treasurer. The treasurer is responsible for the corporation's funds, receipts, and disbursements; takes in money paid to the corporation; deposits corporate funds in bank accounts; disburses authorized funds; and keeps records of the corporation's financial transactions and accounts.

There may also be additional officers, such as more than one vice president and one or more assistant secretaries or assistant treasurers. Sometimes officers have titles such as chief executive officer or chief operating officer, which carry with them whatever duties and powers the board of directors authorizes. However,

CORPORATION REQUIREMENTS

Requirement	Complexity
At least one director, a president, and a secretary. One person can run the whole corporation by being the sole shareholder and the lone director and by appointing himself or herself the president and secretary.	Low
At least one director and one or more of the following: president, vice president, secretary, and treasurer. One person cannot hold all of the required corporate offices.	Moderate
Two or three directors and one or more of the following: president, vice president, secretary, and treasurer. One person cannot hold all of the required corporate offices.	High

these additional officers aren't required by law. The corporation is only required to have one or more of the four principal corporate officers: president, vice president, secretary, and treasurer. In some states, it's easy: The corporation only has to have a president. Or if both a president and a secretary are required, they can be the same person. In other states, however, it gets a bit more complicated. There may be limitations on whether one person can hold more than one corporate office. For small businesses, where only one or two people will be running the corporation, this can be a serious problem.

The box on this page reviews the range of existing state requirements for corporate officers and directors. As far as shareholders are concerned, a corporation can have as many as or as few as it wants.

Is a Corporation Right for You? The Advantages and Disadvantages of Corporations

If the disadvantages of forming a corporation outweigh its advantages, perhaps another form of business entity is more appropriate for you, such as a partnership, Subchapter S corporation, or limited liability company. These are explained in the next two chapters. Or, particularly if you are self-employed, it may be that *no* form of business entity fits your needs. In this case, you may want to conduct business as an individual in a sole proprietorship. To determine if a corporation is right for you, let's examine the benefits and drawbacks of incorporation.

Advantages of a Corporation

- *Limited liability.* Subject to certain exceptions, discussed in Chapter 4, the individuals who own and run the corporation are not liable for the corporation's debts, losses, and other legal liabilities.
- *Legal entity.* The corporation is a legal entity with its own name, its own independent existence, the power to own property and hold funds in its own name, and so forth. This has the advantage of allowing the persons involved to remain anonymous if they wish to. Further, the corporation can have a name that helps promote business. For example, The Christianson Corporation sounds much more impressive than Steve's Store.
- *Perpetual existence.* The corporation goes on even when a shareholder, officer, or director dies. However, a corporation can be terminated in a process called **liquidation** or **dissolution.**
- *Easy to buy and sell ownership.* Subject to some state and federal regulations, such as the securities laws, corporate stock can be bought and sold fairly easily between two people. On the other hand, buying and selling partnership interests is more difficult and legally complicated, and buying and selling Subchapter S corporation stock is subject to limits on who can own stock.
- *Tax benefits.* In general, certain tax benefits are available to corporations that are not available to individuals.

Disadvantages of a Corporation

- *Additional legal and accounting responsibilities.* There have to be stockholders, directors, and officers; meetings called; minutes and records kept; annual reports filed; and so forth. Failing to comply with the legal requirements can result in the loss of some or all of the advantages of a corporation. Further, there are additional federal, state, and local tax obligations and form-filing requirements.
- *Tax disadvantages.* The most significant is the double taxation of income. Corporate profits are first taxed at the corporate tax rate. Then, when profits are distributed as dividends to stockholders, stockholders must pay income tax on those dividends. Partnerships, Subchapter S corporations, and sole proprietorships have their income taxed only to the individual or individuals who receive it.
- *Additional responsibilities.* This applies if the corporation does business in more than one state. For example, if a corporation does business in states other than the one in which it was incorporated, it has to file forms and pay fees in order to transact business in those states.

How to Incorporate

Here's a chronological description of how a typical corporation is incorporated. The documents described are usually, but not always, prepared by attorneys. The tax matters are usually, but not always, taken care of by accountants. This is a summary list; it does not include every detail for every situation, but it does describe the basic steps.

First, the people who want to create a corporation (incorporators) decide in what state they want to incorporate. Incorporating in one's own state is easiest, of course, but there may be reasons for incorporating in other states. Many large corporations are incorporated in Delaware, even though only a tiny portion of their business is done in that state. Why? Because Delaware corporate law is very favorable in such areas as limited liability. But incorporating out of state means that the corporation will have to qualify to do business in its home state.

Second, the incorporators file articles of incorporation with the proper state agency (see page 18). Articles of incorporation contain information that becomes public record for all to see, such as the name of the corporation, the business's principal address, the name(s) and address(es) of the incorporator(s), the purposes of the business, the name(s) and address(es) of the initial director(s), the name and address of the registered agent upon whom legal papers can be served, a statement that the corporation will have perpetual existence (unless the incorporators set a date of termination), the number of shares that may be issued and sold, and other legal matters that can be inserted in the articles if the incorporators want to. Even though this process seems quite formal, articles of incorporation aren't written in stone. They can be amended at virtually any time after the corporation begins, with the proper approval of the directors and the shareholders. The fee for incorporating is generally less than $100.00.

Third, after the articles of incorporation are filed and accepted by the state, the state sends the incorporators a certificate of incorporation.

Fourth, the incorporators purchase what's called a corporate book. A corporate book is a fancy binder, usually leather or vinyl and about $8^{1}/_{2}$" by 11", that holds corporate papers, beginning with the certificate of incorporation. The state doesn't sell corporate books, and in fact there's no legal requirement that the corporation get one. But most corporations do buy one because they are easy to find at business-products suppliers; cost less than $100.00; and contain virtually everything the new corporation needs, such as preprinted stock certificates, a stock transfer ledger, a corporate seal, preprinted forms for bylaws, and preprinted forms for minutes and notices of meetings.

Fifth, the incorporators, or the initial directors if they were named in the articles of incorporation, have an organizational meeting. This meeting is generally required to be held by the end of the year in which the corporation was incorporated, but requirements vary. What happens at one of these meetings? If there are no directors, the incorporators appoint directors. Remember, there are no shareholders yet, so at this stage—and never again—the incorporators can appoint directors. Then bylaws are adopted. Bylaws are lengthy documents, usually 15-30 pages, that spell out in detail the duties of the corporate officers, the formal requirements for giving notice of meetings, and so forth. Finally, other matters, such as opening corporate bank accounts, are authorized.

Sixth, shortly after the organizational meeting, the board of directors meets for its first meeting as the board. At this meeting, the directors elect the officers. Typically, the directors also decide who gets to purchase how many shares of stock at what price so that the corporation has some stockholders.

At this point, most boards sell only a few shares, usually to the key people.

Seventh, the corporation gets its affairs in order with the proper federal, state, and local authorities. This includes getting an employer identification number (EIN) from the Internal Revenue Service and all the proper state and local permits and licenses.

Obviously, this chapter has only touched upon the most basic aspects of corporate law. You may have more questions and may want to know more about the particular requirements of your state. Try calling your state government for further information. The following state agencies are in charge of articles of incorporation and other corporate filings:

Alabama
Corporations Records Supervisor
524 State Office Building
Montgomery, AL 36130
(205) 261-5324

Alaska
Division of Banking
Securities and Corporations
P.O. Box D
Juneau, AK 99811
(907) 465-2530

Arizona
Corporation Commission
P.O. Box 6019
Phoenix, AZ 85005
(602) 542-3026

Arkansas
Corporations Division
State Capitol Building
Little Rock, AR 72201
(501) 682-1010

California
Chief of Corporations
1230 J Street
Sacramento, CA 95814
(916) 445-0620

Colorado
Division of Commercial Recordings
1560 Broadway, Suite 200
Denver, CO 80202
(303) 894-2251

Connecticut
Corporations Division
30 Trinity Street
Hartford, CT 06106
(203) 566-7143

Delaware
Secretary of State
Corporations Division
Townsend Building
Dover, DE 19901
(302) 736-4111

District of Columbia
Department of Consumer
 and Regulatory Affairs
Superintendent of Corporations
614 H Street, NW Room 407
Washington, DC 20013
(202) 727-7278

Florida
Secretary of State
Capitol 2
Tallahassee, FL 32301
(904) 487-6000

Georgia
Business Services & Regulations
West Tower, Suite 315
2 Martin Luther King Jr. Drive
Atlanta, GA 30334
(404) 656-6478

Hawaii
Commerce & Consumer Affairs
1010 Richards Street
Honolulu, HI 96813
(808) 548-6521

Idaho
Secretary of State
Statehouse, Room 203
Boise, ID 83720
(208) 334-2300

Illinois
Department of Business Services
330 Centennial Building
Springfield, IL 62756
(217) 782-6961

Indiana
Secretary of State
State House, Room 155
Indianapolis, IN 46204
(317) 232-6591

Iowa
Secretary of State
Corporations Division
Hoover State Office Building, 2d Floor
Des Moines, IA 50319
(515) 281-8363

Kansas
Secretary of State
Attention: Corporations Filings
Capitol Building, 2d Floor
Topeka, KS 66612
(913) 296-2236

Kentucky
Director of Corporations
State Capitol Building, Room 150
Frankfort, KY 40601
(502) 564-2848

Louisiana
Secretary of State
Attention: Corporations
P.O. Box 94125
Baton Rouge, LA 70804
(504) 342-4716

Maine
Secretary of State
Division of Public Administration
Augusta, ME 04333
(207) 289-1090

Maryland
Department of Assessments
  and Taxation
301 West Preston Street
Baltimore, MD 21201
(301) 225-1330

Massachusetts
Secretary of State
Corporations Division
Ashburton Place
Room 1712
Boston, MA 02108
(617) 727-2853

Michigan
Department of Commerce
Corporations and Securities Bureau
6546 Mercantile Way
Lansing, MI 48909
(517) 334-6302

Minnesota
Secretary of State
Attention: Business Services
180 State Office Building
St. Paul, MN 55155
(612) 296-9215

Mississippi
Secretary of State
Attention: Corporations
P.O. Box 136
Jackson, MS 39205
(601) 359-1333
(609) 530-6412

Missouri
Secretary of State
Attention: Corporations
P.O. Box 778
Jefferson City, MO 65102
(314) 751-1812

Montana
Secretary of State
Corporations Bureau
State Capitol, Room 225
Helena, MT 59601
(406) 444-3666

Nebraska
Secretary of State
Corporations Division
State Capitol, Suite 2304
Lincoln, NE 68509
(402) 471-4079

Nevada
Secretary of State
Attention: Corporate Filings
Capitol Complex
Carson City, NV 89710
(702) 885-5203

New Hampshire
Secretary of State
Corporations Division
State House Annex, 3d Floor
Concord, NH 03301
(603) 271-3244

New Jersey
Secretary of State
Division of
  Commercial Recording
820 Bear Tavern Road, CN 308
Trenton, NJ 08625

New Mexico
Corporate Commission
State Corporation Department
P.O. Drawer 1269
Santa Fe, NM 87504
(505) 827-4504

New York
New York Department of State
Division of Corporations
162 Washington Avenue
Albany, NY 12231
(518) 473-2492

Chapter 1: Corporations 21

North Carolina
Secretary of State
Attention: Corporations
300 N. Salisbury Street
Raleigh, NC 27611
(919) 733-4201

North Dakota
Secretary of State
Corporations Division
State Capitol
Bismarck, ND 58505
(701) 224-4286

Ohio
Secretary of State
Corporations Director
30 E. Broad Street, 14th Floor
Columbus, OH 43266
(614) 466-1145

Oklahoma
Secretary of State
101 State Capitol
Oklahoma City, OK 73105
(405) 521-3911

Oregon
Secretary of State
Corporate Division
158 12th Street NE
Salem, OR 97310
(503) 378-4383

Pennsylvania
Secretary of State
Corporations Bureau
308 North Office Building
Harrisburg, PA 17120
(717) 787-1978

Rhode Island
Director of Corporations
100 No. Main Street
Providence, RI 02903
(401) 277-3040

South Carolina
Director of Corporations
P.O. Box 11350
Columbia, SC 29211
(803) 734-2161

South Dakota
Secretary of State
Capitol Building, 2d Floor
Pierre, SD 57501
(605) 773-3537

Tennessee
Secretary of State
Attention: Corporations
18th Floor, James K. Polk Building
505 Deaderick Street
Nashville, TN 37219
(615) 741-0529

Texas
Secretary of State
Corporations Section
1019 Brazos, 2d Floor
Earl Rudder Building
Austin, TX 78711
(512) 463-5585

Utah
Department of Commerce
Attention: Corporations
P.O. Box 45801
Salt Lake City, UT 84145
(801) 530-6024

Vermont
Secretary of State
Attention: Corporations
Pavilion Office Building
109 State Street
Montpelier, VT 05602
(802) 828-2371

Virginia
State Corporation Commission
Jefferson Building
1220 Bank Street
Richmond, VA 23219
(804) 786-3733

Washington (state)
Secretary of State
Corporations Division
Republic Building, 2d Floor
505 E. Union Avenue
Olympia, WA 98504
(206) 753-7120

West Virginia
Secretary of State
Corporations Division
State Capitol
Charleston, WV 25305
(304) 342-8000

Wisconsin
Secretary of State
Corporations Division
P.O. Box 7848
Madison, WI 53707
(608) 266-8888

Wyoming
Secretary of State
The Capitol
Cheyenne, WY 82002
(307) 777-7311

Addresses and phone numbers change frequently, so if your call or letter doesn't go through, try Directory Assistance for your state capitol.

CHAPTER TWO

Partnerships

KEY TERMS

contributions
distributions

general partnerships
goodwill

limited partnership
unlimited personal liability

A partnership is a legal relationship—usually spelled out in a written partnership agreement—between two or more people who agree to go into business together and split the profits or losses from that business. Under the Uniform Partnership Act (which as of the date of this book has been enacted by every jurisdiction except Louisiana and Puerto Rico), a partnership is defined as "an association of two or more persons to carry on as co-owners a business for profit." Partnerships are one of the oldest forms of conducting business, dating back thousands of years to when human beings first began to build organized societies with cities. By comparison, corporations are relative newcomers, having existed in the law for only a couple of centuries.

General Partnerships

General partnerships are the most common, basic, and least complicated form of partnership. There is usually no limit on how many people can be in a general partnership. The partners are the owners of the business, and they also run the business. Thus, a general partnership is very different from a corporation, because in a corporation the shareholders are the owners, but the officers and directors run the business. The financial structure of a partnership is also much simpler. There is no double taxation of income. The partnership pays no taxes on the profits from the business, although it does have to file returns with the taxing authorities for informational purposes only. Instead, the profits are passed through to the individual partners in proportion to their ownership interest in the business. The individual partners then must pay income tax on those profits. Conversely, if the partnership loses money, the partners bear those losses in proportion to their ownership interest in the business. To understand all this, let's look at the following business arrangement:

> Steve, Rich, and Bob go into business together. They decide that Steve, who will be doing most of the work, will own 50 percent of the partnership. Rich and Bob will each own 25 percent. Business is good the first year, and the partnership makes $100,000 after expenses and employee salaries. The partnership's accountant files informational returns with the IRS and the state authorities. Steve has $50,000 in taxable income, and Rich and Bob each have $25,000 in taxable income. Unfortunately, at Tom and Rob's partnership down the street, things weren't so good last year. The business lost $100,000. Because Tom and Rob each own 50 percent of the partnership, they each have to bear $50,000 in losses. If the partnership doesn't have any accumulated capital or profits, Tom and Rob will have to take money out of their own pockets to pay off the creditors.

In a general partnership, the partners have **unlimited personal liability** for partnership debts and legal obligations, and they usually face unlimited personal liability for the actions of the other partners. This unlimited personal liability is discussed further in Chapter 4, and it is perhaps the single most significant drawback in joining a partnership. Partners also have important legal obligations to each other that constitute fiduciary duties. These fiduciary duties frequently include the following:

- Partners are like trustees in that the same high standards of conduct, good faith, integrity, loyalty, and due care are imposed on partners in their dealings with each other and the partnership. A partner must act in the best interests of the partnership and his or her fellow partners.
- Partners generally cannot compete directly with the partnership. Thus, a partner in a dry-cleaning business cannot moonlight by setting up another dry-cleaning establishment across town. If that partner wanted to invest in a candy store, however, it would probably be acceptable, since candy stores don't normally compete with dry cleaners for business.
- If there are business opportunities that the partnership may wish to take advantage of, individual partners cannot appropriate those opportunities for their own personal profit.
- Partners cannot make a personal profit or otherwise "self-deal" with the partnership unless permitted to do so in writing by the partnership agreement. A partner in a butcher shop can't start taking prime rib home for the family unless his partners permit it.
- Partners cannot divert partnership assets for nonpartnership uses.

General partners also have important rights, protected by the Uniform Partnership Act:

- The right to participate in the management of the partnership

- The right to receive their share of partnership distributions of profits
- The right to repayment of their **contributions,** that is, money or property paid into the partnership to get the business started or to keep the business operating
- The right to repayment and to be indemnified by the partnership for costs and liabilities incurred in the course of conducting partnership business

Unless the partners agree otherwise, each partner has an equal voice in the running of the business. Of course, those partners who own more of the business or who are more critical to the successful functioning of the business will tend to have more weight in management decisions. Most management decisions are made by a simple majority vote. Some decisions, however, are deemed by statute to be so important that all the partners must agree. Those issues that may require unanimous approval include

- Admitting new partners
- Engaging in acts that would make it impossible to continue business
- Submitting to arbitration
- Disposing of partnership **goodwill**—an accounting term that generally means the potential for repeat business
- Amending the partnership agreement
- Assigning partnership property to third parties

Partners in a general partnership also have extensive rights concerning access to general partnership records and files. These rights are related to their right to participate in management and their duty to stay informed about partnership business. Every partner has the right to inspect and copy the partnership's books and cannot be denied access to these books. In addition, because of the fiduciary duties already discussed, the partnership and the other partners may be obligated to disclose important information to an ignorant partner, even if he or she has not yet requested such information.

In the majority of partnerships, the partners are able to work together and resolve their differences without resorting to legal action. If legal problems do develop, however, the law may not permit a partner to sue his or her fellow partners concerning partnership business. Instead, the law may require a unique procedure called an action for an accounting. An accounting is basically an extensive, court-supervised review of the partnership's business, records, and financial transactions.

The law also treats a partnership differently than a corporation with respect to how long the partnership can exist. A corporation is a distinct legal entity. Although its stockholders, officers, and directors may come and go, the corporation can exist indefinitely. A partnership, however, is partly a legal entity and partly just a word used to describe the relationship between several people. Partnerships, therefore, are inherently personal relationships. If a partner dies or withdraws from the partnership, there are legal consequences. The law may deem that the partnership has been dissolved. Or that the heirs of a deceased partner now have an interest in the partnership. Or that the remaining partners will now have to adjust their ownership interests. Because of the legal issues involved, those forming partnerships need to consider several questions:

- If a partner dies, do the remaining partners, assuming that there are more than one, want the partnership to continue? If so, the partnership agreement should state this.
- If a partner withdraws from the partnership and wants to sell his or her partnership interest to another partner or to a third party, do the remaining partners want to permit this? If they don't, the partnership agreement should say so and should give the remaining partners the right to buy out the withdrawing partner's interest. But what if the remaining partners don't have enough money to pay for the withdrawing partner's interest right away? The partnership agreement should anticipate this and should provide for making buy-out payments over a term of several years.
- If a partner leaves, can the remaining partners continue to use the partnership name? In the previous example, if Steve leaves the partnership, can Rich and Bob still use the name "Steve, Rich, and Bob"? The answer is yes IF the partnership agreement gives this right.
- When a partner leaves, how will the remaining partners split their interests in the partnership? Assume our friends Steve, Rich, and Bob each own one-third of the partnership. If any one of them dies or withdraws, the two remaining partners would most likely split the ownership of the partnership 50-50—if they don't admit any new partners. But what if the proportions aren't equal? Say Steve owns 50 percent, and Rich and Bob own 25 percent apiece. Bob dies. Do the two remaining partners now become equal 50-50 partners? Or does Steve now become the dominant partner over Rich? There are no quick answers. Partners with unequal ownership interests need to think about these problems in advance, decide what they want to do, and put that decision in the partnership agreement.

Is a Partnership Right for You? The Advantages and Disadvantages of Partnerships

Before deciding whether a partnership is right for your business, you need to study your situation and your goals. And you need to weigh the pluses of forming a partnership against the minuses.

Advantages of a Partnership

- *No double taxation of income.* No taxes are paid on the profits from the business. All profits are passed on to the partners, who then pay taxes on their income.
- *Less formality.* None of the multiple roles of officers, directors, and shareholders that are present in a corporation exist in a partnership.

Disadvantages of a Partnership

- *No limited liability.* Partners are *personally* responsible for debts incurred by the business.
- *Harder to buy and sell interests.* It is more difficult to transfer interest in a partnership than it is to buy or sell stock in a corporation.

Limited Partnerships

General partnerships have existed in the law for many centuries, but their primary drawback has always been that the general partners face potentially unlimited personal liability for the debts and obligations of the partnership. One answer to that problem is to form a corporation, but then there's the problem of the double taxation of income. There are three major ways in which businesses can preserve the tax advantages of a partnership but limit the owners' personal liability. The first two ways are Subchapter S corporations and limited liability companies, discussed in Chapter 3. The other way to limit liability is with a **limited partnership.**

In a limited partnership, there are two kinds of partners. First, there are the limited partners: those who buy limited partnership interests and whose money the partnership uses to run the business. Normally, a limited partnership can have as many or as few limited partners as it wants. The limited partners are entitled to receive a share of the partnership's profits; those shares are called **distributions.** The individual limited partner must pay income taxes on his or her distributions, but the limited partnership itself pays no taxes, so there is no double taxation. If business is bad and there are large losses, or if the limited partnership loses a large lawsuit, the limited partners may lose all of the money they invested. But they will *never* have to come up with additional money to pay off partnership debts, so their liability is limited.

The second partner in a limited partnership is the general partner. Normally, a limited partnership must have at least one general partner. The general partner runs the business and has the same kind of potentially unlimited personal liability as he or she would have in a general partnership. The following example illustrates the relationships and obligations found in a limited partnership:

> Jane, Steve, and Barbara decide to go into business together, believing that they can make a fortune in the wedding-reception catering business. Jane has worked in the restaurant business for years and is ready to plunge into this new venture. Steve and Barbara, on the other hand, don't have much free time to commit, and they also want to limit their risk, so they decide to become passive investors. The three agree to set up a limited partnership: Steve and Barbara will each invest $10,000 in the limited partnership, get a limited partnership interest in return, and receive a certain percentage of the profits. Jane will be the general partner; she'll run the business and also get a certain percentage of the profits. The three go to a lawyer and get the proper documents written and filed with the state. Unfortunately, business is bad. Jane fails to show up at a certain reception, and the irate client sues. By the time the limited partnership goes out of business, it owes $100,000 in debts and lawsuits. How is this $100,000 loss divided between Jane, Steve, and Barbara? Answer: Steve and Barbara lose their entire investment in the limited partnership (2 × $10,000 = $20,000). Jane is personally liable for the remaining $80,000.

Did you notice something interesting about the above example? It was the sentence "The three go to a lawyer and get the proper documents written and filed with the state." With a *general partnership,* when two or more people go into business together with the intention of sharing profits and losses, that's often enough under the law to create the presumption of a general partnership. (Although people should consult a lawyer about getting a written partnership agreement and complying with all applicable state laws. They should also consult an accountant about tax matters.) With a *limited partnership,* however, all 50 states, the District of Columbia, and Puerto Rico have special statutes that permit the creation of limited partnerships. And these statutes are very specific about how these partnerships must be created.

If the statutes are not followed, there is no limited partnership, even if the people involved—such as Jane, Steve, and Barbara—have agreed to create one. Therefore, people usually get a lawyer to do the paperwork, which includes preparing a limited partnership agreement for the general partner(s) and limited partner(s) to review and sign, and filing the required certificate of limited partnership with the state authorities. There is another good reason for consulting an attorney. In a general partnership, the general partners are active participants in the business; thus, the protections of the securities laws generally do not apply to them. (See Chapter 11 for an overview of securities law.) In a limited partnership, however, limited partners are more like passive investors—somewhat similar to people who buy stocks and bonds and other investments—so both the state and federal securities laws may be involved. These laws may place obligations on the general partner as well. Only an attorney can give you a precise answer.

So, let's highlight the major aspects of a general partnership and a limited partnership:

General Partnerships
- There are two or more general partners.
- General partners have potentially unlimited personal liability.
- There is no double taxation of income, unlike a corporation.

Limited Partnerships
- There is at least one general partner.
- General partner(s) has potentially unlimited personal liability, just as in general partnerships.
- There is at least one limited partner.
- Limited partner(s) has limited liability and can only lose what he or she invested.
- There is no double taxation of income, unlike a corporation.
- There must be compliance with state limited partnership statutes.
- State and federal securities laws may be involved.

Now, let's go back over the principle of limited liability again, since limited liability is the key reason why people form limited partnerships. Since most limited partnerships are small, involving only a handful of people, it's not surprising that the general partner(s) and limited partner(s) usually know each other and work with each other on business matters. But if a limited partner participates in the management of the business too much, the law may decide that he or she has lost his or her limited liability protection—that he or she is

RULPA and Limited Partner Third-Party Liability

(a) Except as provided in subsection (d), a limited partner is not liable for the obligations of a limited partnership unless he or she is also a general partner or, in addition to the exercise of his or her rights and powers as a limited partner, he or she participates in the control of the business. However, if the limited partner participates in the control of the business, he or she is liable only to persons who transact business with the limited partnership reasonably believing, based upon the limited partner's conduct, that the limited partner is a general partner.

(b) A limited partner does not participate in the control of the business within the meaning of subsection (a) solely by doing one or more of the following:

(1) being a contractor for or an agent or employee of the limited partnership or of a general partner or being an officer, director, or shareholder of a general partner that is a corporation [Note to reader: The law usually permits a corporation to be the general partner of a limited partnership],

(2) consulting with and advising a general partner with respect to the business of the limited partnership;

(3) acting as surety for the limited partnership or guaranteeing or assuming one or more specific obligations of the limited partnership;

(4) taking any action required or permitted by law to bring or pursue a derivative action in the right of the limited partnership;

(5) requesting or attending a meeting of partners;

(6) proposing, approving, or disapproving, by voting or otherwise, one or more of the following matters: (i) the dissolution and winding up of the limited partnership; (ii) the sale, exchange, lease, mortgage, pledge, or other transfer of all or substantially all of the assets of the limited partnership; (iii) the incurrence of indebtedness by the limited partnership other than in the ordinary course of its business; (iv) a change in the nature of the business; (v) the admission or removal of a general partner; (vi) the admission or removal of a limited partner; (vii) a transaction involving an actual or potential conflict of interest between a general partner and the limited partnership or the limited partners; (viii) an amendment to the partnership agreement or certificate of limited partnership; or (ix) matters related to the business of the limited partnership not otherwise enumerated in this subsection (b), which the partnership agreement states in writing may be subject to the approval or disapproval of limited partners;

(7) winding up the limited partnership pursuant to [the RULPA]; or

(8) exercising any right or power permitted to limited partners under this Act and not specifically enumerated in this subsection (b).

(c) The enumeration in subsection (b) does not mean that the possession or exercise of any other powers by a limited partner constitutes participation by him or her in the business of the limited partnership.

(d) A limited partner who knowingly permits his or her name to be used in the name of the limited partnership, except under [certain narrow situations permitted by the RULPA] is liable to creditors who extend credit to the limited partnership without actual knowledge that the limited partner is not a general partner.

acting more like a general partner than a passive investor. The reason for this distinction is that the law doesn't want anyone to hide behind limited partner status if he or she takes an active general-partner role in the business. In other words, the law doesn't want anyone to be able to hide from his or her financial responsibilities. State law usually specifies how involved a limited partner can become in limited partnership management without losing the limited liability protection. Most states have enacted some version of the Revised Uniform Limited Partnership Act (RULPA). One section of the RULPA (reproduced on page 29) establishes the liability of a limited partner to third parties. It is a helpful guide, but your particular state's version of the RULPA, or other limited partnership statutes, may have important changes that permit more limited partner involvement or that require less limited partner involvement in order to avoid losing limited liability.

CHAPTER THREE

Subchapter S Corporations and Limited Liability Companies

KEY TERMS

affiliated group
articles of organization
limited liability company
managers
members
Subchapter S corporation

In Chapters 1 and 2, we discussed the two oldest and most common legal forms of business: corporations and partnerships. Corporations and partnerships each have their own advantages and disadvantages. With a corporation, there is the advantage of limited liability, but the trade-off is the double taxation of income. With a partnership, the trade-off is reversed: There is the advantage of no double taxation of income but the disadvantage of no limited liability.

Toward the end of Chapter 2, we discussed one way the law has tried to offer a compromise solution to these trade-offs: the limited partnership. But limited partnerships have their drawbacks, too: There must be at least one general partner in the limited partnership, the tax rules can be complicated and confusing, the legal principles involved can change from state to state, and so on. This chapter discusses two other ways in which the law offers a compromise: the Subchapter S corporation and the limited liability company. Before we get into this discussion, however, let's go over the basic legal mechanisms through which people conduct business and their alternatives:

Basic Legal Mechanisms
- *Corporation* (see Chapter 1). Has limited liability but also double taxation.
- *Partnership* (see Chapter 2). Has no double taxation but also no limited liability.
- *Sole proprietorship.* It is not a legal form at all; it is just conducting business as an individual. Has no double taxation and no limited liability.

Basic Alternatives
- *Limited partnership* (see Chapter 2). May offer both limited liability and no double taxation.
- *Subchapter S corporation* (this chapter). May offer both limited liability and no double taxation.
- *Limited liability company* (this chapter). May offer both limited liability and no double taxation.

You may be asking: So, which of these three basic alternatives is the best, the one I should use? There's no answer to that question in a book of this size. Each of the three basic alternatives has its own requirements and may or may not be available to you; much depends on the federal tax laws, each state's laws, and each business's organizational needs and particular circumstances. This book gives an overview of the principles involved in these three basic alternatives, but it cannot recommend a choice between the three. That's what lawyers and accountants are for.

What Is a Subchapter S Corporation?

As discussed in Chapter 1, a corporation is created by incorporating under the laws of one of the 50 states. It is state law that gives a corporation limited liability. When it comes to paying federal income taxes, however, the IRS has certain rules and regulations that may permit a corporation to be taxed like a partnership. In other words, a corporation may be able to avoid paying income tax, and only its shareholders will have to pay income tax on their share of the profits.

The IRS rules and regulations on this are in Subchapter S of the federal Internal Revenue Code; thus, a corporation that qualifies under these rules and regulations is called a **Subchapter S corporation.**

In order for a business to qualify to become a Subchapter S corporation, it must meet five basic requirements:

- It must have 35 or fewer shareholders. Only corporations with a small number of shareholders can qualify. So as long as it has no more than 35 shareholders, even a multimillion-dollar corporation can qualify.
- It must be a corporation formed in the United States. Thus, a Mexican corporation or other non-U.S. corporation cannot qualify.
- It must have only one class of stock.
- Only individuals, certain estates, and certain trusts may be shareholders in the corporation. Partnerships or other corporations cannot be shareholders.
- All of the shareholders must be citizens or resident aliens of the United States.

Certain corporations cannot become Subchapter S corporations. They are

- Corporations that are part of an **affiliated group.** Essentially, a corporation may be part of an affiliated group if it owns 80 percent or more of the total voting power and 80 percent or more of the total stock value of another corporation.
- Certain corporations called domestic international sales corporations.
- Most insurance corporations.
- Certain financial institutions.
- Corporations that take advantage of cer-

Chapter 3: Subchapter S Corporations and Limited Liability Companies 33

Form **2553** (Rev. September 1993) Department of the Treasury Internal Revenue Service	**Election by a Small Business Corporation** (Under section 1362 of the Internal Revenue Code) ▶ For Paperwork Reduction Act Notice, see page 1 of instructions. ▶ See separate instructions.	OMB No. 1545-0146 Expires 8-31-96

Notes: 1. *This election, to be an "S corporation," can be accepted only if all the tests are met under* **Who May Elect** *on page 1 of the instructions; all signatures in Parts I and III are originals (no photocopies); and the exact name and address of the corporation and other required form information are provided.*

2. *Do not file* **Form 1120S,** *U.S. Income Tax Return for an S Corporation, until you are notified that your election is accepted.*

Part I — Election Information

SAMPLE

Please Type or Print

Name of corporation (see instructions)	**A** Employer identification number (EIN)
Number, street, and room or suite no. (If a P.O. box, see instructions.)	**B** Date incorporated
City or town, state, and ZIP code	**C** State of incorporation

D Election is to be effective for tax year beginning (month, day, year) . . . . ▶ / /

E Name and title of officer or legal representative who the IRS may call for more information

F Telephone number of officer or legal representative ( )

G If the corporation changed its name or address after applying for the EIN shown in **A**, check this box . . . . ▶ ☐

H If this election takes effect for the first tax year the corporation exists, enter month, day, and year of the **earliest** of the following: (1) date the corporation first had shareholders, (2) date the corporation first had assets, or (3) date the corporation began doing business . . . . ▶ / /

I Selected tax year: Annual return will be filed for tax year ending (month and day) ▶ ----------------------
If the tax year ends on any date other than December 31, except for an automatic 52-53-week tax year ending with reference to the month of December, you **must** complete Part II on the back. If the date you enter is the ending date of an automatic 52-53-week tax year, write "52-53-week year" to the right of the date. See Temporary Regulations section 1.441-2T(e)(3).

J Name and address of each shareholder, shareholder's spouse having a community property interest in the corporation's stock, and each tenant in common, joint tenant, and tenant by the entirety. (A husband and wife (and their estates) are counted as one shareholder in determining the number of shareholders without regard to the manner in which the stock is owned.)	**K** Shareholders' Consent Statement. Under penalties of perjury, we declare that we consent to the election of the above-named corporation to be an "S corporation" under section 1362(a) and that we have examined this consent statement, including accompanying schedules and statements, and to the best of our knowledge and belief, it is true, correct, and complete. (Shareholders sign and date below.)*	**L** Stock owned		**M** Social security number or employer identification number (see instructions)	**N** Shareholder's tax year ends (month and day)
	Signature / Date	Number of shares	Dates acquired		

*For this election to be valid, the consent of each shareholder, shareholder's spouse having a community property interest in the corporation's stock, and each tenant in common, joint tenant, and tenant by the entirety must either appear above or be attached to this form. (See instructions for Column K if a continuation sheet or a separate consent statement is needed.)

Under penalties of perjury, I declare that I have examined this election, including accompanying schedules and statements, and to the best of my knowledge and belief, it is true, correct, and complete.

Signature of officer ▶   Title ▶   Date ▶

See Parts II and III on back.   Cat. No. 18629R   Form **2553** (Rev. 9-93)

34 PART 1. BUSINESS ENTITIES

Form 2553 (Rev. 9-93)　　　Page **2**

Part II　Selection of Fiscal Tax Year (All corporations using this part must complete item O and one of items P, Q, or R.)

O Check the applicable box below to indicate whether the corporation is:
　1. ☐ A new corporation adopting the tax year entered in item I, Part I.
　2. ☐ An existing corporation retaining the tax year entered in item I, Part I.
　3. ☐ An existing corporation changing to the tax year entered in item I, Part I.

P Complete item P if the corporation is using the expeditious approval provisions of Revenue Procedure 87-32, 1987-2 C.B. 396, to request: **(1)** a natural business year (as defined in section 4.01(1) of Rev. Proc. 87-32), or **(2)** a year that satisfies the ownership tax year test in section 4.01(2) of Rev. Proc. 87-32. Check the applicable box below to indicate the representation statement the corporation is making as required under section 4 of Rev. Proc. 87-32.

　1. Natural Business Year ▶ ☐ I represent that the corporation is retaining or changing to a tax year that coincides with its natural business year as defined in section 4.01(1) of Rev. Proc. 87-32 and as verified by its satisfaction of the requirements of section 4.02(1) of Rev. Proc. 87-32. In addition, if the corporation is changing to a natural business year as defined in section 4.01(1), I further represent that such tax year results in less deferral of income to the owners than the corporation's present tax year. I also represent that the corporation is not described in section 3.01(2) of Rev. Proc. 87-32. (See instructions for additional information that must be attached.)

　2. Ownership Tax Year ▶ ☐ I represent that shareholders holding more than half of the shares of the stock (as of the first day of the tax year to which the request relates) of the corporation have the same tax year or are concurrently changing to the tax year that the corporation adopts, retains, or changes to per item I, Part I. I also represent that the corporation is not described in section 3.01(2) of Rev. Proc. 87-32.

Note: *If you do not use item P and the corporation wants a fiscal tax year, complete either item Q or R below. Item Q is used to request a fiscal tax year based on a business purpose and to make a back-up section 444 election. Item R is used to make a regular section 444 election.*

Q Business Purpose—To request a fiscal tax year based on a business purpose, you must check box Q1 and pay a user fee. See instructions for details. You may also check box Q2 and/or box Q3.

　1. Check here ▶ ☐ if the fiscal year entered in item I, Part I, is requested under the provisions of section 6.03 of Rev. Proc. 87-32. Attach to Form 2553 a statement showing the business purpose for the requested fiscal year. See instructions for additional information that must be attached.

　2. Check here ▶ ☐ to show that the corporation intends to make a back-up section 444 election in the event the corporation's business purpose request is not approved by the IRS. (See instructions for more information.)

　3. Check here ▶ ☐ to show that the corporation agrees to adopt or change to a tax year ending December 31 if necessary for the IRS to accept this election for S corporation status in the event: (1) the corporation's business purpose request is not approved and the corporation makes a back-up section 444 election, but is ultimately not qualified to make a section 444 election, or (2) the corporation's business purpose request is not approved and the corporation did not make a back-up section 444 election.

R Section 444 Election—To make a section 444 election, you must check box R1 and you may also check box R2.

　1. Check here ▶ ☐ to show the corporation will make, if qualified, a section 444 election to have the fiscal tax year shown in item I, Part I. To make the election, you must complete **Form 8716**, Election To Have a Tax Year Other Than a Required Tax Year, and either attach it to Form 2553 or file it separately.

　2. Check here ▶ ☐ to show that the corporation agrees to adopt or change to a tax year ending December 31 if necessary for the IRS to accept this election for S corporation status in the event the corporation is ultimately not qualified to make a section 444 election.

Part III　Qualified Subchapter S Trust (QSST) Election Under Section 1361(d)(2)**

Income beneficiary's name and address	Social security number
Trust's name and address	Employer identification number

Date on which stock of the corporation was transferred to the trust (month, day, year) . . . . ▶　/　/

In order for the trust named above to be a QSST and thus a qualifying shareholder of the S corporation for which this Form 2553 is filed, I hereby make the election under section 1361(d)(2). Under penalties of perjury, I certify that the trust meets the definitional requirements of section 1361(d)(3) and that all other information provided in Part III is true, correct, and complete.

_____　　_____
Signature of income beneficiary or signature and title of legal representative or other qualified person making the election　　Date

**Use of Part III to make the QSST election may be made only if stock of the corporation has been transferred to the trust on or before the date on which the corporation makes its election to be an S corporation. The QSST election must be made and filed separately if stock of the corporation is transferred to the trust after the date on which the corporation makes the S election.

Printed on recycled paper

Chapter 3: Subchapter S Corporations and Limited Liability Companies   35

Department of the Treasury
Internal Revenue Service

Instructions for Form 2553
(Revised September 1993)
Election by a Small Business Corporation

Section references are to the Internal Revenue Code unless otherwise noted.

SAMPLE

Paperwork Reduction Act Notice.—We ask for the information on this form to carry out the Internal Revenue laws of the United States. You are required to give us the information. We need it to ensure that you are complying with these laws and to allow us to figure and collect the right amount of tax.

The time needed to complete and file this form will vary depending on individual circumstances. The estimated average time is:

Recordkeeping . . . . . 6 hr., 13 min.
Learning about the law or the form . . . . 2 hr., 59 min.
Preparing, copying, assembling, and sending the form to the IRS . . . . 3 hr., 13 min.

If you have comments concerning the accuracy of these time estimates or suggestions for making this form more simple, we would be happy to hear from you. You can write to both the **Internal Revenue Service,** Attention: Reports Clearance Officer, T:FP, Washington, DC 20224; and the **Office of Management and Budget,** Paperwork Reduction Project (1545-0146), Washington, DC 20503. **DO NOT** send the tax form to either of these offices. Instead, see **Where To File** below.

General Instructions

Purpose.—To elect to be an "S corporation," a corporation must file Form 2553. The election permits the income of the S corporation to be taxed to the shareholders of the corporation rather than to the corporation itself, except as provided in Subchapter S of the Code. For more information, get **Pub. 589,** Tax Information on S Corporations.

Who May Elect.—A corporation may elect to be an S corporation only if it meets **all** of the following tests:

1. It is a domestic corporation.

2. It has no more than 35 shareholders. A husband and wife (and their estates) are treated as one shareholder for this requirement. All other persons are treated as separate shareholders.

3. It has only individuals, estates, or certain trusts as shareholders. See the instructions for Part III regarding qualified subchapter S trusts.

4. It has no nonresident alien shareholders.

5. It has only one class of stock (disregarding differences in voting rights). Generally, a corporation is treated as having only one class of stock if all outstanding shares of the corporation's stock confer identical rights to distribution and liquidation proceeds. See Regulations section 1.1361-1(l) for more details.

6. It is not one of the following ineligible corporations:

a. A corporation that owns 80% or more of the stock of another corporation, unless the other corporation has not begun business and has no gross income;

b. A bank or thrift institution;

c. An insurance company subject to tax under the special rules of Subchapter L of the Code;

d. A corporation that has elected to be treated as a possessions corporation under section 936; or

e. A domestic international sales corporation (DISC) or former DISC.

7. It has a permitted tax year as required by section 1378 or makes a section 444 election to have a tax year other than a permitted tax year. Section 1378 defines a permitted tax year as a tax year ending December 31, or any other tax year for which the corporation establishes a business purpose to the satisfaction of the IRS. See Part II for details on requesting a fiscal tax year based on a business purpose or on making a section 444 election.

8. Each shareholder consents as explained in the instructions for Column K.

See sections 1361, 1362, and 1378 for additional information on the above tests.

Where To File.—File this election with the Internal Revenue Service Center listed below.

If the corporation's principal business, office, or agency is located in	Use the following Internal Revenue Service Center address
New Jersey, New York (New York City and counties of Nassau, Rockland, Suffolk, and Westchester)	Holtsville, NY 00501
New York (all other counties), Connecticut, Maine, Massachusetts, New Hampshire, Rhode Island, Vermont	Andover, MA 05501
Illinois, Iowa, Minnesota, Missouri, Wisconsin	Kansas City, MO 64999
Delaware, District of Columbia, Maryland, Pennsylvania, Virginia	Philadelphia, PA 19255
Florida, Georgia, South Carolina	Atlanta, GA 39901
Indiana, Kentucky, Michigan, Ohio, West Virginia	Cincinnati, OH 45999
Kansas, New Mexico, Oklahoma, Texas	Austin, TX 73301
Alaska, Arizona, California (counties of Alpine, Amador, Butte, Calaveras, Colusa, Contra Costa, Del Norte, El Dorado, Glenn, Humboldt, Lake, Lassen, Marin, Mendocino, Modoc, Napa, Nevada, Placer, Plumas, Sacramento, San Joaquin, Shasta, Sierra, Siskiyou, Solano, Sonoma, Sutter, Tehama, Trinity, Yolo, and Yuba), Colorado, Idaho, Montana, Nebraska, Nevada, North Dakota, Oregon, South Dakota, Utah, Washington, Wyoming	Ogden, UT 84201
California (all other counties), Hawaii	Fresno, CA 93888
Alabama, Arkansas, Louisiana, Mississippi, North Carolina, Tennessee	Memphis, TN 37501

When To Make the Election.—Complete and file Form 2553 **(a)** at any time before the 16th day of the third month of the tax year, if filed during the tax year the election is to take effect, or **(b)** at any time during the preceding tax year. An election made no later than 2 months and 15 days after the beginning of a tax year that is less than 2½ months long is treated as timely made for that tax year. An election made after the 15th day of the third month but before the end of the tax year is effective for the next year. For example, if a calendar tax year corporation makes the election in April 1994, it is effective for the corporation's 1995 calendar tax year. See section 1362(b) for more information.

Acceptance or Nonacceptance of Election.—The Service Center will notify the corporation if its election is accepted and when it will take effect. The corporation will also be notified if its election is not accepted. The corporation should generally receive a determination on its election within 60 days after it has filed Form 2553. If box Q1 in Part II is checked on page 2, the corporation will receive a ruling letter from the IRS in Washington, DC, that either approves or denies the selected tax year. When box Q1 is checked, it will generally take an additional 90 days for the Form 2553 to be accepted.

Do not file Form 1120S until the corporation is notified that its election has been accepted. If the corporation is now required to file **Form 1120,** U.S. Corporation Income Tax Return, or any other applicable tax return, continue filing it until the election takes effect.

Care should be exercised to ensure that the IRS receives the election. If the corporation is not notified of acceptance or nonacceptance of its election within 3 months

Cat. No. 49978N

PART 1. BUSINESS ENTITIES

of date of filing (date mailed), or within 6 months if box Q1 is checked, please take follow-up action by corresponding with the Service Center where the corporation filed the election. If the IRS questions whether Form 2553 was filed, an acceptable proof of filing is: **(a)** certified or registered mail receipt (timely filed); **(b)** Form 2553 with accepted stamp; **(c)** Form 2553 with stamped IRS received date; or **(d)** IRS letter stating that Form 2553 has been accepted.

End of Election.— Once the election is made, it stays in effect for all years until it is terminated. During the 5 years after the election is terminated under section 1362(d), the corporation (or a successor corporation) can make another election on Form 2553 only with IRS consent. See Regulations section 1.1362-5 for more details.

Specific Instructions
Part I

Part I must be completed by all corporations.

Name and Address of Corporation.— Enter the true corporate name as set forth in the corporate charter or other legal document creating it. If the corporation's mailing address is the same as someone else's, such as a shareholder's, please enter "c/o" and this person's name following the name of the corporation. Include the suite, room, or other unit number after the street address. If the Post Office does not deliver to the street address and the corporation has a P.O. box, show the box number instead of the street address. If the corporation changed its name or address after applying for its EIN, be sure to check the box in item G of Part I.

Item A. Employer Identification Number.— If the corporation has applied for an employer identification number (EIN) but has not received it, enter "applied for." If the corporation does not have an EIN, it should apply for one on **Form SS-4,** Application for Employer Identification Number, available from most IRS and Social Security Administration offices.

Item D. Effective Date of Election.— Enter the beginning effective date (month, day, year) of the tax year requested for the S corporation. Generally, this will be the beginning date of the tax year for which the ending effective date is required to be shown in item I, Part I. For a new corporation (first year the corporation exists) it will generally be the date required to be shown in item H, Part I. The tax year of a new corporation starts on the date that it has shareholders, acquires assets, or begins doing business, whichever happens first. If the effective date for item D for a newly formed corporation is later than the date in item H, the corporation should file Form 1120 or Form 1120-A, for the tax period between these dates.

Column K. Shareholders' Consent Statement.— Each shareholder who owns (or is deemed to own) stock at the time the election is made must consent to the election. If the election is made during the corporation's tax year for which it first takes effect, any person who held stock at any time during the part of that year that occurs before the election is made, must consent to the election, even though the person may have sold or transferred his or her stock before the election is made. Each shareholder consents by signing and dating in column K or signing and dating a separate consent statement described below.

An election made during the first 2½ months of the tax year is effective for the following tax year if any person who held stock in the corporation during the part of the tax year before the election was made, and who did not hold stock at the time the election was made, did not consent to the election.

If a husband and wife have a community interest in the stock or in the income from it, both must consent. Each tenant in common, joint tenant, and tenant by the entirety also must consent.

A minor's consent is made by the minor or the legal representative of the minor, or by a natural or adoptive parent of the minor if no legal representative has been appointed.

The consent of an estate is made by an executor or administrator.

If stock is owned by a trust that is a qualified shareholder, the deemed owner of the trust must consent. See section 1361(c)(2) for details regarding qualified trusts that may be shareholders and rules on determining who is the deemed owner of the trust.

Continuation sheet or separate consent statement.— If you need a continuation sheet or use a separate consent statement, attach it to Form 2553. The separate consent statement must contain the name, address, and employer identification number of the corporation and the shareholder information requested in columns J through N of Part I.

If you want, you may combine all the shareholders' consents in one statement.

Column L.— Enter the number of shares of stock each shareholder owns and the dates the stock was acquired. If the election is made during the corporation's tax year for which it first takes effect, do not list the shares of stock for those shareholders who sold or transferred all of their stock before the election was made. However, these shareholders must still consent to the election for it to be effective for the tax year.

Column M.— Enter the social security number of each shareholder who is an individual. Enter the employer identification number of each shareholder that is an estate or a qualified trust.

Column N.— Enter the month and day that each shareholder's tax year ends. If a shareholder is changing his or her tax year, enter the tax year the shareholder is changing to, and attach an explanation indicating the present tax year and the basis for the change (e.g., automatic revenue procedure or letter ruling request).

If the election is made during the corporation's tax year for which it first takes effect, you do not have to enter the tax year of any shareholder who sold or transferred all of his or her stock before the election was made.

Signature.— Form 2553 must be signed by the president, treasurer, assistant treasurer, chief accounting officer, or other corporate officer (such as tax officer) authorized to sign.

Part II

Complete Part II if you selected a tax year ending on any date other than December 31 (other than a 52-53-week tax year ending with reference to the month of December).

Box P1.— Attach a statement showing separately for each month the amount of gross receipts for the most recent 47 months as required by section 4.03(3) of Revenue Procedure 87-32, 1987-2 C.B. 396. A corporation that does not have a 47-month period of gross receipts cannot establish a natural business year under section 4.01(1).

Box Q1.— For examples of an acceptable business purpose for requesting a fiscal tax year, see Revenue Ruling 87-57, 1987-2 C.B. 117.

In addition to a statement showing the business purpose for the requested fiscal year, you must attach the other information necessary to meet the ruling request requirements of Revenue Procedure 93-1, 1993-1 I.R.B. 10 (updated annually). Also attach a statement that shows separately the amount of gross receipts from sales or services (and inventory costs, if applicable) for each of the 36 months preceding the effective date of the election to be an S corporation. If the corporation has been in existence for fewer than 36 months, submit figures for the period of existence.

If you check box Q1, you must also pay a user fee of $200 (subject to change). Do not pay the fee when filing Form 2553. The Service Center will send Form 2553 to the IRS in Washington, DC, who, in turn, will notify the corporation that the fee is due. See Revenue Procedure 93-23, 1993-19 I.R.B. 6.

Box Q2.— If the corporation makes a back-up section 444 election for which it is qualified, then the election must be exercised in the event the business purpose request is not approved. Under certain circumstances, the tax year requested under the back-up section 444 election may be different than the tax year requested under business purpose. See **Form 8716,** Election To Have a Tax Year Other Than a Required Tax Year, for details on making a back-up section 444 election.

Boxes Q2 and R2.— If the corporation is not qualified to make the section 444 election after making the item Q2 back-up section 444 election or indicating its intention to make the election in item R1, and therefore it later files a calendar year return, it should write "Section 444 Election Not Made" in the top left corner of the 1st calendar year Form 1120S it files.

Part III

Certain Qualified Subchapter S Trusts (QSSTs) may make the QSST election required by section 1361(d)(2) in Part III. Part III may be used to make the QSST election only if corporate stock has been transferred to the trust on or before the date on which the corporation makes its election to be an S corporation. However, a statement can be used in lieu of Part III to make the election.

Note: *Part III may be used only in conjunction with making the Part I election (i.e., Form 2553 cannot be filed with only Part III completed).*

The deemed owner of the QSST must also consent to the S corporation election in column K, page 1, of Form 2553. See section 1361(c)(2).

Page 2

tain tax benefits for doing business in Puerto Rico and other U.S. possessions.

There are two additional matters to consider when becoming a Subchapter S corporation. First, there will be many accounting changes, so your accountant will be an important part of the process. Second, once a corporation becomes a Subchapter S corporation, it must make sure that it doesn't lose that privilege: It must watch how many and what kind of people become shareholders.

Subchapter S Forms

In order to apply for Subchapter S corporation status, all that is necessary is a properly completed IRS Form 2553. On pages 33-36 are copies of Form 2553 and the instructions. Both of these are stamped SAMPLE because the IRS periodically changes them, and only the most current forms can be used. Both Form 2553 and the instructions can be obtained from the IRS by calling 1-800-TAX-FORM.

What Is a Limited Liability Company?

We have now discussed both limited partnerships (in Chapter 2) and Subchapter S corporations, entities that combine a corporation's advantage of limited liability with a partnership's advantage of no double taxation of income. Both limited partnerships and Subchapter S corporations have been around for decades and can be used by any business—assuming the business meets the requirements in any state. Within the past few years, however, a new form of business entity has emerged: the **limited liability company.** It is growing so fast in popularity that it may one day replace both limited partnerships and Subchapter S corporations. But judging its success is a bit like analyzing a new car model. Because it has no track record, you can't be sure all the bugs have been worked out.

A limited liability company is formed by filing **articles of organization** with the state. Articles of organization are similar to a corporation's articles of incorporation (see Chapter 1). Depending on state law, the articles of organization may have to include the following:

- The name of the limited liability company. The name may have to include the words "limited liability company" or an abbreviation such as "L.l.c."
- The purpose of the limited liability company.
- The address of the limited liability company.
- The most remote date on which the limited liability company may dissolve. Unlike corporations, limited liability companies usually don't have perpetual existence; they are legally terminated or dissolved if certain things happen.

When formed, a limited liability company is owned by its **members,** which are like shareholders or partners. Most states require at least two members but do not restrict the maximum number of members. And membership is generally open to corporations, partnerships, and other business entities in addition to individuals. You'll note that these rules are much more liberal than those governing Subchapter S corporations, which can't have more than 35 stockholders and which have several restrictions on who can be stockholders. Also, no member is required to be a general partner, as in a limited partnership. Nevertheless, all of the members are protected by limited liability, and this limited liability is available even if some or all of the members actively participate in the business. (Remember the limited partnership discussion in Chapter 2?) The people who manage a limited liability company are the **managers;** they have the role that officers and directors have in a corporation or general partners have in a general or limited partnership. There is usually no limit on how many members may be managers: A few, most, or even all of the members can be managers.

In 1977, Wyoming became the first state to pass laws permitting limited liability companies. Florida passed similar laws in 1982. Six years later, in 1988, the federal Internal Revenue Service issued an important decision entitled Revenue Ruling 88-76, which stated that a Wyoming limited liability company would be taxed like a partnership under the Internal Revenue Code. Thus, a limited liability company's members could avoid the double taxation of a corporation, still enjoy limited liability, and take advantage of a business entity that was more flexible and liberal than both limited partnerships and Subchapter S corporations. Since 1988, the IRS has issued several decisions concerning limited liability companies in various states and has generally held that they will be treated as partnerships under federal tax law. Whether the IRS will continue to treat limited liability companies as partnerships in future years is not known: There are legal matters that the IRS has yet to rule on, and Congress may change the tax laws. Nevertheless, after the IRS issued its 1988 decision, 16 states rushed to enact limited liability company laws. As of the writing of this book, you could form a limited liability company in the following 18 states: Arizona, Colorado, Delaware, Florida, Illinois, Iowa, Kansas, Louisiana, Maryland, Minnesota, Nevada, Oklahoma, Rhode Island, Texas, Utah, Virginia, West Virginia, and Wyoming.

By the time you read this book, your state may well have enacted a limited liability company law. Virtually every state either has limited liability company laws pending before its legislature or under study by a legislative committee. Whether limited liability companies will become as commonplace as limited partnerships or Subchapter S corporations remains to be seen. It is worth noting, however, that the principle of the limited liability company has long been accepted in the international community. The legal equivalents of limited liability companies are widespread in Latin America and Western Europe.

CHAPTER FOUR

Basic Principles of Business Entity Liability

KEY TERMS

piercing the corporate veil *plaintiff* *scope of employment*

Let us now take a look at issues of liability that could affect your business.

Liability for the Acts of Employees

In certain circumstances, a business entity can be held liable for the wrongful conduct of its employees. In general, in order for someone suing a business entity to prove that it is financially liable for the wrongful conduct of an employee, the **plaintiff** (person suing) must prove the following:

1. The employee was actually responsible for the unlawful harm allegedly inflicted on the plaintiff.
2. What the employee did, or failed to do, was the direct cause of that unlawful harm.
3. The employee was, in fact, an employee of the business entity at the time that the wrongful conduct occurred.
4. The wrongful act was committed within the scope of the employee's employment; that is, the wrongful act was a contemplated or foreseeable aspect of the employee's job and/or the employee's conduct on behalf of the business entity.

These four requirements are just the basics, of course. Every type of lawsuit has additional specific legal issues: the burden of proof, defenses, procedural requirements, state statutes and legal principles, etc. But to see how these requirements come into play, let's take a look at Bob the Z-Mart employee.

At the Z-Mart Store, Lynne, the owner, tells Bob, the employee, to clean the floor but says, "Don't spend too much time on it," because she wants Bob to finish stocking the shelves. As a result, Bob does a sloppy job cleaning the floor. Tom enters the store and slips on a piece of debris. Tom might be able to sue the Z-Mart Store for negligence and recover slip-and-fall damages. Why? 1) Bob was responsible for Tom's injury because Bob didn't clean the floor well. 2) What Bob did was the direct cause of Tom's harm. 3) Bob was Z-Mart's employee when he cleaned the floor and Tom was injured. 4) Bob's job duties, his **scope of employment,** included cleaning the floor. This is just the start of Tom's legal battle, however, because he has to comply with his state's requirements for bringing a negligence/slip-and-fall lawsuit.

Personal Liability of Individuals in Business Entities

As we know from Chapters 1, 2, and 3, there are three basic ways of conducting business. First, there's the sole proprietorship: a person who runs a business without using any type of business entity. Obviously, if a sole proprietor does something wrong and gets sued, he or she may face personal legal liability. Therefore, there's no further discussion about the potential personal legal liability of sole proprietors in this book. The second way of doing business is the corporation. The next section discusses when the officers, directors, and shareholders of a corporation may be personally liable for acts relating to corporate business. The third way of doing business is the general or limited partnership. Under what circumstances general partners and limited partners may face personal liability is discussed at the end of this chapter. Limited liability companies (see Chapter 3) are not discussed; they are too recent and too new for a meaningful analysis.

Potential Personal Liability of the Officers, Directors, and Shareholders of a Corporation

This discussion applies to both normal corporations and Subchapter S corporations (see Chapter 3), because as far as personal liability is concerned, there is no significant difference between the two.

Officers. A corporation's officers—including the president, vice president(s), treasurer, and secretary—run the day-to-day operations of the corporation. One thing that corporate officers often do is sign contracts for the corporation. If the contract does not clearly indicate that the contract is on behalf of the corporation, the officer may be personally liable for any breach of the contract. For example, let's say that Jim is president of the K Corporation. If Jim signs a contract with a signature line that reads, "The K Corporation by Jim, President," it's pretty clear that Jim was acting as the K Corporation's president and not in a personal capacity. If the contract's signature line just says, "By Jim," then Jim may face personal legal liability. Under certain circumstances, federal and state laws may hold corporate officers liable for corporate crimes, taxes, and other obligations if the corporate officer knew or should have known of the corporation's activities. In addition, corporate officers may be personally liable if they act outside their corporate authorization or if they agree to personally guaranty a corporation's obligations. Finally, the law frequently permits a corporation to indemnify a corporate officer for legal liabilities incurred in the course of the corporation's business. Because of this, many officers purchase what is known as directors' and officers' liability insurance to protect themselves.

Directors. A director who breaches his or her legal duties risks personal liability. If the director does not live up to his or her duties to act honestly and in the best interests of the corporation and the shareholders, he or she may be sued by the shareholders. Also, because of their responsibility for corporate actions, directors may face lawsuits and even criminal prosecution if they knowingly were—or should have known that they were—involving the corporation in activities that violated state and/or federal laws. As with corporate officers, the law frequently permits a corporation to indemnify a corporate director for legal liabilities incurred in the course of the corporation's business. To guard against this, directors may purchase directors' and officers' liability insurance.

Shareholders. Shareholders are the owners of a corporation. Generally, a shareholder has no potential liability beyond what he or she paid for the shares in the corporation. This is true whether the corporation is large or small. Let's say Susan invests $10,000 by buying stock in IBM. Ron also invests $10,000, but he buys stock in a small incorporated business that runs a local auto-body shop. In a bizarre and unrelated coincidence, both IBM and the local auto-body shop go out of business. Susan and Ron have each lost their $10,000 investments. Fortunately, neither Susan nor Ron has legal liability to any creditors of the failed businesses because of the principle of limited liability we discussed in Chapter 1.

There *are* some exceptions to shareholder limited liability, however. First, if the corporation was not properly incorporated, or if its corporate status has not been properly maintained, then there may not be a corporate legal liability shield. How can this happen? If the articles of incorporation were not properly filed, the corporation's incorporation may be defective. Or if proper papers were not filed with the state, then the corporation may lose its corporate status. Second, and this happens primarily in small corporations, if the corporation makes dividends or other distributions to shareholders that cause the corporation to go out of business, the shareholders may have to turn those dividends or other distributions over to creditors. Third, there is the legal doctrine of **piercing the corporate veil,** which also happens primarily in small corporations, particularly those with only one or just a few shareholders. This occurs when a corporation is formed, but its separate legal identity is ignored. This is illustrated in the following example:

> Clarence opens an adult video store in a residential area. He has complied with all applicable zoning laws and so forth but is still afraid that he will be sued by some irate neighbor in the future. So he incorporates the video store. In compliance with his state's laws, Clarence becomes the corporation's one and only director;

elects himself both president and secretary of the corporation, as is permitted by state law; and is the only shareholder, again, as is permitted by state law. But Clarence doesn't treat the corporation as a separate entity. He doesn't keep the corporate book up-to-date and doesn't write up any corporate minutes. He doesn't get a corporate checking account separate from his personal checking account and doesn't keep corporate expenses separate from his personal expenses. He cashes checks made payable to the corporation and spends the money for personal uses. Sure enough, a neighbor sues Clarence and the video store. In court, the lawsuit goes badly for Clarence, and he faces some serious financial liability. Clarence claims that the plaintiff can't get at anything more than what the corporation owns, but he may be WRONG. If the court decides to pierce the corporate veil, Clarence may face personal financial liability for the lawsuit, because he ignored the corporation's separate legal status.

There are other less common exceptions to shareholder limited liability in addition to the ones mentioned. These exceptions differ from state to state.

Potential Personal Liability of General Partners and Limited Partners

In a general partnership, there are only general partners. In a limited partnership, there are limited partners and at least one general partner. The discussion below on general partners applies to both general partners in a general partnership and in a limited partnership.

General partners. As discussed in Chapter 2, general partners have unlimited personal liability for partnership debts and legal obligations, and they usually face unlimited personal liability for the actions of the other partners. There are other matters for which general partners may face personal financial and legal liability, such as the following:

- *Debts and legal liabilities caused by previous partners.* If a person becomes a new partner in a partnership, he or she may face personal financial and legal liability for the conduct of a *previous* partner.
- *Debts and legal liabilities after leaving a partnership.* Even if someone has left a partnership and is no longer a general partner in that partnership, he or she may still be liable for partnership debts and legal liabilities.
- *Debts and liabilities incurred by other general partners.*

Limited partners. As discussed in Chapter 2, limited partners generally enjoy limited liability protection for the debts and legal liabilities of a limited partnership. They must be careful, however, about participating in the management of the limited partnership, or they may lose that limited liability.

PART TWO

BUSINESS TRANSACTIONS AND ACTIVITIES

CHAPTER FIVE

Contracts

KEY TERMS

acceptance
actual damages
adhesion contract
anticipatory breach of contract
breach of contract

conditional offers
consideration
contract
expectancy
meeting of the minds

offer
punitive damages
reliance
restitution
statute of limitations

A **contract** is a type of agreement. If two people say to each other, "Let's go to the store and buy some potato chips," that's a type of agreement. Obviously, it's not a very important type of agreement, so if one person changes his or her mind and decides not to go to the store after all, the consequences are not very great.

When agreements are important and there are disputes, the courts and the law may become involved. In fact, the legal system has been involved in contract disputes for thousands of years. The courts of the Roman Empire developed legal principles concerning contracts that survived into England's Middle Ages. And since England colonized America, we have both English and Roman roots in our contract laws. Today, the American legal system has certain basic principles that underlie those agreements that qualify as contracts. It is best if contracts are in writing, but contracts can also be verbal. There are many types of contracts and many laws that affect their enforceability.

For an agreement to be a contract, there has to be an agreement between two or more people to do specified things in exchange for other specified things. For example:

Shirley wants to go to the store to buy some potato chips, but she doesn't have a car. So Shirley says to Rich, "I will pay you a dollar to take me to the store to buy some potato chips." Rich agrees and takes Shirley to the store. This is a type of contract: Shirley and Rich agreed to do a specified thing (have Shirley pay Rich a dollar) in exchange for another specified thing (have Rich take Shirley to the store).

The Elements of a Contract: Offer, Acceptance, and Consideration

In order for an agreement to be a contract, there are three basic requirements under the law: First, there has to be an offer. Then, there has to be acceptance of that offer. And finally, there has to be consideration.

Offer

An **offer** is a basically a proposal, an expression by one person that he or she is willing to do something for certain terms. For example:

Betsy goes into Manami's wholesale video store and says to Manami, "I want to buy 1,000 videotapes of the movie *Cannibal Holocaust* from you. I will pay you $15 for each videotape." This is an offer to form a contract.

There is more than one type of offer, however. There can be an offer to form a contract that has one or more conditions attached to it. These types of offers are called **conditional offers.**

Betsy goes into Manami's wholesale video store and says to Manami, "I want to buy 1,000 videotapes of the movie *Cannibal Holocaust* from you. I will pay you $15 for each videotape IF you deliver them to my place of business on February 1." This is a type of conditional offer.

Acceptance

Consenting to or agreeing to a contractual offer is called **acceptance.** Acceptance can be *verbal,* such as by saying yes, or it can be *written* in the form of a document. When someone signs a contract, that is a form of acceptance. For example:

Betsy goes into Manami's wholesale video store and says to Manami, "I want to buy 1,000 videotapes of the movie *Cannibal Holocaust* from you. I will pay you $15 for each videotape." This is an offer to form a contract. Manami says, "Yes. You have a deal." There has now been both an offer and an acceptance of the offer.

The offer and the acceptance generally have to match. If they match, then there's an agreement leading up to a contract. If they don't match, it's more like a negotiation: an offer, to which someone responds with a counteroffer rather than an acceptance, which continues until both sides reach an agreement or **meeting of the minds.**

Betsy goes into Manami's wholesale video store and says to Manami, "I want to buy 1,000 videotapes of the horror movie *Cannibal Holocaust* from you. I will pay you $15 for each videotape." This is an offer to form a contract. Manami says, "I will sell you 1,000 videotapes at $15 a videotape, but all I have is an action movie called *Ultradome.*" Manami's acceptance does not match Betsy's offer, so there is no meeting of the minds.

Without a meeting of the minds, there is no contract. Still, the contract process can continue until offers, counteroffers, and so forth result in an offer and acceptance that constitutes a meeting of the minds.

Betsy goes into Manami's wholesale video store and says to Manami, "I want to buy 1,000 videotapes of the horror movie *Cannibal Holocaust* from you. I will pay you $15 for each videotape." This is an offer to form a contract. Manami says, "I will sell you 1,000 videotapes at $15 a videotape, but all I have is an action movie called *Ultradome.*" Betsy says, "Yes, that's fine." Manami's acceptance did not match Betsy's offer, so it was more like a counteroffer. Betsy accepted the counteroffer; thus, there was a meeting of the minds, which makes Manami's counteroffer and Betsy's acceptance of that counteroffer the basis for Betsy and Manami's contract. In other words, their deal is now that Betsy will pay $15 a videotape for 1,000 videotapes of the movie *Ultradome.*

Consideration

Unlike offer and acceptance, **consideration** is more theoretical. Consideration has nothing to do with being considerate, nice to people, whatever. In contract law, it means something of value in the formation of the contract that gives the contract legal validity. The law has required consideration for centuries, but it has never been able to say exactly what it is or what it is not. Thus, consideration can sometimes be something of an anachronism and a mere formality. But it is, nevertheless, important; for without it, there may not be a valid contract. In the business world, mutual promises in a contract of sale, whether express or implied, are generally sufficient consideration.

Betsy goes into Manami's wholesale video store and says to Manami, "I want to buy 1,000 videotapes of the movie *Cannibal Holocaust* from you. I will pay you $15 for each videotape." Manami says, "OK." Betsy made an offer; Manami has accepted the offer. There has also been consideration. Betsy's consideration is express: She promised to pay $15 per tape. Manami's consideration is implied: By saying "OK," she implied that she promised to sell Betsy 1,000 tapes for $15 apiece.

When is there no consideration? See the following exchange between Betsy and Manami:

Betsy goes into Manami's wholesale video store. Betsy says to Manami, "I will pay you $20,000 if there is no earthquake in the next 20 seconds." Manami says, "It's a deal." There is no earthquake. Does Betsy now have to pay Manami $20,000? No. Unlike buying and selling videotapes, nothing of real value has been exchanged or promised between Betsy and Manami.

In the business world, promises in connection with offers, counteroffers, and acceptance go back and forth every day. In this bargaining process, consideration usually flows naturally from the actions and promises of the parties, as was shown in the previous examples. You may, however, see language in contract documents that says something like "in consideration of the sum of one dollar..." before the document goes on to say what the contract is about. Are the parties to the contract really entering the contract for $1? Of course not. Such language is a formality, but it is put in the contract to make sure the lawyers don't trip up in court over the requirement of consideration and have a judge declare the contract invalid. Other times a contract may say, "in consideration of the promises set forth herein and other good and valuable consideration..." This is a more truthful statement of what's going on: The parties have entered the contract because of what they've committed themselves to do for each other.

Liability for Breach of Contract

What happens if someone who enters into a contract doesn't do what they were supposed to do in that contract? They might be sued for **breach of contract.** Essentially, breach of contract is when someone cannot or will not perform their contract obligations, and there is no valid legal justification or excuse for this failure.

Manami's wholesale video store and Betsy now have a valid contract. Betsy has promised to buy 1,000 videotapes for $15 apiece, and Manami has promised to deliver them to Betsy's place of business on February 1. However, Manami never shows up. Manami may be liable for breach of contract.

Sometimes, but not always, the law lets people sue without having to wait for the contract to actually be breached.

On January 1, Betsy and Manami's wholesale video store form a valid contract. Betsy promises to buy 1,000 videotapes for $15 apiece, and Manami promises to deliver them to Betsy's place of business on December 31, almost a year later. However, on January 2, Manami calls Betsy and tells her that she won't deliver the tapes, because she has suddenly decided to close her business and move to Japan. Betsy runs a retail video business, and with this particular store Betsy has to plan her inventory well in advance. Therefore, long before December 31, Betsy calls another wholesaler. Betsy has to pay the other wholesaler more than she agreed to pay Manami for the videotapes, so Betsy now wants to sue Manami. Can she?

Maybe. Contract law differs from state to state, but in many states the law may permit people such as Betsy to sue for **anticipatory breach of contract.** In an anticipatory breach of contract, one party to a contract can sue a second party to a contract before the second party has committed any breach or default, if the second party has positively and unequivocally stated that he, she, or it will not or cannot do what is required under the contract by the specified due date. Here, Manami's conduct has been positive and unequivocal, and under the law of contracts in Betsy's state, Manami's conduct may well constitute anticipatory breach of contract.

If one person sues another person for breach of contract and wins, the court may award him or her damages. This means that the victorious plaintiff gets the right to collect money from the defendant as compensation for the plaintiff's losses from the breach of contract. In contract law, however, the winning plaintiff is generally limited to **actual damages.** Actual damages represent losses that are real, known, or can be estimated. Actual damages are different from **punitive damages,** in which extra money over and above actual damages must be paid by the losing defendant to the plaintiff as punishment for the defendant's particularly bad behavior. Punitive damages are generally not permitted in contract lawsuits, but many states have exceptions in cases where the defendant has committed fraud or breached a fiduciary duty or where the lawsuit involves a statute that specifically permits punitive damages.

When actual damages are calculated, there are three factors that go into the calculation. (The actual process is more complex, but the legal details and requirements are too numerous to list in this book.)

- **Restitution.** Money the plaintiff actually paid to the defendant in connection with the contract
- **Reliance.** Money that the plaintiff lost because he or she was relying on the contract, depending on the defendant to live up to the defendant's obligations under the contract
- **Expectancy.** Money the plaintiff was hoping to gain from the contract

Back at Manami's video store...

Manami's wholesale video store and Betsy had a valid contract. Betsy promised to buy 1,000 videotapes for $15 apiece, and Manami promised to deliver them to Betsy's place of business. Betsy gave Manami $2,000 as a downpayment on the delivery. Betsy also spent $5,000 building new shelves in her retail video store to hold the tapes. Finally, Betsy expected to make a profit of $20,000 after expenses from selling and/or renting the tapes to her customers. However, Manami never delivers the tapes, and Betsy sues for breach of contract. Betsy wants $27,000 in actual damages: $2,000 in restitution damages for Betsy's loss of the $2,000 downpayment, $5,000 in reliance damages for the $5,000 Betsy spent building new shelves, and $20,000 in expectancy damages for the $20,000 in profits Betsy expected to make from having the 1,000 videotapes.

Enforcing a Contract

In certain situations the law will not enforce a contract. Here's a list of the most common situations in which a contract, or some of the provisions in a contract, might not be enforced by a court in a lawsuit.

Unconscionable Contracts

When a contract, or the terms in a contract, are very unfair or oppressive, a court in good conscience will not enforce it. Judges generally have the power, as the administrators of justice, to declare contracts unconscionable "in the interests of justice." One type of potentially unconscionable contract is the so-called **adhesion contract.** An adhesion contract is a standardized, often preprinted form of contract that consumers dealing with large companies often have to either accept or reject on a take-it-or-leave-it basis. There is a famous case in law where a consumer bought a car that turned out to be defective, but the sales contract was a preprinted form with wording in fine print that made it impossible for the consumer to win against the car company. When the consumer sued, the court held that the contract was unconscionable: The contract was an adhesion contract because the consumer didn't have the sophistication or bargaining power to negotiate over the terms. And the fine print was so unfair to the consumer that the court would not enforce it. There are other situations in which a contract, whether or not it is an adhesion contract, may be unconscionable. There are no firm guidelines, though, about when a court might decide "in the interests of justice" to hold that a contract is unconscionable.

Fraudulent Contracts

If a seller misrepresents material facts to the buyer, the seller may have committed fraud, and the contract may be unenforceable.

The Statute of Frauds

A popular term for those statutes, enacted in one form or another in virtually every state, require certain types of contracts and other transactions to be in writing, or they cannot be enforced. Contracts concerning real estate, for example, are frequently required to be in writing. If a real estate contract is verbal, it may not be enforceable.

Illegal Contracts

A court will not enforce a contract in which people have agreed to do something illegal.

Lack of Capacity

The law may say that certain people don't have the capacity to enter into enforceable contracts. These people may include children under the age of 18, people being forced under threats or other situations of coercion to sign contracts, people under the influence of drugs or alcohol, and mentally insane or incapacitated people.

Statute of Limitations

People suing for breach of contract must sue within a certain time period. Every state has a law or legal principle, called the **statute of limitations,** that says how long you can wait to sue before you lose your right to sue. The statute of limitations may be anywhere from 1 year to 20 years or more; every state is different. However, most states provide a lengthier statute of limitations for written contracts than they do for verbal contracts.

Violation of Consumer Protection Laws

The federal government has passed a variety of consumer protection laws, which are enforced largely through the Federal Trade Commission (FTC). There are also state consumer protection laws. Consumer protection laws require various disclosures.

They may require certain contract provisions and may forbid others. For instance, a sales contract may 1) be required to disclose the applicable interest rate and all finance charges if the sale is on credit, 2) be required to contain a provision permitting the consumer to return the product, and 3) be prevented from containing any provision limiting the seller's liability for personal injuries resulting from product defects. There can also be specific consumer protection laws and regulations for businesses that are widely blamed for fraud and deception. For example, the FTC has issued specific regulations concerning the used-car industry.

For further information concerning state consumer protection laws, contact your local consumer protection agency. For further information about federal laws, contact the FTC:

Federal Trade Commission
Sixth and Pennsylvania Avenue NW
Washington, DC 20580
(202) 326-2222

CHAPTER SIX

The Uniform Commercial Code and Business Transactions

KEY TERMS

affirmation of fact
express warranty
financing statement

Implied warranty
risk of loss
security interest
specific performance

UCC-1
UCC-3
Uniform Commercial Code

In modern times, we take for granted that there is a certain level of fairness and predictability in the legal system, no matter where a business transaction takes place. Throughout most of history, however, this was far from true. The law would differ from nation to nation, province to province, and city to city. Even in the United States, every state had, and still does have, the power to enact its own laws concerning business transactions. However, beginning in the 1950s, a national editorial board composed of legal scholars drafted the **Uniform Commercial Code** (UCC), a body of laws concerning business transactions. The UCC is intended to make business transactions regular and predictable throughout the country and to reduce state-by-state variations. The UCC has been adopted, with some variations, in every jurisdiction except Louisiana and Puerto Rico.

The UCC consists of the following 11 parts, called articles:

- *Article One* consists of general introductory provisions.
- *Article Two* concerns the sale of goods and products.
- *Article Three* concerns transactions in commercial paper, such as bank checks, and liability for indorsements.

- *Article Four* concerns bank deposits.
- *Article Five* concerns letters of credit, which are financial instruments issued by banks and other financial institutions.
- *Article Six* concerns bulk transfers, such as when a business sells its assets and inventory to another business.
- *Article Seven* concerns warehouse receipts, bills of lading, and other documents representing title to goods.
- *Article Eight* concerns transfers in investment securities, such as indorsing stock certificates when they are sold.
- *Article Nine* concerns secured transactions.
- *Articles Ten and Eleven* concern technical matters, such as the effective date of enactment of that state's UCC, some transitional provisions, etc.

There is also a new article, called Article Two-A, that concerns leases of personal property. As of this date, some, but not all, of the states have incorporated Article Two-A into their UCC.

Many law books and law review articles have been written about the UCC, but basically the two most important articles are Article Two, concerning the sale of goods, and Article Nine, concerning secured transactions. They are summarized below.

Sale of Goods

Under the UCC and Article Two, there are many legal implications surrounding the purchase and sale of goods. The four most basic are warranties, risk of loss, seller's rights, and buyer's rights. In reading the discussion below, remember that the Uniform *Commercial* Code is just that: essentially a legal code for merchants and businesspeople. In retail sales, consumer protection laws may impose additional requirements (see Chapter 5).

Warranties

There are several types of warranties that the UCC recognizes or imposes on sellers of goods in commercial transactions.

Express warranty. An express warranty can be a warranty that is written in a contract of sale or that is a verbal **affirmation of fact** or promise in connection with a deal.

Fred's bakery needs flour, so Fred goes to Lenny's Flour Power Mill. Lenny says that he has a shipment of Grade A flour ready to sell. Lenny says that the shipment is all Grade A flour, and he gives a sample of the flour to Fred to inspect. The sample is fine Grade A flour. Fred buys the flour, pursuant to a contract of sale for "Grade A flour." However, when the shipment arrives at the bakery, it is not Grade A flour; it is spoiled and full of worms. Fred can probably sue Lenny for violating an express warranty that the flour was Grade A flour: The contract said the shipment would be Grade A flour, and Lenny made an affirmation of fact when he told Fred that the shipment was Grade A flour. Further, the sample of flour was an express warranty that the rest of the flour would be as good as the sample.

Warranty of title and against infringement. A seller generally warrants that the goods he or she is selling don't have any liens against them. In other words, in the above example, the UCC says that Lenny warrants to Fred that the flour is Lenny's to sell.

Implied warranty of fitness for a particular purpose. Article Two says that "when the seller at the time of contracting has reason to know of any particular purpose for which the goods are required and that the buyer is relying on the seller's skill or judgment to select or furnish suitable goods, there is unless excluded or modified...an implied warranty that the goods shall be fit for such purpose." The following example illustrates how this provision might apply in Fred's business dealings:

> Fred goes to buy an industrial air-conditioning unit for his bakery. He goes to Mark's Air-Conditioning Supply Company. Fred describes the size of his bakery, the amount of heat produced by the machinery, how cool he wants to keep the facility, and so forth. Mark recommends the NotSoHot 1000, and Fred buys it. The machine turns out to be inadequate: It can't keep the bakery cool, and it blows out after a few days. Fred may be able to sue Mark for breach of the implied warranty of fitness for a particular purpose, since Mark had reason to know that Fred was buying an air conditioner for the particular purpose of keeping the bakery cool and that Fred relied on Mark's skill and judgment to select a suitable machine.

Implied warranty of merchantability. Article Two says that unless excluded or modified, "a warranty that the goods shall be merchantable is implied in a contract for their sale if the seller is a merchant with respect to goods of that kind." This means that people who are in the business of selling certain products give an implied warranty to their customers that the products are of "fair average quality."

> Fred's bakery sells 10,000 glazed doughnuts to Dot. Dot runs a retail business called Dot's Donut Dollies that sells coffee, doughnuts, and other breakfast items. The doughnuts turn out to have been mistakenly glazed with salt instead of sugar and, as a result, are repugnant to the taste. Dot may be able to sue Fred for breach of an implied warranty of merchantability, since Fred's bakery is a merchant with respect to doughnuts and the doughnuts were certainly not of fair average quality.

In order to exclude or modify one or more of the above four types of UCC Article Two warranties, a disclaimer may not be effective unless it is in writing, is conspicuous, is reasonable, and specifically names the type of warranty being excluded or modified.

Risk of Loss

At some point in a commercial transaction, the person who buys goods takes over the potential **risk of loss.** In other words, the goods could be damaged or stolen, and the buyer (or the buyer's insurance company) must bear the expense involved. Here are some of the UCC's most basic rules concerning risk of loss.

- The risk of loss is with the seller until it passes to the buyer.
- The buyer and seller can agree in their contract as to when in the transaction the risk of loss becomes the buyer's rather than the seller's.

- If the seller is to ship goods by a third-party carrier, but the seller is not required to deliver the goods to a specific place (just to take the goods to the carrier), the risk of loss becomes the buyer's when the goods are delivered to the carrier.
- If the seller is required to ship goods to a specific place, the risk of loss becomes the buyer's when the goods are delivered to that specific place.
- If the goods are held by a third party who is responsible for their storage, such as a commercial warehouse, the risk of loss becomes the buyer's when the buyer receives certain documents of title or the third party acknowledges the buyer's right to take the goods.
- If the goods are defective, the risk of loss does not become the buyer's unless the defects are fixed or the buyer agrees to accept the defective goods.

Seller's Rights

The UCC and Article Two give the seller of goods various legal rights in the event of wrongful conduct by the buyer. These rights include

- The right to sue the buyer for the purchase price of the goods if the buyer fails or refuses to pay for them. This is basically a breach of contract lawsuit. However, if there are still goods in the seller's possession, the buyer may be required to try to resell the goods for a fair price in order to offset what the buyer owes.
- The right to recover reasonable costs and expenses incurred if the seller has to resell goods that the buyer will not pay for.
- The right to compensation for additional costs and expenses incurred by reason of the buyer's wrongful conduct.

Buyer's Rights

The UCC and Article Two give the buyer of goods various legal rights in the event of wrongful conduct by the seller:

- Under certain circumstances, the right to completely reject defective goods that the seller cannot repair within a reasonable time. The buyer has responsibilities with respect to seller goods in the buyer's possession.
- The right to sue for breach of contract.
- The right to revoke acceptance of goods under certain circumstances if the buyer discovers defects in the goods.
- If the buyer can prove that it is absolutely necessary, the right to a court order forcing the seller to deliver the goods. This is called **specific performance.**
- Under certain circumstances, the right to recover any extra expense incurred for having to purchase replacement goods from another seller.
- Under certain circumstances, the right to recover costs and expenses such as injuries to people or property caused by a breach of warranty, inspection costs, storage costs, return shipment costs, etc.

Secured Transactions

Article Nine of the UCC concerns secured transactions. A secured transaction is a financial transaction that is secured by giving the lender or creditor a legal interest in collateral, namely some type of property of the debtor. This legal interest in collateral is called a **security interest.** A security interest gives the lender or creditor the right to take that collateral and sell it in order to pay off the debt. Secured transactions help businesses get credit when they otherwise might not be able to. For example:

> Ross runs a small business. He has never run a business before, has no personal assets of substantial value, and cannot be too sure of making a profit in his business. The local bank is willing to take a chance and give Ross a small loan, but it needs some assurance that the loan can be repaid. Therefore, the bank takes a security interest in the property of Ross's business. If Ross cannot repay the loan, the bank can sell the collateral in order to pay off the loan.

There are nine basic types of property that can be collateral for a security interest:

- *Consumer goods.* Namely, goods used for family and household purposes.
- *Farm products.* Namely, livestock, crops, and supplies used or produced in agriculture.
- *Inventory.* Namely, most items that a business holds out as being for sale.
- *Equipment.* Namely, goods bought for, or used primarily in, business.
- *Financial instruments.* Such as stocks, bonds, and promissory notes.
- *Documents.* Namely, such items as warehouse receipts, bills of lading, and other documents of title.
- *Chattel paper.* This refers to financial documents covering personal property, particularly leases of personal property. For example, a car dealership probably has chattel paper for the cars it has leased to customers, so that chattel paper might be collateral for a security interest.
- *Accounts.* This refers primarily to accounts receivable, which basically means money that the business is waiting to receive from customers and other sources.
- *General intangibles.* This includes many types of financial interests not included in the above items, such as copyright royalties.

The above classifications are not set in stone. For example, when an item of inventory (see "Inventory" above) is sold, it can become an account receivable ("Account"). Therefore, many security interests include "proceeds" of collateral, in order to cover such changes in classification.

With some exceptions, the evidence of a security interest is typically a document called a **financing statement** that is filed and recorded in public records. Usually the financing statement is a preprinted form called a **UCC-1.** The creditor, not the debtor, usually takes care of filing the UCC-1 financing statement, because the statement protects the creditor, so it is in the creditor's interest to make sure that the legal requirements are taken care of.

A UCC-1 financing statement is generally good for five years, after which it has to be renewed in order to stay valid. The renewal form is called a UCC-3. The UCC-3 is also the standard form used for another important matter: terminating the security interest when the debt has been repaid. Just as the UCC-1 has to be filed in public records, so too must the UCC-3 be, or there is no public notice that the debt has been terminated.

CHAPTER SEVEN

Intellectual Property

KEY TERMS

copyrights
design patents
intellectual property

patent
patent infringement
secondary meaning

servicemarks
trademarks
utility patents

The phrase **intellectual property** covers a wide variety of subjects in the business world. This chapter summarizes the legal principles behind the three major types of intellectual property, namely, patents, trademarks and servicemarks, and copyrights.

Patents

A **patent** is a privilege granted by the federal government under the Constitution that gives the holder of the patent the exclusive right to profit from the use of "any new and useful process, machine, manufacture or composition of matter or any new and useful improvement thereof."

This definition covers most types of inventions and new machines. There are two basic types of patents:

- **Utility patents.** A utility patent protects the substantive, functional nature of a new invention and gives the holder of the patent 17 years of exclusive rights.
- **Design patents.** A design patent protects ornamental, nonsubstantive creations for 14 years.

In addition, there is a special type of patent called a plant patent, which gives the inventors of new, asexually reproduced plants 17 years of exclusive rights. As biotechnology grows, organically related patents such as the plant patent will probably multiply.

There are certain things, however, that cannot be patented. These include

- Newly discovered scientific principles
- New ideas or mental processes
- Newly discovered elements or other natural substances
- New methods of conducting business
- Items that should be protected under other federal laws, such as writings, which fall under the federal copyright laws

The U.S. Patent and Trademark Office (PTO) regulates the issuance of patents. A patent application is filed by a lawyer who specializes in patent law and who represents the inventor. The patent application includes various technical specifications concerning the invention, and the PTO may require additional technical submissions before it issues its final decision. It can take several years for the PTO to process a patent application and grant a patent. Until a patent is granted, there is very little that an inventor can do to prevent others from imitating the new invention.

Once the PTO grants a patent, the holder of the patent has exclusive rights to the invention until the patent expires. If the patent holder's rights are violated, the patent holder can sue for **patent infringement.** The patent holder can sue if the other party does one of two things:

- Uses the patent holder's new invention without the patent holder's consent
- Uses technology that is marginally different from the patent holder's new invention but is, in essence, equivalent

So, the patent holder can sue someone for copying or, in effect, imitating the patent holder's invention. In any such patent infringement lawsuit, the defendant can be held liable to the patent holder for

- Direct infringement, namely, illegally using or selling a machine or invention
- Active inducement to infringement, namely, aiding and abetting another party's act of patent infringement
- Contributory infringement, namely, cooperating in the sale of components of the patented machine, device, or other item

Further information concerning patents and patent applications can be obtained from the following address:

Patent and Trademark Office
2021 Jefferson Davis Highway
Arlington, VA 22202
(703) 557-4636

Trademarks and Servicemarks

In addition to patents, the Patent and Trademark Office is the agency responsible for the registration of federally protected trademarks and servicemarks. There are state laws that provide for trademark and servicemark registration with state agencies, but those state laws do not give nearly as much protection as federal law.

A **trademark** is "any word, name, symbol, device, or any combination thereof" used to identify goods and distinguish them from those manufactured and sold by others. A **servicemark** is "any word, name, symbol, device, or any combination thereof" used to identify services offered and distinguish them from those offered by others. Thus, trademarks are for goods, and servicemarks are for services. For example, Planter's Peanuts is a well-known name for goods, namely, cocktail peanuts and the like. Continental Airlines Peanut Fares, however, is a well-known name for services, namely, discount air flights. Trademarks and servicemarks aren't just names, they can also be business logos and other distinctive designs.

Most of the famous brand names that you can think of are protected. For goods, brands such as Coca-Cola, Maytag, and Buick are probably trademarked. For services, brands such as Hertz and Orkin Pest Control are probably servicemarked. What these brand names have in common, and what most trademarks and servicemarks have in common, is that they are "fanciful and arbitrary." This means that they are made-up words that have no real meaning except in relation to the product or service. The English language contained no such word as *Coca-Cola* until a soft drink was invented and given that name. If a name is not fanciful and arbitrary, it may not be entitled to registration. There is a sizable list of items that cannot be trademarked or servicemarked:

- Generic words and phrases, such as *beer* or *white bread*.
- Words and phrases that are merely descriptive of the product or service. For example, *Idaho potatoes* and *German beer* cannot be trademarked because they only describe where the products come from, and that's so broad that no one should have the right to exclusive use of those words. There are some exceptions, however, for descriptive phrases that have acquired **secondary meaning.** Take the phrase *T-bone steaks*. Normally, that would merely be a descriptive phrase that no one could trademark. However, suppose a nationwide chain of steak houses opens, calling itself T-bone Steaks. The chain advertises often, and soon the public begins to recognize the name T-bone Steaks and identify it with that steak-house chain, in addition to the cut of meat. The steakhouse chain may be able to register its name as a trademark that has acquired secondary meaning—in addition to a literal, dictionary meaning—that the public associates with a product from a unique source.
- Obscenities.
- Flags, coats of arms, and other emblems of the United States, a state, or a foreign country.
- The name, picture, or signature of a living person who has not given his or her consent. The name, picture, or signature of a dead president cannot be used while his wife is still alive, unless she consents.
- Words and phrases that are confusingly similar to existing trademarks and servicemarks.

If a business is using a word or phrase for its products or services that falls within one of these nonregistrable categories, it does not necessarily mean that the name cannot be used in business. However, there will be no federally protected right to exclusive use of that name.

A registered trademark or servicemark entitles the owner to file a lawsuit in federal court against people who illegally use or infringe on the mark. The court has various powers in such a case, including the power to impose triple damages against the defendant. Unlike patents, there is no time limit on how long a federal trademark or servicemark lasts. The mark can last forever, so long as the owner of the mark files paperwork, called an application for renewal, every 10 years. Marks registered before November 16, 1989, only have to be renewed every 20 years. There are ways, however, in which a trademark or servicemark can be lost:

- If an application for renewal is not filed on time or is not filed properly, or other paperwork periodically required by the PTO is not filed or is not filed properly.
- If the owner stops using the mark in commerce.
- If the owner fails to stop others from illegally using the mark.
- If the mark becomes so much a part of the English language that it becomes generic and thus unprotectable. Coca-Cola, for example, is very concerned that the word *coke* will become a generic English term for a type of soft drink and will no longer be Coca-Cola's exclusive property.

Finally, when someone gets a trademark or servicemark, they can protect that mark by using a circle around the letter *R* (for registered) after the mark. If a person obtained a trademark for Christianson Premium Beer, he could use the words "Christianson Premium Beer®" on the beer containers, on the packaging, in advertising, and so forth. The ® symbol gives public notice of trademark protection.

Copyrights

A **copyright** gives the owner of the copyright protection against the illegal use of his or her original works. Most people only think of books and other literary works when they think of copyrights. But the federal copyright laws will also protect

- Musical and dramatic works
- Choreographies
- Pictoral, graphic, and sculptural works
- Computer software
- Movies
- Audiovisual works and sound recordings

A copyright lasts for a very long time, and unlike trademarks or servicemarks, the owner is not required to use the copyrighted material in commerce or to file renewal papers. There are three basic rules concerning the life of a copyright:

- After January 1, 1978, a copyright lasts for the life of the author plus 50 years.
- Copyrights before January 1, 1978, generally cannot last longer than 75 years. Thus, there is no protection for works copyrighted and published before January 1, 1920 (75 years ago, as of the writing of this book).
- There is a special rule for certain original works that are written or otherwise created after January 1, 1978, by one person for another, known generically as works for hire. Such works are protected for 75 years from the date they are first published or 100 years from the year they are created, whichever expires first.

Unlike patents and trademarks, copyright registration is handled by the Copyright Office, which is a part of the Library of Congress. Copyright registration is technically not required, but the procedures are so easy and inexpensive (again, unlike patents and trademarks) that there is no good reason not to take advantage of federal copyright protection. Finally, like trademarks and servicemarks, there is a way to protect the copyright by giving public notice of its existence. The form of copyright notice is a circle around the letter C, along with the year of publication and the name of the owner of the copyright. For example: Copyright © 1993 by Stephen G. Christianson. If a copyright notice such as this is to be completely effective, it must be published on each and every copy of the work.

For further information, contact:

Copyright Office
Library of Congress
Washington, DC 20559
(202) 479-0700

A Final Comment

This chapter has covered the three major areas of intellectual property law—patents, trademarks and servicemarks, and copyrights—and has summarized the different legal principles involved. In the course of business, it's not uncommon that a company will seek more than one type of federal protection for its products or services, as is illustrated below:

> Barbara, Susan, and Jennifer go into the computer business together. Barbara designs and builds a new type of computer. Susan creates a new type of software. Jennifer handles the marketing and comes up with a clever name for the new device. Assuming that all the legal requirements are met, Barbara, Susan, and Jennifer may want to get three types of federal protection for their business. First, they may need patent protection for Barbara's new computer design. Second, they may need copyright protection for Susan's new software. Third, they may need trademark protection for Jennifer's clever new name.

PART THREE

EMPLOYMENT LAWS AND REGULATIONS

CHAPTER EIGHT

Hiring and Firing

KEY TERMS

Americans with Disabilities Act
discrimination

employment agreement
employment at will

There are many federal, state, and local laws and legal principles that affect the hiring and firing of employees. Most of these laws concern some sort of **discrimination** that has been made illegal. At the state and local level, the laws are usually enforced by a state department of labor, state equal employment opportunity agency, state or local human rights commission, or some other authority. (See Chapter 9 for a directory of state departments of labor.) As for federal antidiscrimination laws, most of them are enforced by the Equal Employment Opportunity Commission and/or the Department of Justice. For specific problems, these agencies can be reached at the following addresses:

Equal Employment Opportunity
  Commission
1801 L Street NW
Washington, DC 20507
(202) 663-4264

U.S. Department of Justice
  Civil Rights Division
10th and Constitution NW
Washington, DC 20530
(202) 514-2000

Proper Hiring Procedures: Antidiscrimination Laws and Regulations

Here is a checklist of subjects and questions that should be avoided in the hiring process, whether on job application forms, in personal interviews, or when making hiring decisions. Otherwise, an employer may be sued.

- *Race.* Obviously, it is illegal to discriminate against a job applicant on the basis of the applicant's race.
- *Citizenship.* Employers cannot discriminate against people such as permanent resident aliens, who have the right to work in the United States, unless being a U.S. citizen is necessary for a security clearance or some other legitimate job qualification. Note that employers *can* and *should* ask if the applicant has the right to accept employment in the United States. It is illegal to knowingly hire aliens who don't have documents proving that they can lawfully work in the U.S.
- *Sex or sexual orientation.* There are very few situations when an individual's sex is a legitimate job requirement, such as in modeling. Also, many jurisdictions have laws that make it illegal to discriminate against gays and lesbians.
- *Religion.* Employers cannot discriminate on the basis of religious beliefs. Further, employers must make reasonable accommodations for an employee's religious beliefs. For example, an employer might have to be flexible about requiring an employee to work on Sundays or certain religious holidays.
- *Height and weight.* Unless strictly relevant to the job, there should be no minimum height and weight requirements. Such requirements might be construed as a disguised attempt to discriminate against applicants on the basis of sex (typically women) or national origin (for example, Asian-Americans). There have been some recent legal developments that indicate that discrimination on the basis of obesity may constitute grounds for a lawsuit.
- *Number of children.* The number of children that an applicant has is usually not a legitimate hiring consideration. Questions about children, and how they are being taken care of, can be construed as discrimination against women.
- *Marital status.* Employers cannot discriminate on the basis of marital status, whether someone is married, single, divorced, widowed, or separated.
- *Age.* Under federal law, it is illegal to discriminate against anyone over the age of 40. State and local laws may also make it illegal to discriminate against any age group at all. However, employers can ask applicants if they are legally old enough to work.
- *Skin color, hair color, eye color, facial characteristics, and other bodily characteristics.* Any questions on an application form relating to these matters could be construed as racially motivated.
- *Previous workers' compensation claims.*
- *Lie detector tests.* The Employee Polygraph Protection Act of 1988 places severe restrictions on the use of lie detector tests and whether job applicants must consent to such tests. There may be additional restrictions under state law.
- *Substance abuse.* Generally, an employee's prior history of and treatment for drug abuse or alcoholism is not a permissible area of inquiry for employers.
- *Prior work absences due to illness.* However, an employer can state its policy

concerning sick leave and ask if the job applicant will be able to comply with that policy.

- *Arrest history.* Some minorities are arrested more often than the Caucasian majority. Thus, questions about prior arrests may illegally discriminate against minorities by discouraging them from applying for a job.
- *Prison history.* Usually, an employer can only ask about job-related convictions, which may indicate unsuitability for the job.
- *Discharges from military service.* Specifically, whether the job applicant got an honorable, general, or dishonorable discharge from any branch of the armed services. As with arrest history above, some minorities get the less desirable general and dishonorable discharges more frequently than the Caucasian majority. Therefore, questions about military discharges may illegally discriminate against minorities by discouraging them from applying for a job.
- *Other personal matters.* Common sense should be the guide here. An employer should not question a job applicant about something unless that matter is relevant to the job opening. Otherwise, the question might be considered an attempt at illegal discrimination or an attempt to obtain forbidden information. Under federal, state, and local laws, such personal matters may include political affiliation, credit history, bankruptcy history, and length of residency in the state or locality.

Finally, in special circumstances, there may be additional legal requirements respecting the hiring process. For example, government contractors are subject to specific hiring requirements. And state and local laws may require certain statements and disclosures on job application forms.

Appendix 1 contains fact sheets published by the EEOC concerning various types of illegal discrimination. These fact sheets don't necessarily cover all of the possible forms of illegal activity under federal and state laws, however. The EEOC, state authorities, and/or a lawyer may have to be consulted, and there may be changes in the applicable laws and regulations.

Americans with Disabilities Act

The **Americans with Disabilities Act** imposes certain restrictions on employers. Basically, the act prohibits employers from discriminating against job applicants on the basis of physical disability, unless no reasonable accommodation can be made to enable the job applicant to perform the necessary job tasks. The act generally forbids *asking* about disabilities on job application forms, in reference checks, and in personal interviews. Employers also can't require medical examinations as part of the application process, in order to eliminate people with disabilities.

So, how does an employer find out whether a job applicant has the necessary abilities to perform the job without asking about disabilities? What the employer has to do is describe what the job involves, ask whether the applicant can do the job and all the necessary tasks, and then make a decision based on the applicant's responses.

However, an employer cannot automatically reject a job applicant if the applicant has a disability but could perform the job with reasonable accommodations.

Appendix 2 contains a copy of EEOC information concerning the ADA. Again, this information doesn't necessarily cover all of the possible forms of illegal activity under federal and state laws. The EEOC, state authorities, and/or a lawyer may have to be consulted, and there may be changes in the applicable laws and regulations.

Employment Agreements

An **employment agreement** is a type of contract between an employer and an employee who want to set down the terms of employment in writing. Usually, when an employer hires an employee, there is no employment agreement. This situation is normally regarded as **employment at will.** Subject to certain limitations (see end of this chapter), the employer can fire the employee at any time. Executives, professionals, senior managers, and other upper-level employees are different, however. They take on more responsibilities for the employer and in turn receive a higher salary and more privileges. Both the employer and the upper-level employee being hired may have an incentive to use an employment agreement, so that there is no misunderstanding about job responsibilities, salary, commissions, bonuses, benefits, employer secrets, severance pay, and other matters. If there is a valid employment agreement, then there is no employment at will. The employer's right to fire the employee, or the employee's right to quit, depends on the terms of the employment agreement as negotiated between the employer and the employee (or between their lawyers).

Employment agreements should always be in writing. They can be long or short, simple or complex, but if they are not in writing, they are likely not enforceable in any court proceedings. Remember Chapter 5 on contracts and the discussion concerning the Statute of Frauds? As a type of contract, employment agreements may be required under state law to be in writing.

See an example of an employment agreement on pages 71-74. Each clause is followed by a comment in brackets explaining its significance and meaning. This example is NOT intended for use as a "standard form," since so much depends on the negotiations and bargaining power in each situation. For example, if the potential employee has skills that are in high demand, he or she may be in a superior bargaining position and may be able to get better terms. Conversely, if the economy is bad and there are plenty of job applicants, the potential employee may have to make concessions with respect to severance pay, benefits, and other clauses.

Limitations on the Employment at Will Doctrine

As stated above, if there is no employment agreement, a person is usually hired for employment at will. The employer can fire the employee at any time, and the employee can quit at any time. However, the principle of employment at will is rid-

EMPLOYMENT AGREEMENT

THIS AGREEMENT, entered into this day of _____, 19___, is by and between _____ (the "Employee") and _____ (the "Employer").

[This is the standard preface to an employment agreement. It should state the exact date on which the agreement was signed; the employee's full, legal name; and the full, legal name of the employer.]

WITNESSETH:

WHEREAS, the Employer wishes to employ the Employee and the Employee wishes to be employed by the Employer, and

WHEREAS, the parties have decided to set forth the terms upon which the Employer will employ the Employee in this Agreement;

NOW, THEREFORE, in consideration of the promises set forth herein and other good and valuable consideration, the receipt and sufficiency of which is hereby acknowledged by the Employer and the Employee, the parties hereto agree as follows:

[These are called the recitals. They usually don't involve anything substantive but exist to satisfy the legal doctrine of consideration, which is a prerequisite to any legally enforceable contract. See Chapter 5.]

Section 1: Employment. Subject to the terms and conditions set forth herein, the Employer hereby employs the Employee and the Employee hereby accepts such employment. The Employee shall perform the following services: _____
_____

[This section should describe in reasonable detail the employee's work duties and his or her official title.]

Section 2: Term of Employment. The Employee will report to the place of work on _____, 19__ (the "Starting Date"). Unless otherwise terminated earlier pursuant to the provisions of this Agreement, the term of the Employee's employment shall be for ___ year/s, commencing on the Starting Date. This Agreement shall automatically renew from year to year thereafter unless terminated upon written notice by either Employer or Employee not less than 30 calendar days prior to the expiration of this Agreement or prior to the expiration of any renewal period.

[Generally, an employee cannot sue his or her employer for wrongful termination unless the employment agreement specifically says that the employee was hired for a specified term of a number of years. An automatic renewal clause such as this means that if an employee wants to stay with an employer, and the employer wants the employee to stay, they don't have to sign a new employment agreement.]

Section 3: Salary. For services performed, the Employer shall pay the Employee a salary of $_____ a year. The Employee's compensation shall be paid in such manner as salaries are normally paid to other comparable employees of the Employer. The Employee shall be entitled to an annual compensation review, and shall be entitled to participate in any life, accident and health insurance, incentive and profit-sharing, pension, 401(k), retirement or other plan or benefit provided by the Employer to its employees generally or to employees with duties comparable to the Employee's in particular.

[If an employee is to be paid by the hour instead of by a salary, the agreement should state 1) how much he or she is to be paid per hour, 2) how many hours a week he or she must work, and 3) how much he or she will be paid for hours of overtime.]

Section 4: Exclusivity and Confidentiality. The Employee agrees to devote his or her full-time best efforts and attention to duties with the Employer and not to enter into any outside employment or engage in any other business activities without the Employer's express prior written consent.

Employee shall not, directly or indirectly, whether during the term of this Agreement or at any time thereafter, disclose or cause to be disclosed any confidential information of the Employer's. Confidential information includes any information that might be used in a manner adverse to the Employer's interests, including but not limited to trade secrets, patents, marketing research, client lists, client information, business methods, assets, finances, contracts, product research, and technical data. Upon leaving the Employer's employment, Employee shall return any and all written material, computer disks, and other items containing confidential information in tangible form. Confidential material does not include information 1) learned or acquired by the Employee independently of his employment with the Employer, 2) disclosed to the Employee by a third party not affiliated with or employed by the Employer, or 3) that becomes disclosed by means or by causes that do not violate the terms of this Agreement.

[An employer may ask an employee to not work for anyone else or pursue independent business activities during the term of employment. The employer may also ask the employee to not disclose any confidential information. The confidentiality clause may also contain a "stipulation to injunctive relief," which says that the employee agrees that the employer shall have the right to get a court order preventing the employee from disclosing any confidential information.]

Section 5: Rights to Intellectual Property. The Employer shall be deemed the owner of all right, title and interest in and of any patentable process, invention, improvements in methods or business operations, discovered by the Employee in connection with his employment with the Employer during the term of this agreement. The Employee shall execute such documents and perform such acts as may reasonably be required by the Employer to give effect to this section.

[With this type of clause, an employer can claim ownership to any new inventions and other discoveries that the employee makes while on the job. It is a common clause in employment agreements for scientific, research, and technical personnel, since such personnel are using the employer's facilities and working on their time.]

Section 6: Vacations. The Employee is entitled to __ weeks of vacation per calendar year, at full pay, to be taken at such times as the Employee and the Employer shall mutually agree upon. For partial calendar years, the __ weeks of vacation shall be prorated accordingly. The Employee may not carry over more than __ week/weeks of unused vacation time from any previous calendar year or years into any succeeding calendar year. In addition to vacation time, the Employee shall be entitled to take __ holiday days off, at full pay, to be taken at such times as the Employee and the Employer shall mutually agree upon.

Section 7: Termination With Cause. The Employer may discharge the Employee at any time prior to the expiration of this Agreement for 1) fraud, gross negligence, wanton and willful misconduct and/or incompetency, or 2) a material breach of the terms of this Agreement. If the Employee is terminated for cause, the Employee shall be entitled to receive ___ (weeks/months) salary as severance pay.

[This type of clause helps avoid wrongful termination litigation by spelling out when the Employer can fire an Employee for cause and what severance pay the Employee gets in such a situation.]

Section 8: Termination Without Cause. The Employer may, at any time, and upon __ days prior written notice, discharge the Employee without cause. If the Employee is terminated without cause, the Employee shall be entitled to receive ___ (weeks/months) salary as severance pay.

[Employers typically reserve the right to fire employees without cause so that they can eliminate personality conflicts, institute organizational reforms, and so forth. The amount of severance pay in this situation is a matter of negotiation, but it is usually only fair that the Employer pay more than it would if it fired the Employee for cause.]

Section 9: Termination By Employee. The Employee may, at any time, and upon __ days prior written notice, terminate this Agreement for any reason. In the event of such termination by the Employee, the Employer shall have no further obligations to the Employee other than to pay any and all sums then currently due and owing to the Employee, including wages to the date of termination.

[This type of clause preserves an employee's right to quit for any reason]

Section 10: Invalidity. The invalidity or unenforceability of any particular provision of this Agreement shall not affect the other provisions hereof, and this Agreement shall be construed in all respects as if such invalid or unenforceable provision were omitted.

[Very common. This type of clause means that any invalid or illegal clause doesn't throw out the whole agreement.]

Section 11: Modification and Waiver. No change, modification or waiver of this Agreement shall be valid unless the same is in writing and signed by both Employer and Employee. The failure of any party at any time to insist upon strict performance of any term, covenant, condition or promise set forth herein shall not be construed as a waiver of performance of the same term, covenant, condition or promise at a future time.

[Very common. This type of clause means that all changes to the agreement will be in writing and that neither the employer nor the employee will inadvertently waive any rights.]

Section 12: Complete Agreement. This Agreement sets forth and is intended to be a complete integration of all of the promises, agreements, conditions, understandings, covenants, warranties and representations among the parties with respect to the subject matter hereof and there are no promises, agreements, conditions, understandings, covenants, warranties or representations, oral or written, express or implied, among the parties, with respect to the subject matter hereof other than as set forth herein.

[Very common. This type of clause says that this employment agreement constitutes the complete deal between the employer and the employee, so no one can claim otherwise at a later date. It is intended to prevent fraud, so no one can claim, "Oh, but they promised me…, but didn't put it in writing in the contract."]

Section 13: Multiple Counterparts. This Agreement may be executed in multiple counterparts, each one of which shall be deemed to be an original, and all of which together shall constitute one and the same Agreements.

[Very common. Means that both the employer and the employee can keep a signed copy of the contract for their records and that each copy will be legally just as good as an original.]

Section 14: Choice of Law. This Agreement shall be governed by, and construed in accordance with, the laws of the state of _____.

[Very common. This type of clause says what state's laws control the agreement, which can be important since contract and employment laws vary from state to state. If this clause says that a certain state's laws are controlling, but the employee neither lives in that state nor works there, then this clause may not be legally enforceable.]

Executed and acknowledged by the parties hereto as of the date set forth above.

[Below are the parties' signature lines]

EMPLOYEE:_____

EMPLOYER: _____

[Below is an example of an employer's signature line if the employer is a corporation. Typically, the president signs on the corporation's behalf, but other officers may sign if they are authorized to sign by the board of directors.]

EMPLOYER:

_____, Inc. a _____ [name of state] corporation

By:_____, its _____

[Example: "By: John Doe, its President." Doe signs his name in the space following "By."]

[Below is an example of an employer's signature line if the employer is a partnership. Typically, a general partner signs on the general partnership's or the limited partnership's behalf.]

EMPLOYER:

_____, a [general/limited] partnership

By: _____ Position: _____

[Example: "By: John Doe. Position: General Partner." Doe signs his name after "By."]

dled with exceptions created by federal, state, and local antidiscrimination laws. These exceptions far exceed the list of 17 hiring no-nos listed previously. In brief, an employer may be sued if it does any one of the following:

- Fires an employee for any discriminatory reason, such as race, religion, national origin, sex, age, etc. In some instances, such as with disabilities, an employee can be fired if no reasonable accommodation can be made for that employee in order to get the necessary job tasks done.
- Fires a union employee in violation of a collective bargaining agreement with the union or applicable labor laws.
- Fires an employee for failing to consent to, or cooperate in, illegal activity.
- Fires an employee for exercising his or her legal rights, such as voting for a particular political candidate, or for insisting upon his or her legal rights, such as any right to be paid extra for overtime work.
- Fires an employee in retaliation for cooperating with government authorities in an investigation or for making lawful claims with government authorities, such as for workers' compensation.
- Fires an employee for personal conduct outside of work hours and the workplace, unless such conduct has sufficient work-related consequences that it justifies termination.

Here's a list of reasons that DO permit an employer to fire an employee without violating the limitations on employment at will. However, the following reasons cannot be used as a disguise for illegal discrimination or any form of illegal job termination as discussed above.

- Wanting to cut the number of employees in order to improve profitability because of slow business, poor economic conditions, etc.
- Inability to perform the required job tasks or incompetency in performing those required job tasks
- Committing a crime in connection with employment
- Negligence or neglect of duty
- Intoxication or drug abuse on the job or that affects on-the-job performance
- Disobedience
- Violating reasonable work rules and regulations
- Unexcused failure to report to work and/or unexcused failure to report to work on time
- Disrespect to the employer, other employees, or customers
- Personality conflicts, quarreling, and attitude problems
- Lying or other dishonest conduct
- Inability to function well with customers and/or clients
- Endangering customers, clients, or fellow workers
- Failing to measure up to reasonable job performance standards
- Inability to retain necessary job qualifications, such as professional licenses or security clearances

CHAPTER NINE

Obligations of Employers

KEY TERMS

income tax witholding
independent contractor

self-employment tax
Social Security taxes

unemployment compensation
workers' compensation

Federal, state, and local laws place numerous legal obligations on employers. This chapter summarizes the major legal obligations, but to satisfy many of them, there is simply no substitute for professional help. For example, to comply with federal and state withholding rules (see below), most businesses will need to hire a payroll preparation service and/or a bookkeeper.

Federal and State Withholdings

Every business faces a variety of potential tax and withholding obligations. The major ones are set forth below. Since the details of tax law are outside the scope of this book, businesses just getting started should become acquainted with the federal tax rules for small businesses. Appendix 3 contains excerpts from a helpful IRS booklet called *Publication 334, Tax Guide for Small Business*. The booklet is updated annually and can be obtained by calling the IRS at 1-800-TAX-FORM. Your state and local authorities may also have some helpful information concerning their respective rules and regulations.

○ *Federal, state, and local **income tax witholding.*** Every employee's estimated federal income tax liability must be withheld from each biweekly paycheck. Depending on state income tax legislation and even city and county income tax ordinances, there may be additional income tax withholdings as well. These withholdings must be paid to the appropriate federal, state, and local taxing authorities, then an IRS W-2 Form must be sent to each employee by January 31 of the following year, listing the total federal, state, and local taxes withheld (also the amount of FICA taken, see below).

o *Social security taxes.* The Federal Insurance Contributions Act (FICA) requires employers to withhold **Social Security taxes** from employee paychecks and pay those taxes over to the Social Security Administration. There is also a payroll tax: Employers must pay a FICA tax to the Social Security Administration based on employee wages, and employers cannot pass this tax on to employees or otherwise force employees to pay the payroll tax portion of FICA. However, if an employer uses independent contractors instead of employees, then there is no FICA payroll tax. The independent contractor bears the whole social security tax obligation when he or she pays the federal **self-employment tax** as part of his or her federal tax obligations.

o *Garnishments.* If an employee has had a legal judgment rendered against him or her, then his or her wages may be garnished. If the employer receives a garnishment notice that a portion of the employee's wages must be paid over to some third party, then the employer must do so or risk being sued.

o *Child custody and other support awards.* As with garnishments, discussed above, an employer may be required by law to pay over a certain portion of an employee's wages to some third party who has child custody or other support rights.

Workers' Compensation

If an employee is injured on the job, he or she is generally not required to sue the employer or pursue other litigation in order to get compensation for lost work time, medical expenses, and other costs stemming from the injury. Instead, the injured employee makes a claim under state **workers' compensation** laws. There are two basic requirements:

o The employee's injury must be in the course of employment. This means that the injury must have occurred during working hours or while in transit to the business premises or work site, as long as the employee was clearly "on the job" when the injury took place.
o The employee's injury must arise out of the employment relationship. In other words, the injury must be work-related, so injuries caused by nonwork matters, such as fighting and brawling, are typically not covered.

Workers' compensation is funded largely by mandatory workers' compensation insurance. The workers' compensation insurance requirement may include paying into a fund administered by state authorities, having to get workers' compensation insurance from a private insurance company, or setting up a "self-insurance" plan.

Unemployment Compensation

Unemployment compensation is temporary assistance provided to people who have lost their jobs through no fault of their own. Thus, people who are laid off due to bad economic conditions are generally entitled to unemployment compensation, but people who quit a job without being required or forced to do so are generally not entitled to unemployment compensation. Unemployment compensation is financed by federal and state taxes on the employer's payroll. These federal and state taxes go into a state fund that pays the unemployment compensation benefits.

The Difference Between an Employee and an Independent Contractor

If a worker is an **independent contractor** rather than an employee, the employer is freed from many of the above obligations. The employer doesn't have to pay most payroll taxes, doesn't have to pay FICA, isn't liable for unemployment compensation, and so forth. In the 1990s, many companies seeking to cut expenses have fired employees, only to later rehire them as "independent contractors." To be a legitimate independent contractor, however, the worker has to have real independence over how the job is performed and not be subject to the same sort of supervision and control that employees are. In other words, an independent contractor is hired to get a job done with little regard for when or where it is done, but an employee is hired to work fixed hours at a fixed place and so forth. The IRS is very concerned about the abuse of independent contractor relationships, and it looks at an extensive number of factors in determining whether a person is an employee or an independent contractor. A person is more likely to be deemed an employee than an independent contractor if

- The person is given instructions about how, when, and where to work rather than left to his or her own initiative
- The person is trained for a specific assignment or given job training on a regular basis
- The person is required to perform the job personally
- The person is compensated for any expenses or support personnel that he or she may need on the job
- The person does not supply his or her own equipment, tools, and other supplies necessary for the job
- There is no specific contract for each particular job that the person does, but instead there is a broader contract or a more extensive course of dealing that resembles a permanent employer-employee relationship
- The person must do the job during regular working hours rather than whenever he or she wishes to
- The person is required to work full-time
- The person must comply with standard personnel rules and regulations
- The person must make regular reports concerning work progress
- The person is paid wages and not a commission or by the assignment
- The person has no investment at risk and no independent business entity or organization

These 12 factors are only guidelines. There is a way, however, to determine whether a person is an employee or an independent contractor. Both employers and employees (or independent contractors) can obtain a Form SS-8, "Determination of Employee Work Status for Purposes of Federal Employment Taxes and Income Tax Withholding," from the IRS by calling 1-800-TAX-FORM. The form will arrive in approximately two weeks. The IRS's decision is not always binding, however. Also, even if a worker is determined to be an independent contractor, the employer is not necessarily free from legal liability for any wrongful conduct by the worker.

A copy of Form SS-8 appears on pages 81–84. The form is stamped SAMPLE because the IRS periodically changes it, and only the most current form can be used.

Federal Labor Laws

The federal government has a host of labor laws and labor-related legislation. Here is a summary of the most important ones (space prohibits listing every labor-related law):

- *ERISA.* ERISA stands for the Employee Retirement Income Security Act of 1974. Congress enacted ERISA in order to give employees the right to obtain information from their employer about employee pension plans. ERISA involves fiduciary duties, employee participation regulations, and other matters that have created a significant amount of litigation. Any employer considering creating a pension plan or revising its existing plan is strongly advised to get professional advice.
- *OSHA.* OSHA stands for the Occupational Safety and Health Administration. OSHA enforces work-safety legislation, such as the Occupational Safety and Health Act, and issues extensive regulations on how the workplace must be maintained. In addition to OSHA regulations, there are state and local safety regulations. All such regulations are enforced by federal, state, and/or local inspectors.
- *The Fair Labor Standards Act.* This act sets the federal minimum wage, which is periodically adjusted by Congress, and it also establishes overtime pay requirements. Most top-level executives and professional employees are not covered under this act: They typically work for an annual salary and are expected to work whatever hours are required in order to get their tasks done.
- *The Labor-Management Relations Act.* This act regulates labor-management relations, primarily where labor unions are involved, and includes protections for union organizers.
- *The Equal Pay Act.* This act prohibits wage and salary discrimination based on sex.
- *The Americans With Disabilities Act.* This act prohibits employer discrimination against employees on the basis of disability. Employers must make reasonable accommodations for disabled employees, unless such accommodations create undue hardships for the employer.
- *The Employee Polygraph Act.* This act places severe restrictions on when employers may require employees to take lie detector tests.
- *The Civil Rights Act of 1964.* Title 7 of the act forbids employers from discriminating against employees or potential employees on the basis of race, color,

Chapter 9: Obligations of Employers   81

Form SS-8
(Rev. July 1993)
Department of the Treasury
Internal Revenue Service

Determination of Employee Work Status for Purposes of Federal Employment Taxes and Income Tax Withholding

OMB No. 1545-0004
Expires 7-31-96

Paperwork Reduction Act Notice

We ask for the information on this form to carry out the Internal Revenue laws of the United States. You are required to give us this information. We need it to ensure that you are complying with these laws and to allow us to figure and collect the right amount of tax.

The time needed to complete and file this form will vary depending on individual circumstances. The estimated average time is: **recordkeeping,** 34 hr., 55 min., **learning about the law or the form,** 6 min. and **preparing and sending the form to IRS,** 40 min. If you have comments concerning the accuracy of these time estimates or suggestions for making this form more simple, we would be happy to hear from you. You can write to both the **Internal Revenue Service,** Attention: Reports Clearance Officer, T:FP, Washington, DC 20224; and the **Office of Management and Budget,** Paperwork Reduction Project (1545-0004), Washington, DC 20503. **DO NOT** send the tax form to either of these offices. Instead, see **General Information** for where to file.

Purpose

Employers and workers file Form SS-8 to get a determination as to whether a worker is an employee for purposes of Federal employment taxes and income tax withholding.

General Information

This form should be completed carefully. If the firm is completing the form, it should be completed for **ONE** individual who is representative of the class of workers whose status is in question. If a written determination is desired for more than one class of workers, a separate Form SS-8 should be completed for one worker from each class whose status is typical of that class. A written determination for any worker will apply to other workers of the same class if the facts are not materially different from those of the worker whose status was ruled upon.

Please return Form SS-8 to the Internal Revenue Service office that provided the form. If the Internal Revenue Service did not ask you to complete this form but you wish a determination on whether a worker is an employee, file Form SS-8 with your District Director.

*Caution: Form SS-8 is **not** a claim for refund of social security and Medicare taxes or Federal income tax withholding. Also, a determination that an individual is an employee does not necessarily reduce any current or prior tax liability. A worker must file his or her income tax return even if a determination has not been made by the due date of the return.*

SAMPLE

Name of firm (or person) for whom the worker performed services	Name of worker
Address of firm (include street address, apt. or suite no., city, state, and ZIP code)	Address of worker (include street address, apt. or suite no., city, state, and ZIP code)
Trade name	Telephone number (include area code) ( )	Worker's social security number - -
Telephone number (include area code) ( )	Firm's taxpayer identification number -	

Check type of firm for which the work relationship is in question:
☐ **Individual** ☐ **Partnership** ☐ **Corporation** ☐ **Other** (specify) ▶

Important Information Needed to Process Your Request

This form is being completed by: ☐ Firm   ☐ Worker

If this form is being completed by the worker, the IRS **must** have your permission to disclose your name to the firm.

Do you object to disclosing your name and the information on this form to the firm? . . . .   ☐ Yes   ☐ No
If you answer "Yes," the IRS cannot act on your request. **DO NOT complete the rest of this form unless the IRS asks for it.**

Under section 6110 of the Internal Revenue Code, the information on this form and related file documents will be open to the public if any ruling or determination is made. However, names, addresses, and taxpayer identification numbers must be removed before the information can be made public.

Is there any other information you want removed? . . . .   ☐ Yes   ☐ No
If you check "Yes," we cannot process your request unless you submit a copy of this form and copies of all supporting documents showing, in brackets, the information you want removed. Attach a separate statement telling which specific exemption of section 6110(c) applies to each bracketed part.

This form is designed to cover many work activities, so some of the questions may not apply to you. **You must answer ALL items or mark them "Unknown" or "Does not apply."** *If you need more space, attach another sheet.*

Total number of workers in this class. (Attach names and addresses. If more than 10 workers, attach only 10.) ▶ _____

This information is about services performed by the worker from _____ to _____
(month, day, year)   (month, day, year)

Is the worker still performing services for the firm? . . . .   ☐ Yes   ☐ No

If "No," what was the date of termination? ▶ _____
(month, day, year)

Cat. No. 16106T   Form **SS-8** (Rev. 7-93)

Form SS-8 (Rev. 7-93)   Page **2**

1a Describe the firm's business ....
  b Describe the work done by the worker ....
....

2a If the work is done under a written agreement between the firm and the worker, attach a copy.
  b If the agreement is not in writing, describe the terms and conditions of the work arrangement ....
....

  c If the actual working arrangement differs in any way from the agreement, explain the differences and why they occur ....
....

3a Is the worker given training by the firm? . . . . ☐ Yes   ☐ No
     If "Yes": What kind?
     How often? ....
  b Is the worker given instructions in the way the work is to be done (exclusive of actual training in 3a)? . ☐ Yes   ☐ No
     If "Yes," give specific examples. ....
  c Attach samples of any written instructions or procedures.
  d Does the firm have the right to change the methods used by the worker or direct that person on how to
     do the work? . . . . ☐ Yes   ☐ No
     Explain your answer ....
....

  e Does the operation of the firm's business require that the worker be supervised or controlled in the
     performance of the service? . . . . ☐ Yes   ☐ No
     Explain your answer ....
....

4a The firm engages the worker:
     ☐ To perform and complete a particular job only
     ☐ To work at a job for an indefinite period of time
     ☐ Other (explain) ....
  b Is the worker required to follow a routine or a schedule established by the firm? . . . . ☐ Yes   ☐ No
     If "Yes," what is the routine or schedule? ....
....

  c Does the worker report to the firm or its representative? . . . . ☐ Yes   ☐ No
     If "Yes": How often? ....
     For what purpose? ....
     In what manner (in person, in writing, by telephone, etc.)? ....
     Attach copies of report forms used in reporting to the firm.
  d Does the worker furnish a time record to the firm? . . . . ☐ Yes   ☐ No
     If "Yes," attach copies of time records.
5a State the kind and value of tools, equipment, supplies, and materials furnished by:
     The firm ....
....
     The worker ....
....

  b What expenses are incurred by the worker in the performance of services for the firm? ....
....

  c Does the firm reimburse the worker for any expenses? . . . . ☐ Yes   ☐ No
     If "Yes," specify the reimbursed expenses ....

6a Will the worker perform the services personally? . . . . ☐ Yes   ☐ No
  b Does the worker have helpers? . . . . ☐ Yes   ☐ No
     If "Yes": Who hires the helpers?   ☐ Firm   ☐ Worker
     If hired by the worker, is the firm's approval necessary? . . . . ☐ Yes   ☐ No
     Who pays the helpers?   ☐ Firm   ☐ Worker
     Are social security and Medicare taxes and Federal income tax withheld from the helpers' wages? . . ☐ Yes   ☐ No
     If "Yes": Who reports and pays these taxes? ☐ Firm   ☐ Worker
     Who reports the helpers' incomes to the Internal Revenue Service? ☐ Firm   ☐ Worker
     If the worker pays the helpers, does the firm repay the worker? . . . . ☐ Yes   ☐ No
     What services do the helpers perform?

Form SS-8 (Rev. 7-93) Page **3**

 7 At what location are the services performed? ☐ Firm's ☐ Worker's ☐ Other (specify) _____
 8a Type of pay worker receives:
   ☐ Salary   ☐ Commission   ☐ Hourly wage   ☐ Piecework   ☐ Lump sum   ☐ Other (specify) _____
  b Does the firm guarantee a minimum amount of pay to the worker? . . . . ☐ Yes ☐ No
  c Does the firm allow the worker a drawing account or advances against pay? . . . . . ☐ Yes ☐ No
    If "Yes": Is the worker paid such advances on a regular basis? . . . . ☐ Yes ☐ No
  d How does the worker repay such advances? _____
 9a Is the worker eligible for a pension, bonus, paid vacations, sick pay, etc.? . . . . . . ☐ Yes ☐ No
    If "Yes," specify _____
  b Does the firm carry workmen's compensation insurance on the worker? . . . . ☐ Yes ☐ No
  c Does the firm deduct social security and Medicare taxes from amounts paid the worker? . . . ☐ Yes ☐ No
  d Does the firm deduct Federal income taxes from amounts paid the worker? . . . . . . ☐ Yes ☐ No
  e How does the firm report the worker's income to the Internal Revenue Service?
    ☐ Form W-2 ☐ Form 1099-MISC ☐ Does not report ☐ Other (specify) _____
    Attach a copy.
  f Does the firm bond the worker? . . . . ☐ Yes ☐ No
10a Approximately how many hours a day does the worker perform services for the firm? _____
    Does the firm set hours of work for the worker? . . . . ☐ Yes ☐ No
    If "Yes," what are the worker's set hours? _____ am/pm to _____ am/pm (Circle whether am or pm)
  b Does the worker perform similar services for others? . . . . ☐ Yes ☐ No ☐ Unknown
    If "Yes": Are these services performed on a daily basis for other firms? . . . . ☐ Yes ☐ No ☐ Unknown
    Percentage of time spent in performing these services for:
    This firm _____ % Other firms _____ % ☐ **Unknown**
    Does the firm have priority on the worker's time? . . . . ☐ Yes ☐ No
    If "No," explain _____
  c Is the worker prohibited from competing with the firm either while performing services or during any later
    period? . . . . ☐ Yes ☐ No
11a Can the firm discharge the worker at any time without incurring a liability? . . . . . . ☐ Yes ☐ No
    If "No," explain _____
  b Can the worker terminate the services at any time without incurring a liability? . . . . ☐ Yes ☐ No
    If "No," explain _____
12a Does the worker perform services for the firm under:
    ☐ The firm's business name ☐ The worker's own business name ☐ Other (specify) _____
  b Does the worker advertise or maintain a business listing in the telephone directory, a trade
    journal, etc.? . . . . ☐ Yes ☐ No ☐ Unknown
    If "Yes," specify _____
  c Does the worker represent himself or herself to the public as being in business to perform
    the same or similar services? . . . . ☐ Yes ☐ No ☐ Unknown
    If "Yes," how? _____
  d Does the worker have his or her own shop or office? . . . . ☐ Yes ☐ No ☐ Unknown
    If "Yes," where? _____
  e Does the firm represent the worker as an employee of the firm to its customers? . . . . ☐ Yes ☐ No
    If "No," how is the worker represented? _____
  f How did the firm learn of the worker's services? _____
13 Is a license necessary for the work? . . . . ☐ Yes ☐ No ☐ Unknown
    If "Yes," what kind of license is required? _____
    By whom is it issued? _____
    By whom is the license fee paid? _____
14 Does the worker have a financial investment in a business related to the services performed? ☐ Yes ☐ No ☐ Unknown
    If "Yes," specify and give amounts of the investment _____
15 Can the worker incur a loss in the performance of the service for the firm? . . . . . . ☐ Yes ☐ No
    If "Yes," how? _____
16a Has any other government agency ruled on the status of the firm's workers? . . . . . . ☐ Yes ☐ No
    If "Yes," attach a copy of the ruling.
  b Is the same issue being considered by any IRS office in connection with the audit of the worker's tax
    return or the firm's tax return, or has it recently been considered? . . . . ☐ Yes ☐ No
    If "Yes," for which year(s)?

Form SS-8 (Rev. 7-93)   Page **4**

17. Does the worker assemble or process a product at home or away from the firm's place of business? . ☐ Yes ☐ No
    If "Yes":
    Who furnishes materials or goods used by the worker? ☐ Firm ☐ Worker
    Is the worker furnished a pattern or given instructions to follow in making the product? . . . . . ☐ Yes ☐ No
    Is the worker required to return the finished product to the firm or to someone designated by the firm? . ☐ Yes ☐ No

    Answer items 18a through n only if the worker is a salesperson or provides a service directly to customers.

18a. Are leads to prospective customers furnished by the firm? . . . . ☐ Yes ☐ No ☐ Does not apply
  b. Is the worker required to pursue or report on leads? . . . . ☐ Yes ☐ No ☐ Does not apply
  c. Is the worker required to adhere to prices, terms, and conditions of sale established by the firm? . . ☐ Yes ☐ No
  d. Are orders submitted to and subject to approval by the firm? . . . . ☐ Yes ☐ No
  e. Is the worker expected to attend sales meetings? . . . . ☐ Yes ☐ No
     If "Yes": Is the worker subject to any kind of penalty for failing to attend? . . . . ☐ Yes ☐ No
  f. Does the firm assign a specific territory to the worker? . . . . ☐ Yes ☐ No ☐ Does not apply
  g. Who does the customer pay? ☐ Firm ☐ Worker
     If worker, does the worker remit the total amount to the firm? . . . . ☐ Yes ☐ No
  h. Does the worker sell a consumer product in a home or establishment other than a permanent retail establishment? . . . . ☐ Yes ☐ No
  i. List the products and/or services distributed by the worker, such as meat, vegetables, fruit, bakery products, beverages (other than milk), or laundry or dry cleaning services. If more than one type of product and/or service is distributed, specify the principal one. _____
  j. Did the firm or another person assign the route or territory and a list of customers to the worker? . . ☐ Yes ☐ No
     If "Yes," enter the name and job title of the person who made the assignment. _____
  k. Did the worker pay the firm or person for the privilege of serving customers on the route or in the territory? ☐ Yes ☐ No
     If "Yes," how much did the worker pay (not including any amount paid for a truck or racks, etc.)? $ _____
     What factors were considered in determining the value of the route or territory? _____
  l. How are new customers obtained by the worker? Explain fully, showing whether the new customers called the firm for service, were solicited by the worker, or both. _____
  m. Does the worker sell life insurance? . . . . ☐ Yes ☐ No
     If "Yes":
     Is the selling of life insurance or annuity contracts for the firm the worker's entire business activity? . . ☐ Yes ☐ No
     If "No," list the other business activities and the amount of time spent on them _____
     Does the worker sell other types of insurance for the firm? . . . . ☐ Yes ☐ No
     If "Yes," state the percentage of the worker's total working time spent in selling other types of insurance _____ %
     At the time the contract was entered into between the firm and the worker, was it their intention that the worker sell life insurance for the firm: ☐ on a full-time basis ☐ on a part-time basis
     State the manner in which the intention was expressed. _____
  n. Is the worker a traveling or city salesperson? . . . . ☐ Yes ☐ No
     If "Yes": From whom does worker principally solicit orders for the firm? _____
     If the worker solicits orders from wholesalers, retailers, contractors, or operators of hotels, restaurants, or other similar establishments, specify the percentage of the worker's time spent in this solicitation. _____ %
     Is the merchandise purchased by the customers for resale or for use in their business operations? If used by the customers in their business operations, describe the merchandise and state whether it is equipment installed on their premises or a consumable supply. _____

19. Attach a detailed explanation of any other reason why you believe the worker is an independent contractor or is an employee of the firm.

Under penalties of perjury, I declare that I have examined this request, including accompanying documents, and to the best of my knowledge and belief, the facts presented are true, correct, and complete.

Signature ▶   Title ▶   Date ▶

If this form is used by the firm in requesting a written determination, the form must be signed by an officer or member of the firm.
If this form is used by the worker in requesting a written determination, the form must be signed by the worker. If the worker wants a written determination about services performed for two or more firms, a separate form must be completed and signed for each firm.
Additional copies of this form may be obtained from any Internal Revenue Service office or by calling 1-800-TAX-FORM (1-800-829-3676).

religion, national origin, or gender.
- *The Age Discrimination in Employment Act.* This act forbids employers from discriminating against people who are over 40 years old.
- *COBRA (the Comprehensive Omnibus Budget Reconciliation Act).* COBRA requires certain employers who fire their employees to give the terminated employees the right to continue their health insurance benefits for a limited period. COBRA and other health-insurance-related laws may be superseded by more comprehensive health-care legislation.
- *The Fair Credit Reporting Act.* This act imposes disclosure requirements on employers who intend to make credit report inquiries about their employees or credit report inquiries about people who apply for work. Generally, the employer must notify the person involved that the employer has made a credit report request.
- *The Family Medical Leave Act.* This act requires employers with more than 49 employees to give employees the right to a maximum of 12 weeks unpaid leave for certain pregnancy and medical reasons.
- *The Immigration Reform and Control Act.* This act requires all employers to be sure that they are not employing illegal aliens.
- *The Worker Adjustment and Retraining Notification Act.* This act requires employers with 100 or more employees to give a 60-day notice of planned layoffs or factory closings to the employees.

If you have further questions about federal labor laws and regulations, you can contact the following:

Department of Labor
200 Constitution Avenue NW
Washington, DC 20210
(202) 523-8165

Occupational Safety and
  Health Administration
  [a division of the Department of Labor]
200 Constitution Avenue NW
Washington, DC 20210
(202) 523-8017

Here's a list of the state agencies in charge of enforcing state labor laws and regulations:

Alabama
Department of Labor
64 N. Union Street
Montgomery, AL 36130
(205) 242-3460

Alaska
Department of Labor
P.O. Box 1149
Juneau, AK 99802
(907) 465-2700

Arizona
Industrial Commission
800 W. Washington
Phoenix, AZ 85007
(602) 542-4411

Arkansas
Department of Labor
10421 W. Markham
Little Rock, AR 72205
(501) 682-4500

California
Department of
  Industrial Relations
1121 L Street
Sacramento, CA 95814
(916) 324-4163

Colorado
Department of
  Labor & Employment
1313 Sherman Street
Denver, CO 80203
(303) 866-2782

Connecticut
Department of Labor
200 Folly Brook Boulevard
Wethersfield, CT 06109
(203) 566-4384

Delaware
Department of Labor
820 N. French Street
Wilmington, DE 19801
(302) 571-2710

District of Columbia
Department of
  Employment Services
500 C Street NW
Washington, DC 20001
(202) 639-1000

Florida
Department of Labor &
  Employment Security
Tallahassee, FL 32399
(904) 488-8641

Georgia
Department of Labor
148 International Boulevard
Atlanta, GA 30303
(404) 656-3011

Hawaii
Department of Labor &
  Industrial Relations
830 Punchbowl Street
Honolulu, HI 96813
(808) 548-3150

Idaho
Labor & Industrial
  Services Department
277 N. Sixth Street
Boise, ID 83720
(208) 334-3950

Illinois
Department of Labor
State Capitol Plaza
Springfield, IL 62702
(217) 782-6206

Indiana
Division of Labor
State Office Building
Indianapolis, IN 46204
(317) 232-2663

Iowa
Division of Labor Services
Department of Employment Services
1000 E. Grand
Des Moines, IA 50319
(515) 281-8067

Kansas
Department of
Human Resources
401 SW Topeka Boulevard
Topeka, KS 66603
(913) 296-7474

Kentucky
Labor Cabinet
U.S. 127
South Frankfort, KY 40601
(502) 564-3070

Louisiana
Department of Labor
P.O. Box 94094
Baton Rouge, LA 70804
(504) 342-3011

Maine
Department of Labor
State House Station Number 54
Augusta, ME 04333
(207) 289-3786

Maryland
Division of Labor & Industry
Licensing & Regulation Department
501 St. Paul Place
Baltimore, MD 21202
(301) 333-4179

Massachusetts
Department of Labor & Industries
Executive Office of Labor
100 Cambridge Street
Boston, MA 02202
(617) 727-3455

Michigan
Department of Labor
7310 Woodward Avenue
Detroit, MI 48202
(313) 876-5000

Minnesota
Department of
 Labor & Industry
443 Lafayette Road
St. Paul, MN 55101
(612) 296-2342

Missouri
Department of Labor &
 Industrial Relations
421 E. Dunklin
Jefferson City, MO 65104
(314) 751-4091

Montana
Department of
 Labor & Industry
Capitol Station
Helena, MT 59620
(406) 444-2723

Nebraska
Department of Labor
550 S. 16th Street
P.O. Box 94600
Lincoln, NE 68509

Nevada
Labor Commission
505 E. King Street
Carson City, NV 89710
(702) 885-4850

New Hampshire
Department of Labor
19 Pillsbury Street
Concord, NH 03301
(603) 271-3171

New Jersey
Department of Labor
CN 110
Trenton, NJ 08625
(609) 292-2323

New Mexico
Labor & Industrial Division
230 W. Manhatten
Santa Fe, NM 87501
(505) 827-6875

New York
Department of Labor
State Office Building
Albany, NY 12240
(518) 457-2741

North Carolina
Department of Labor
4 W. Edenton Street
Raleigh, NC 27601
(919) 733-7166

North Dakota
Department of Labor
State Capitol
600 East Boulevard
Bismarck, ND 58505
(701) 224-2661

Ohio
Department of Industrial Relations
2323 W. Fifth Avenue
Columbus, OH 43266
(614) 466-3271

Oklahoma
State Department of Labor
1315 Broadway Place
Oklahoma City, OK 73103
(405) 521-2461

Oregon
Bureau of Labor & Industries
1400 SW Fifth Avenue
Portland, OR 97201
(503) 229-5737

Pennsylvania
Department of Labor & Industry
1700 Labor & Industry Building
Harrisburg, PA 17120
(717) 787-3756

Rhode Island
Department of Labor
220 Elmwood Avenue
Providence, RI 02907
(401) 277-2741

South Carolina
Department of Labor
3600 Forest Drive
Landmark Center
Columbia, SC 29204
(803) 734-9600

South Dakota
Department of Labor
Kneip Building
Pierre, SD 57501
(605) 773-3101

Tennessee
Department of Labor
501 Union Boulevard
Nashville, TN 37219
(615) 741-2582

Texas
Department of
 Labor & Standards
Capitol Station
Austin, TX 78711
(512) 463-5520

Utah
Industrial Commission
P.O. Box 45802
Salt Lake City, UT 84145
(801) 530-6800

Vermont
Department of
Labor & Industry
7 Court Street
Montpelier, VT 05602
(802) 828-2286

Virginia
Department of
 Labor & Industry
P.O. Box 12064
Richmond, VA 23219
(804) 786-2377

Washington (the state)
Department of
 Labor & Industries
General Administration Building
Olympia, WA 98504
(206) 753-6307

West Virginia
Division of Labor
State Capitol Complex
Charleston, WV 25305
(304) 348-7890

Wisconsin
Industrial Labor &
 Human Relations
201 E. Washington Avenue
P.O. Box 7946
Madison, WI 53707
(608) 266-7552

Wyoming
Department of
 Labor & Statistics
Herschler Building
Cheyenne, WY 82002
(307) 777-7261

Addresses and phone numbers change frequently, so if your call or letter doesn't go through, try Directory Assistance for your state capitol.

PART FOUR

OTHER LAWS AND REGULATIONS AFFECTING BUSINESSES

CHAPTER TEN

Zoning and Environmental Law

KEY TERMS

comprehensive plan *EPA* *nonconforming use*
environmental impact statements *NEPA* *variance*

Every business, big or small, has a place of work. This place of work may be an office, a store, a factory, or whatever. Obviously, having a place of business also involves the use of land, whether that land is owned or rented. This chapter summarizes two major areas of the law that concern businesses and their use of land.

Zoning

The federal government leaves the regulation of land use mostly up to the states. There are several exceptions, however, such as

- Historic landmarks
- National parks and wildlife preserves
- Federal lands
- Military bases

Every state has legislation that delegates the job of regulating land use to local authorities. So ultimately, the power to establish zoning regulations and ordinances generally rests with the county, city, township, or other municipal authorities.

Within each county or other local jurisdiction, there is typically a **comprehensive plan,** or other similar item, for land use within the jurisdiction. The comprehensive plan is like a map, and every part of the county or city has a permitted land-use designation. The most basic types of zoning designations are

- Agricultural, such as farms and pastures
- Commercial, such as stores and shopping centers
- Industrial, such as factories
- Residential, such as houses and apartment buildings

There can also be many variations within each of these designations. For example, a lot might be classified as "light industrial" instead of simply "industrial," and building a warehouse on it might be permissible, but not building a steel mill. Or a residential zoning classification might permit building single-family homes on large lots, but not higher-density housing such as townhouses. A comprehensive plan serves a variety of purposes and interests. Local politics may lead the authorities to prevent industrial and commercial development in residential areas, and economic development interests may lead to zoning that encourages business growth. Within the comprehensive plan, the zoning regulations and ordinances can be very detailed and can cover situations right down to each particular neighborhood and business, deciding such things as the number of seats permitted in a restaurant, the size of a convenience store parking lot, and what kinds of billboards can be erected.

Zoning laws and the comprehensive plan are intended to be flexible, because of the constantly changing nature of land usage, economic pressures, and local politics. Thus, although an area or a particular piece of land may be zoned for a specific permitted use, there are exceptions. The two major forms of exceptions are nonconforming uses and variances.

Nonconforming Uses

A **nonconforming use** is an exception that is granted to the owner of a particular piece of land that permits him or her to use the land in a manner that would otherwise be inconsistent with the zoning designation for that area. Nonconforming uses often occur when an area's zoning designation is changed, and rather than inflict hardship on people who depend on the old designation, certain properties are granted nonconforming uses—a type of "grandfather" privilege.

Example:

Roberta has a small business, Roberta's Wine Shoppe, which is one of a handful of businesses in a growing suburban neighborhood. Roberta opened the store years ago, when the area was still largely rural and when there were few restrictions on where you could run a business. Now, however, the growth in population and development has caused neighborhood residents to petition their local zoning officials, asking them to zone the neighborhood for exclusively residential use. Roberta is concerned since she doesn't want to go out of business. However, Roberta may be able to obtain a nonconforming use for her store and be able to stay in business.

If the locality grants a nonconforming use, the nonconforming use normally "runs with the land." This means that Roberta can sell her store to another person who wants to continue the business. Otherwise, Roberta would have no market for the sale of her business and property, because if anyone bought that land all he or she could do would be to convert the store into a residence. There are ways, however, in which businesspeople like Roberta can lose their nonconforming use rights.

○ If the owner of the property quits the

nonconforming use. For example, if Roberta closes her store or is forced to go out of business.
- If the owner of the property attempts a substantial change in the nature of the nonconforming use—i.e. if Roberta turned her Wine Shoppe into an adult video store.

Variance

A **variance** is basically a request for an exception to the zoning laws. It is like a nonconforming use, but the reasons for granting a variance are not limited to pre-existing land use. The reasons for requesting a variance depend completely on the local regulations and each case's specific circumstances. Much depends on the local zoning board's discretion.

Example:

Steve runs a small store on a road that leads into a residential area. There is a sign out front that reads, Steve's Store. In compliance with the zoning ordinance, the sign is 20 feet back from the road. Large trees on other properties, however, obscure the view of Steve's sign from drivers on the road. Steve goes to the local zoning board and asks for a variance. He wants to move the sign to within 10 feet of the road, so drivers can see it. Will Steve get his variance?

The answer is maybe. The zoning board will probably have a public hearing on Steve's variance request. At a public hearing, the person requesting a variance presents his or her case to the zoning officials. Members of the public are free to attend. Local residents who don't want billboards along the road in front of Steve's business could go to the public hearing and object to Steve's variance request. But if Steve or his attorney makes a good presentation to the zoning board, and there is no significant public objection, Steve will probably get his variance, since his request is reasonable.

Environmental Law

Until 1969, there was very little government regulation over environmental matters, other than legislation to preserve certain areas as national parks and wildlife preserves. Growing public concern over air and water pollution prompted Congress to pass the National Environmental Policy Act of 1969 (**NEPA**). NEPA created the federal Council on Environmental Quality. In 1970, the federal Environmental Protection Agency (**EPA**) was created. The EPA oversees the enforcement of federal environmental laws and coordinates environmental protection activities with state and local authorities. For example, the EPA supervises the filing and review of **environmental impact statements,** which are lengthy disclosure documents required for certain major projects—such as building large factories—that may have a significant impact on the environment. In addition, the EPA enforces the major environmental laws that have been passed by Congress. These laws can affect businesses in many ways, depending on the nature of the business.

Example:

The EPA enforces the Resource Conservation and Recovery Act. This act requires that solid wastes and hazardous wastes be safely disposed of, and there are special requirements for highly toxic substances. The act covers people who create the waste, people who transport the waste, and people who dispose of the waste. People who store or dispose of certain wastes must obtain an EPA permit. Also, the people involved in the creation, transportation, and disposal of waste may be subject to extensive record-keeping requirements. But at Lynne's Gas Station and Auto-Body Shop, no one knows or cares about the act or EPA regulations. In the back lot, waste products—used automotive fluids, old tires, waste chemicals from auto body machinery—have been accumulating for years. Soon the amount of junk in the back lot begins to annoy Lynne, and she decides to take action. She gets her brother Scott to truck the wastes to her friend Mary's house. Mary lives near the river. At night, Mary dumps the wastes into the river. If the EPA hears of this activity, do Lynne, Scott, and Mary have any potential liability under the act?

Answer: Yes. Lynne, Scott, and Mary may all face potential liability under the Resource Conservation and Recovery Act, since they have respectively been involved in the creation, transportation, and disposal of waste.

In addition to the Resource Conservation and Recovery Act, the EPA enforces the following environmental legislation:

- *The Comprehensive Environmental Response, Compensation, and Liability Act (CERCLA),* which concerns hazardous waste spills and authorizes the EPA to see that spills are cleaned up and that the responsible parties pay the cleanup costs.
- *The Water Pollution Control Act,* which governs the discharge of sewage, hazardous wastes, pesticides, oil, and other pollutants from industrial facilities into water.
- *The Clean Air Act,* which governs air pollution from automobiles, industrial chemicals, factories, and other sources. Among other things, the Clean Air Act requires the safe treatment and disposal of chlorofluorocarbons, which are produced by chemicals in appliances such as refrigerators and air conditioners.
- *The Marine Protection, Research, and Sanctuaries Act,* which severely restricts dumping waste in ocean waters.
- *The Oil Pollution Act,* which concerns spills of petroleum products and petroleum waste.
- *The Safe Drinking Water Act,* which governs drinking water and determines what levels of organic material, chemical waste, and other foreign substances are acceptable.
- *The Lead Contamination Control Act,* which concerns the use of lead in connection with products that dispense drinking water, specifically lead-lined watercooler tanks.

State and Local Environmental Laws and Regulations

In addition to federal laws and EPA regulations, there are state and local environmental laws and regulations that affect businesses. The state and local laws and regulations may include the following:

- *Mandatory recycling.* It is usually the local authorities who establish the requirements concerning the recycling of newspapers, paper products, glass, aluminum cans, plastic products, and other wastes. The local authorities dictate how recyclables must be separated and presented for recycling, what the fines for noncompliance are, and how businesses must comply with the rules and regulations.
- *State and local waste disposal requirements.* These are requirements over and above the federal requirements for certain chemicals and petroleum products. There may be fines and other legal consequences if businesses simply pour wastes down the drain or don't arrange for the wastes to be collected and disposed of by the local sanitation authorities.
- *Garbage dumps and other landfills.* There are restrictions on what can be disposed of at such sites, but these restrictions vary from state to state and locality to locality. Thus, people and businesses with waste that can't be disposed of in their state or locality may try to dispose of this waste in other states or localities, where the rules are more permissive. But looking for another state, city, or county in which to deposit your waste could cause legal conflicts and may not be permissible.

If you have further questions about federal environmental laws and regulations, the Environmental Protection Agency can be reached at the following address:

401 M Street SW
Washington, DC 20460
(202) 260-2090

State agencies in charge of enforcing state environmental laws and regulations are listed below:

Alabama
Environmental Health
 Administration
State Office Building
Montgomery, AL 36130
(205) 242-5004

Alaska
Department of
 Environmental Conservation
P.O. Box O
Juneau, AK 99811
(907) 465-2600

Arizona
Department of
 Environmental Quality
2005 N. Central
Phoenix, AZ 85004
(602) 257-6917

Arkansas
Department of
 Pollution Control and Ecology
8001 National Drive
Little Rock, AR 72209
(501) 562-7444

California
Department of
  Environmental Affairs
1102 Q Street
Sacramento, CA 95814
(916) 322-5840

Colorado
Department of Health
4210 E. 11th Avenue
Denver, CO 80220
(303) 331-8500

Connecticut
Division of
  Environmental Quality
Environmental Protection
Department
165 Capitol Avenue
Hartford, CT 06106
(203) 566-2110

Delaware
Department of
  Natural Resources
  & Environmental Control
89 Kings Highway
Dover, DE 19901
(302) 736-4403

District of Columbia
Housing & Environmental
  Regulations Administration
Department of Consumer
  and Regulatory Affairs
614 H Street NW
Washington, DC 20001
(202) 727-7395

Florida
Environmental
  Regulation Department
Twin Towers
2600 Blairstone Road
Tallahassee, FL 32399
(904) 488-4805

Georgia
Department of
  Natural Resources
205 Butler Street SW
Floyd Towers
Atlanta, GA 30334
(404) 656-3500

Hawaii
Environmental Protection &
  Health Services
Department of Health
1250 Punchbowl Street
Honolulu, HI 96813
(808) 548-4139

Idaho
Division of the Environment
Department of Health
  and Welfare
450 W. State Street
Boise, ID 83720
(208) 334-5840

Illinois
Environmental
  Protection Agency
2200 Churchill Road
Springfield, IL 62708
(217) 782-3397

Indiana
Department of
  Environmental Management
105 S. Meridian Street
Indianapolis, IN 46206
(317) 232-8162

Iowa
Air Quality and
  Solid Waste Bureau
Department of
  Natural Resources
Wallace State Office Building
Des Moines, IA 50319
(515) 281-8852

Kansas
Department of Health &
  Environment
Forbes Field
Topeka, KS 66620
(913) 296-1535

Kentucky
Natural Resources &
  Environmental Protection
Capitol Plaza
Frankfort, KY 40601
(502) 564-3350

Louisiana
Department of
  Environmental Quality
P.O. Box 44066
Baton Rouge, LA 70804
(504) 342-1266

Maine
Department of
  Environmental Protection
State House Station No. 17
Augusta, ME 04333
(207) 289-2811

Maryland
Department of Environment
2500 Broening Highway
Baltimore, MD 21224
(301) 631-3084

Massachusetts
Executive Office of
  Environmental Affairs
100 Cambridge Street
Boston, MA 02202
(617) 727-9800

Michigan
Environmental
  Protection Bureau
Department of
  Natural Resources
P.O. Box 30028
Lansing, MI 48909
(517) 373-7917

Minnesota
Pollution Control Agency
520 Lafayette Road
St. Paul, MN 55155
(612) 296-6300

Mississippi
Pollution Control Bureau
Commission on
 Environmental Quality
Southport Mall
Jackson, MS 39209
(601) 961-5100

Missouri
Division of
 Environmental Quality
Department of Natural
 Resources
P.O. Box 176
Jefferson City, MO 65102
(314) 751-4810

Montana
Environmental Sciences Division
Capitol Station
Helena, MT 59620
(406) 444-3948

Nebraska
Department of
 Environmental Control
301 Centennial Mall S.
P.O. Box 94877
Lincoln, NE 68509
(402) 471-2186

Nevada
Environmental
 Protection Division
Conservation and Natural
 Resources   Department
201 S. Fall Street
Carson City, NV 89710
(702) 885-4670

New Hampshire
Department of
 Environmental Services
6 Hazen Drive
Concord, NH 03301
(603) 271-3503

New Jersey
Department of
 Environmental Protection
CN 402
Trenton, NJ 08625
(609) 292-2885

New Mexico
Department of
 Health & Environment
P.O. Box 968
Santa Fe, NM 87504
(505) 827-2850

New York
Department of
 Environmental Conservation
50 Wolf Road
Albany, NY 12233
(518) 457-3446

North Carolina
Department of
 Natural Resources
 and Community Development
512 N. Salisbury Street
Raleigh, NC 27604
(919) 733-4984

North Dakota
Environmental Health Section
Department of Health
1200 Missouri Avenue
Bismarck, ND 58501
(701) 224-2374

Ohio
Environmental
 Protection Agency
1800 Watermark Drive
Columbus, OH 43266
(614) 481-7050

Oklahoma
Department of
 Pollution Control
1000 NE 10th Street
P.O. Box 53504
Oklahoma City, OK 73152
(405) 271-4677

Oregon
Department of
 Environmental Quality
811 SW Sixth Avenue
Portland, OR 97204
(503) 229-5696

Pennsylvania
Department of
 Environmental Resources
9th Floor, Fulton Building
Harrisburg, PA 17120
(717) 787-2814

Rhode Island
Department of
 Environmental Management
9 Hayes Street
Providence, RI 02908
(401) 277-2771

South Carolina
Division of Environmental
 Quality Control
Department of Health &
 Environmental Control
2600 Bull Street
Columbia, SC 29201
(803) 734-5360

South Dakota
Division of Environmental Health
Water & Natural Resources
 Department
Foss Building
Pierre, SD 57501
(605) 773-3151

Tennessee
Bureau of Environment
Department of
 Health & Environment
1st Floor, TERRA Building
Nashville, TN 37219
(615) 741-3657

Texas
Department of Health
1100 W. 49th Street
Austin, TX 78756
(512) 458-7541

PART 4. OTHER LAWS AND REGULATIONS AFFECTING BUSINESSES

Utah
Division of
 Environmental Health
Department of Health
288 N. 1460 W.
P.O. Box 16690
Salt Lake City, UT 84116
(801) 538-6121

Vermont
Agency of
 Natural Resources
103 S. Main Street
Waterbury, VT 05676
(802) 244-7347

Virginia
Council on the
 Environment
Ninth Street Office Building
Richmond, VA 23219
(804) 786-4500

Washington (state)
Department of Ecology
300 Desmond Drive
Lacy, WA 98504
(206) 407-6000

West Virginia
Division of
 Natural Resources
1800 Washington Street
Charleston, WV 25305
(304) 348-2754

Wisconsin
Division of
 Environmental Quality
Department of
 Natural Resources
P.O. Box 7921
Madison, WI 53707
(608) 266-1099

Wyoming
Department of
 Environmental Quality
Herschler Building
Cheyenne, WY 82002
(307) 777-7938

Addresses and phone numbers change frequently, so if your call or letter doesn't go through, try Directory Assistance for your state capitol.

CHAPTER ELEVEN

Federal and State Securities Laws

KEY TERMS

blue sky laws
securities

Securities Act
Securities and Exchange Commission

Securities Exchange Act
Uniform Securities Act

Before the Great Depression, the nation's stock markets and bond markets were mostly unregulated. The stock market crash of October 1929, however, forced the federal government to begin regulating the securities markets. In 1933, Congress passed the Securities Act of 1933. The **Securities Act** imposes registration and disclosure requirements on securities offered for sale to the public. It also forbids fraud, manipulation, and deception in connection with the sale of securities. In 1934, Congress passed the Securities Exchange Act of 1934. The **Securities Exchange Act** regulates securities traded on the various stock markets throughout the country, and it regulates the network of brokerage houses that buy and sell securities, or the over-the-counter market. The act also imposes registration requirements on stock exchanges, stock brokers, and stock dealers, and like the Securities Act, it forbids fraud, manipulation, and deception in connection with the sale of securities.

The Securities Act and the Securities Exchange Act established the basic framework of federal securities regulation. Congress has passed additional legislation expanding the scope of securities regulation and investor protection. This additional legislation includes the Public Utility Holding Company Act of 1935, the Trust Indenture Act of 1939, the Investment Company Act of 1940, the Investment Advisors Act of 1940, and the Securities Investor Protection Act of 1970.

The federal securities laws are enforced by the U.S. **Securities and Exchange Commission** (the SEC). In addition, Congress has given the SEC the power to issue regulations in order to further the securities laws' purpose of investor protection. There are many SEC regulations, but the most significant is Rule 10b-5, issued under the authority of the Securities Exchange Act. Rule 10b-5 makes illegal the use of "any manipulative or deceptive device or contrivance" in connection with "the purchase or sale" of any security. Basically, Rule 10b-5 is a broad antifraud regulation. Not only does the SEC enforce Rule 10b-5 violations, but individuals who are the victim of Rule 10b-5 violations can sue the offender without waiting for the SEC to take action.

What Is a Security?

Stocks and bonds are obviously **securities**. There are many types of investments, however, and it is not always clear whether or not an investment is a security covered by the securities laws and regulations.

For example:

Jim and Jane love fast food, and they decide that they want to go into the fast food business. Clog Your Arteries is offering franchises, so Jim and Jane buy the right to open the first Clog Your Arteries in Little Rock, Arkansas. Jim and Jane invest a sizable amount of time, money, and effort into their restaurant, but the business is a failure, and Jim and Jane lose everything. Do Jim and Jane have any protection under federal securities laws?

Answer: Probably not. The federal securities laws generally don't consider franchises to be securities. There are some exceptions for passive investors in franchises, who are relying on others to take care of the business, but Jim and Jane were not passive investors. (They may be protected under applicable franchise laws, however.)

The Securities Exchange Act gives a lengthy definition of what a security is:

"…any note, stock, treasury stock, bond, debenture, certificate of interest or participation in any profit-sharing agreement or in any oil, gas, or other mineral royalty or lease, any collateral-trust certificate, pre-organization certificate or subscription, transferable share, investment contract, voting-trust certificate, certificate of deposit, for a security, any put, call, straddle, option, or privilege on any security, certificate of deposit, or group or index of securities (including any interest therein or based on the value thereof), or any put, call, straddle, option, or privilege entered into on a national securities exchange relating to foreign currency, or in general, any instrument commonly known as a "security"; or any certificate of interest or participation in, temporary or interim certificate for, receipt for, or warrant or right to subscribe to or purchase, any of the foregoing; but shall not include currency or any note, draft, bill of exchange, or banker's acceptance which has a maturity at the time of issuance of not exceeding nine months, exclusive of days of grace, or any renewal thereof the maturity of which is likewise limited."

If a type of investment doesn't fit within the above definition, it might still be a security subject to the federal securities laws. In 1946, in a landmark case, *SEC v. W.J. Howey Co.*, the Supreme Court stated that an investment is a security if that investment is 1) an investment of money, 2) in a common enterprise, 3) with the expectation of profits, 4) solely from the efforts of others.

Using these four elements, courts have found that the federal securities laws apply to limited partnership interests. This is important, since limited partnerships are an important form of business entity (see Chapter 2). In addition, the courts have found that under the four elements of Howey, the federal securities laws may apply to investments in

- Certain types of pension plans
- Passive franchises
- An interest in a cooperative housing complex
- Demand promissory notes issued by a cooperative to its members
- Loans solicited by political organization fund-raisers

The four elements of Howey are just a general formula, however; there has been a great deal of litigation over the details and specific applications of each of the four requirements.

Effect of the Federal Securities Laws

The federal securities laws mean three basic things to business people, especially the owners of businesses. First, if a person who owns a business or plans to start a business wants to raise money by selling stock or other securities, he or she has to comply with the SEC's regulations and registration requirements. These regulations and registration requirements apply even if the stock or other security is not being offered to the general public, but to a small handful of potential investors.

Andrea, Bill, and Carl have a small business. They want to expand the business but need to raise money to do it. They decide that they will turn the business into a corporation or perhaps a limited partnership and sell interests in the business (either stock or limited partnership interests) to other people. They know that the federal securities laws apply if a business sells securities to the general public, but all they want to do is sell to friends and relatives. The potential investors are Andrea's mother, Bill's wife, and Carl's best friend. Do Andrea, Bill, and Carl have to worry about complying with federal securities laws?

Answer: Yes. Since both stock and limited partnership interests are types of securities, the federal securities laws apply. Since the number of potential investors is small, and the amount of money sought to be raised by selling securities is also likely to be small, one of the SEC's many regulations concerning small securities offerings should apply. These regulations are designed principally for small businesses and have easier registration and filing requirements than do regulations for big companies such as IBM and MCI.

The second important aspect of federal securities laws is that there can't be any fraud or misrepresentation in connection with the securities offering, or the business might be sued.

Andrea, Bill, and Carl commence their securities offering and comply with all applicable federal (and state) registration and other legal requirements. Carl, however, tells a potential investor that the business has been making a million dollars a year. Excited by Carl's statement, the investor buys securities in Andrea, Bill, and Carl's business. In fact, Carl lied: The business has barely been making a profit, and it soon goes under. Does the investor have a potential lawsuit under the federal securities laws?

Answer: Yes, since Carl misrepresented the profitability of the business in connection with the sale of the securities.

Finally, there must be full disclosure of all the relevant facts required to be disclosed by the securities laws.

Andrea, Bill, and Carl go to a lawyer to get their securities offering paperwork done. The documents require extensive disclosures about the business. One of the required disclosures is whether or not the business has all of the required state licenses and permits. In fact, one of the business's permits has lapsed, but Andrea, Bill, and Carl don't want to admit it. So they say on the documents that all licenses and permits are valid. Their lie is not discovered during the securities offering by anyone. After the offering, the business has problems with the state over the lapsed permit, and as a result, the investors lose some money. Do the investors have a potential lawsuit under the federal securities laws?

Answer: Yes, since Andrea, Bill, and Carl failed to make a required disclosure.

State Blue Sky Laws

In addition to the federal securities laws, there are state statutes and regulations that apply to the offering and sale of securities. These state statutes and the various state securities regulations are known as **blue sky laws.** State blue sky laws include the following:

○ *Their own registration, disclosure and filing requirements.* Therefore, a securities offering has to comply with not only federal securities laws, but also state blue sky laws. In our example, Andrea, Bill, and Carl would also have to comply with the blue sky laws of their state in order to raise money by selling securities. Important: The blue sky laws of *several* states may be involved, depending on how wide the offering is and where the potential investors live. Obviously, a good lawyer is important here in order to ensure that both federal securities laws and the blue sky laws of one or more states are complied with.

○ *Their own antifraud provisions.* All states have blue sky laws that prohibit fraud in connection with the sale of securities akin to Rule 10b-5 discussed previously. However, some states don't let individuals sue for blue-sky violations independent of whatever action the state securities agency takes. A person can sue for federal securities violations, however, regardless of whether he or she chooses to sue for state blue-sky violations.

Most state securities laws are based on the **Uniform Securities Act.** The Uniform Securities Act includes most of the investor protections provided by the federal securities laws, and sometimes the state blue sky laws will favor the investor in a lawsuit.

A Final Note

You may be slightly confused about all the regulations surrounding the sale of securities. You may be asking, What about the situation in Chapter 1, where people set up a corporation in order to take advantage of limited liability and issue themselves stock through which they own the corporation? Are there federal or blue sky problems here? The answer is no, there usually aren't. In a corporation, the incorporators who are also the initial shareholders and the operators of the business typically do not have to worry about making some additional federal and state securities filings. They can go into business on the strength of their incorporation under state law.

If you have further questions about federal securities laws and regulations, you can contact the Securities and Exchange Commission:

450 Fifth Street NW
Washington, DC 20549
(202) 272-3100

For more information, here's a list of the state agencies in charge of enforcing state blue-sky securities laws and regulations:

Alabama
Securities Commission
166 Commerce Street
Montgomery, AL 36130
(205) 242-2984

Alaska
Banking, Securities and
 Corporations Division
Commerce & Economic
 Development Department
P.O. Box D
Juneau, AK 99811
(907) 465-2521

Arizona
Securities Division
Corporation Commission
1200 W. Washington
Phoenix, AZ 85007
(602) 542-4242

Arkansas
Securities Department
201 E. Marham Street
Little Rock, AR 72201
(501) 682-1011

California
Department of Corporations
1115 11th Street
Sacramento, CA 95814
(916) 445-8200

Colorado
Securities Division
Department of
  Regulatory Agencies
1560 Broadway
Denver, CO 80202
(303) 894-2320

Connecticut
Securities & Business
  Investments
Department of Banking
44 Capitol Avenue
Hartford, CT 06106
(203) 566-4560

Delaware
Department of State
Townsend Building
Dover, DE 19901
(302) 736-4111

District of Columbia
Department of
  Consumer &
  Regulatory Affairs
614 H Street, NW
Washington, DC 20001
(202) 727-7170

Florida
Securities Division
Department of Banking
  and Finance
The Capitol, LL22
Tallahassee, FL 32399
(904) 488-9805

Georgia
Secretary of State
2 Martin Luther King Jr. Drive
Atlanta, GA 30334
(404) 656-2894

Hawaii
Business Registration Division
Commerce & Consumer
  Affairs Department
1010 Richards Street
Honolulu, HI 96813
(808) 548-6521

Idaho
Department of Finance
700 W. State Street
Boise, ID 83720
(208) 334-3313

Illinois
Secretary of State
213 State House
Springfield, IL 62706
(217) 782-2201

Indiana
Securities Commission
1 N. Capitol
Indianapolis, IN 46204
(317) 232-6681

Iowa
Securities Division
Department of Commerce
Lucas State Office Building
Des Moines, IA 50319
(515) 281-4441

Kansas
Securities Commission
900 SW Jackson
Topeka, KS 66612
(913) 296-3307

Kentucky
Financial Institutions
 Department
Public Protection &
 Regulation Cabinet
911 Leawood Drive
Frankfort, KY 40601
(502) 564-3390

Louisiana
Department of the Treasury
P.O. Box 44154
Baton Rouge, LA 70804
(504) 342-0010

Maine
Bureau of Banking
Professional & Financial
 Regulations
State House
Augusta, ME 04333
(207) 289-3231

Maryland
Division of Securities
Office of the Attorney
 General
7 N. Calvert Street
Baltimore, MD 21202
(301) 576-6360

Massachusetts
Securities Division
Office of the Secretary
of the Commonwealth
1 Ashburton Place
Boston, MA 02133
(617) 727-7190

Michigan
Department of Commerce
6546 Mercantile Way
Lansing, MI 48909
(517) 334-6212

Minnesota
Registration and
 Analysis Division
Department of Commerce
5th Floor
Metro Square Building
St. Paul, MN 55101
(612) 296-6325

Mississippi
Securities Division
Office of the Secretary
 of State
401 Mississippi Street
Jackson, MS 39201
(601) 359-1350

Missouri
Division of Securities
Office of the Secretary
 of State
Truman Building
Jefferson City, MO 65102
(314) 751-4136

Montana
Securities Division
Office of the State Auditor
Capitol Station
Helena, MT 59620
(406) 444-2040

Nebraska
Department of
  Banking & Finance
301 Centennial Mall S.
Lincoln, NE 68509
(402) 471-2171

Nevada
Securities Division
Office of the
  Secretary of State
State Capitol
Carson City, NV 89710
(702) 885-5203

New Hampshire
Division of Securities
Department of Securities
169 Manchester Street
Concord, NH 03301
(603) 271-2261

New Jersey
Bureau of Securities
Department of
  Law & Public Safety
80 Mulberry Street, Room 308
Newark, NJ 07102
(201) 648-2040

New Mexico
Securities Division
Regulation & Licensing
  Department
Lew Wallace Building
Santa Fe, NM 87503
(505) 827-7750

North Carolina
Division of Securities
Office of the Secretary of State
300 N. Salisbury Street
Raleigh, NC 27603
(919) 733-3924

North Dakota
Securities Commissioner
State Capitol, 9th Floor
600 E. Boulevard
Bismarck, ND 58505
(701) 224-2910

Ohio
Division of Securities
Department of Commerce
2 Nationwide Plaza
3d Floor
Columbus, OH 43266
(614) 644-7381

Oklahoma
Securities Commission
2401 N. Lincoln Boulevard
Oklahoma City, OK 73152
(405) 521-2451

Oregon
Corporate Securities
Department of
  Insurance & Finance
Labor & Industries Building
Salem, OR 97310
(503) 378-4385

Pennsylvania
Securities Commission
333 Market Street
14th Floor
Harrisburg, PA 17120
(717) 787-6828

Rhode Island
Banking Division
Department of
  Business Regulation
100 N. Main Street
Providence, RI 02903
(401) 277-2405

South Carolina
Secretary of State
Wade Hampton Building
Columbia, SC 29211
(803) 734-2155

South Dakota
Division of Securities
Commerce & Regulations
  Department
910 E. Sioux Avenue
Pierre, SD 57501
(605) 773-3177

Tennessee
Securities Division
Department of
  Commerce & Insurance
614 Tennessee Building
Nashville, TN 37219
(615) 741-2947

Texas
Securities Board
Capitol Station
Austin, TX 78711
(512) 474-2233

Utah
Securities Division
Department of
  Business Regulation
160 East 300 South
Salt Lake City, UT 84145
(801) 530-6607

Vermont
Department of
  Banking & Insurance
120 State Street
Montpelier, VT 05602
(802) 828-3301

Virginia
State Corporation Commission
1220 Bank Street
13th Floor
Richmond, VA 23219
(804) 786-3603

Washington (state)
Securities Division
Department of
  Licensing
1300 Quince Street
Olympia, WA 98504
(206) 753-6928

West Virginia
Securities Division
Office of the
  State Auditor
State Capitol Complex
Charleston, WV 25305
(304) 348-2257

Wisconsin
Office of the
  Commissioner of Securities
111 W. Wilson Street
Madison, WI 53701
(608) 266-3433

Wyoming
Secretary of State
State Capitol
Cheyenne, WY 82002
(307) 777-7378

Addresses and phone numbers change frequently, so if your call or letter doesn't go through, try Directory Assistance for your state capitol.

CHAPTER TWELVE

Bankruptcy Law

KEY TERMS

automatic stay
Bankruptcy Code
bankruptcy court

bankruptcy estate
Chapter 7
Chapter 11
Chapter 13

classes of creditors
exemptions
reorganization plan

It is probably safe to say that every society throughout history has had to decide how to treat people who cannot repay their debts. More often than not, the treatment was harsh. A person might be executed or sold into slavery to pay their debts. In England, people who couldn't pay their debts were often thrown into debtors' prison, leaving their families with no means of support. By the time of the U.S. Revolutionary War, people began to think that perhaps the legal system should do more than just punish people—that bankruptcy should give people a way to start their lives over again. In the Constitution, the founding fathers gave Congress the power to establish nationwide bankruptcy laws. Congress passed the first federal bankruptcy legislation in 1800 and made major revisions in 1803, 1841, 1867, 1898, and 1978. The 1978 Bankruptcy Act, which is periodically amended and revised, established today's **Bankruptcy Code,** which governs the bankruptcy process.

The bankruptcy process starts in a United States **bankruptcy court.** There is at least one bankruptcy court district in every state. The case is begun as either a Chapter 7 case, a Chapter 11 case, or a Chapter 13 case. *Chapter* refers to chapters of the Bankruptcy Code. As the case progresses, there are circumstances under which a case begun under one chapter can be converted into a case under another chapter, but it is important to begin the case under the most appropriate chapter. **Chapter 7** is a liquidation chapter. A business files under Chapter 7 when it cannot pay off its debts and believes that the only thing to do is to sell off all the business's assets and give what it can to the creditors before going out of business. If there's not enough to pay off the debts, the creditors lose. The obvious price of a Chapter 7 case is that the business will have to close up shop. **Chapter 11** is a reorganization chapter. A business files under Chapter 11 when it is having trouble paying its debts and meeting current obligations, but believes that the problems are only temporary or that the problems can be worked out if the debts are restructured. The advantage of Chapter 11 is that the business gets to stay in business once the reorganization is complete. **Chapter 13** is also a reorganization chapter. It is primarily for individuals without a great deal of debt, but it is also open to sole proprietors, so it is briefly discussed in this chapter.

Alternatives to Bankruptcy

Bankruptcy is a haven of last resort. It's a way for people and businesses to get out from under insurmountable debts, but it's not a miracle cure. There are legal consequences, such as to your ability to get credit, that can last for years. Also, you may have heard that going through bankruptcy is not considered immoral or a black mark on one's character anymore. But don't believe everything you hear. There are still plenty of people who believe that honest citizens and honest businesses pay their debts, so bankruptcy can affect a person's and a business's reputation in the community. This may mean problems getting credit, trouble getting referral business, a reluctance by others to bring you into new business opportunities, and so forth. Thus, you may want to explore alternatives to declaring bankruptcy in order to get your personal and/or business debts under control. There are two major non-bankruptcy options:

○ *State law alternatives.* The most common alternative is called an assignment for the benefit of creditors. This means that creditors agree to release the debtor from any further financial obligations if the debtor turns over most or all of the debtor's assets to the creditors. Also, there are state corporate and partnership dissolution proceedings, which involve winding up a business entity's affairs, then dissolving it.

○ *Workouts.* A workout is a term for a private agreement between a creditor or a group of creditors and a debtor. A court of law is typically not involved. The debtor negotiates new payment terms with the creditors and signs agreements to make the deals legal. Workouts are very common with banks, since most banks would rather negotiate a new deal than pay legal fees in a bankruptcy case and/or declare the debt as a bad loan. For example, say a business has taken out a two-year loan from a bank. Business is bad, and the company cannot make the monthly loan payments. Rather than declare bankruptcy, the business may be able to negotiate a workout with the bank, such as restructuring the loan to stretch it out over three years at a lower interest rate. The new loan deal, with its lower monthly payments, may let the business stay out of bankruptcy and help the bank get its money back

Chapter 7 Bankruptcy

Practically any individual or business can file under Chapter 7, the liquidation chapter of the Bankruptcy Code. But there are some technical exceptions.

A Chapter 7 case is begun by filing a Chapter 7 bankruptcy petition. The petition triggers the protection of the Bankruptcy Code and invokes the jurisdiction of the bankruptcy court. In addition to the petition, the debtor files schedules that list its assets, debts, creditors, and so forth. When the petition is filed, there is an **automatic stay.** The automatic stay means that the debtor's creditors must immediately stop any debt collection activities and cannot do any of the following:

- Initiate, or threaten to initiate, legal proceedings outside of the bankruptcy process (such as by suing in state court) in order to collect debts.
- Send threatening letters or make threatening telephone calls to the debtor.
- Foreclose on the debtor's property. For example, a bank cannot foreclose on the debtor's house or a debtor business's real estate and other assets.
- Terminate utility services that they may currently be providing. For example, the telephone, gas, and electric companies cannot cut their service to the debtor.

After the case is begun, the court will appoint a trustee. The trustee supervises the debtor's assets, which are known as the **bankruptcy estate.** The bankruptcy estate, whether it is a person's or a business's, includes the debtor's 1) personal property, such as cash, stocks, bonds, machines, and appliances; 2) real estate, such as land, houses, buildings, and factories; and (3) intangible assets, which are things of value that don't exist in physical form, such as patents, trademarks, and copyrights. Creditors must file a proof of claim in order to establish their right to receive anything from the Chapter 7 liquidation. If a creditor does not file a proof of claim, the creditor may lose the right to recover any money.

Once all of the debts owed to creditors have been determined, the trustee sells off the debtor's property. This is called the liquidation of the bankruptcy estate. If the debtor who filed for bankruptcy is a person and not a corporation, partnership, or other business entity, then not all of the debtor's property is sold off. The Bankruptcy Code lets a person retain many different types of property so that he or she is not left totally destitute after bankruptcy and can make a fresh start in life. These provisions in the Bankruptcy Code are called **exemptions.** These exemptions include

- Up to $7,500 in residential property.
- One automobile, so long as it is not worth more than $1,200.
- Personal items, such as clothes, furniture, and appliances. Up to $4,000 worth of personal items may be exempted by the debtor, but each item must not be

worth more than $200.
- Up to $750 in implements, professional books, and tools of the debtor's trade.
- Certain insurance, pension, annuity, and IRA benefits.
- Social security benefits.
- Unemployment compensation benefits.
- Public assistance benefits.
- Veterans benefits.
- Disability benefits.
- Alimony and support benefits.
- Any right to receive compensation under wrongful death laws.
- Any right to receive benefits under a crime victim's reparation law.
- Any right to receive compensation for loss of future earnings.
- Miscellaneous special exemptions, such as for health aids and burial plots.

These exemptions can vary from state to state, however, because the Bankruptcy Code gives state legislatures the power to "opt out" of the Bankruptcy Code exemptions and enact their own list of exemptions.

If the debtor in a Chapter 7 case is a business entity, such as a corporation or partnership, the end result of the bankruptcy proceedings is dissolution of the business entity. The entity no longer exists. With an individual, such as a sole proprietor in business for himself or herself, there obviously can't be dissolution. You can't dissolve a person. Therefore, a debtor in a Chapter 7 case who is an individual gets a "discharge" for those debts left over after the bankruptcy estate has been used up in paying off creditors. A discharge means that the debtor is freed from all of his or her other debts. There are exceptions, however.

Sometimes an individual can't get a Chapter 7 discharge for certain debts. What does it mean if a Chapter 7 debt is nondischargeable? It means that creditors can recommence collections efforts after the bankruptcy case is over.

Potentially nondischargeable debts include

- Most types of tax debts, including income taxes, payroll taxes, property taxes, and tax penalties.
- Unpaid customs duties imposed on goods brought into the United States.
- Debts due to fraud or misrepresentation. For example, if a person gives a lender false financial statements in order to get credit.
- Consumer debts for luxury goods and services or cash advances.
- Unlisted and unscheduled debts. This means creditors that the debtor does not list in his or her bankruptcy paperwork with the court.
- Debts resulting from acts of embezzlement or larceny by the debtor. Also, debts resulting from certain wrongful acts committed by the debtor while acting as a fiduciary for another.
- Debts for alimony, support, or maintenance.
- Debts caused by willful and malicious injuries inflicted by the debtor on others.
- Fines, penalties, and forfeitures imposed on the debtor in other legal proceedings.
- Student loan obligations.

Once the Chapter 7 proceedings are over, a person cannot declare Chapter 7 bankruptcy again for six years.

Chapter 11 Bankruptcy

Chapter 11 is for business reorganizations. If a business has debts and obligation it cannot meet and must file for bankruptcy, but it does not want to go out of business as with Chapter 7 bankruptcy, then it will file for bankruptcy under Chapter 11 of the Bankruptcy Code. Chapter 11 enables a business to stay in business while it reorganizes its debts so that it will emerge from bankruptcy with manageable payments and obligations. There is an important alternative to Chapter 11 for people with unsecured debts of less than $100,000, secured debts of less than $350,000, and a steady income: It's called Chapter 13 and is summarized later.

Practically any business can file under Chapter 11. Some individuals may also qualify for Chapter 11, but Chapter 11 is primarily intended for businesses. A Chapter 11 case is begun by filing a Chapter 11 bankruptcy petition with the local bankruptcy court. Like a Chapter 7 case, the debtor must file schedules that list its assets, debts, creditors, and so forth. In addition, the debtor must file a list of its 20 biggest creditors, a disclosure statement, and a proposed plan of reorganization. There's more paperwork, because Chapter 11 is the most complicated chapter of the Bankruptcy Code.

When the Chapter 11 petition is filed, there is an automatic stay, just as with Chapter 7. The automatic stay means that the debtor's creditors must immediately stop any debt collection activities. Unlike Chapter 7, however, the court appoints a trustee only in unusual situations, such as when the court suspects the debtor of fraud. The people who ran the business before continue to run the business during the bankruptcy proceedings, although there are financial statements that have to be filed periodically with the court.

The heart of Chapter 11 proceedings is the **reorganization plan.** The reorganization plan starts as a lengthy proposal that the debtor must prepare and propose to the court and the creditors. The debtor categorizes its creditors into different **classes of creditors.** For example, there can be a class of unsecured creditors, a class of secured creditors, a class of shareholder creditors, and so forth. The proposed classes of creditors must be reasonable and fair. Then, the debtor says what it proposes to pay to each class.

Example:

Fred's business has gone into Chapter 11 bankruptcy. It owes money on several two-year loans to various banks, which are secured creditors. It also owes money to a number of suppliers, which are unsecured creditors. After going over its finances and determining what it can pay, Fred's business presents a reorganization plan. The plan has two proposed classes of creditors: the secured creditor banks and the unsecured creditor suppliers. Fred's business proposes to pay the banks two-thirds of the loans due and to pay that over three years instead of two. As for the suppliers, Fred's business proposes to pay them half of what the business owes them.

This is a very simple example, of course: Many Chapter 11 plans have very complicated reorganization proposals. What happens next to Fred's proposed reorganization plan, or any Chapter 11 reorganization plan? It goes to the creditors, which can accept it or reject it. There are complicated rules about the majority of creditors necessary to approve a reorganization plan. However, the court has certain powers, such as the ability to "cram down" a reorganization plan proposal with respect to a class of creditors, to help get a plan through the bankruptcy process. The reorganization plan may undergo many changes in order to satisfy the creditors and the court.

Typically, the Chapter 11 process is over when the court confirms a final reorganization plan. The debtor leaves the bankruptcy process with only those debts contained in the reorganization plan, subject to some exceptions. All the debtor's other debts are discharged. As with Chapter 7 bankruptcies, a business cannot declare Chapter 11 bankruptcy more than once every six years.

Chapter 13 Bankruptcy

Chapter 11 is a valuable reorganization mechanism for businesses in financial trouble, but it is complicated and potentially lengthy. For individuals and sole proprietors, there is a potential alternative: Chapter 13. Debtors other than individuals and sole proprietors generally can't use Chapter 13. In order to qualify for Chapter 13 bankruptcy, the debtor must have

- Less than $100,000 in unsecured debts
- Less than $350,000 in secured debts
- A steady income

The bankruptcy process under Chapter 13 is quicker, less complicated, and generally less expensive than Chapter 11. Chapter 13 permits a debtor with steady income to dedicate a portion of that income to paying off creditors over the next several years. Like Chapter 11, the Chapter 13 debtor must prepare and file a repayment plan, which is subject to review by the creditors and the court. If the plan is confirmed by the court, and the debtor makes all the payments required by the plan over the next several years, then the debtor gets a discharge from those pre-bankruptcy debts that the plan did not require to be repaid.

APPENDIX ONE

EEOC FACT SHEETS

Facts About Pregnancy Discrimination

The Pregnancy Discrimination Act is an amendment to Title VII of the Civil Rights Act of 1964. Discrimination on the basis of pregnancy, childbirth or related medical conditions constitutes unlawful sex discrimination under Title VII. Women affected by pregnancy or related conditions must be treated in the same manner as other applicants or employees with similar abilities or limitations.

Hiring

An employer cannot refuse to hire a woman because of her pregnancy related condition as long as she is able to perform the major functions of her job. An employer cannot refuse to hire her because of its prejudices against pregnant workers or the prejudices of co-workers, clients or customers.

Pregnancy and Maternity Leave

An employer may not single out pregnancy related conditions for special procedures to determine an employee's ability to work. For example, if an employer requires its employees to submit to a doctor's statement concerning their inability to work before granting leave or paying sick benefits, the employer may require employees affected by pregnancy related conditions to submit such statements.

If an employee is temporarily unable to perform her job due to pregnancy, the employer must treat her the same as any other temporarily disabled employee; for example, by providing modified tasks, alternative assignments, disability leave or leave without pay.

Pregnant employees must be permitted to work as long as they are able to perform their jobs. If an employee has been absent from work as a result of a pregnancy related condition and recovers, her employer may not require her to remain on leave until the baby's birth. An employer may not have a rule which prohibits an employee from returning to work for a predetermined length of time after childbirth.

Employers must hold open a job for a pregnancy related absence the same length of time jobs are held open for employees on sick or disability leave.

Health Insurance

Any health insurance provided by an employer must cover expenses for pregnancy related conditions on the same basis as costs for other medical conditions. Health insurance for expenses arising from abortion is not required, except where the life of the mother is endangered.

Pregnancy related expenses should be reimbursed exactly as those incurred for other medical conditions, whether payment is on a fixed basis or a percentage of reasonable and customary charge basis.

The amounts payable by the insurance provider can be limited only to the same extent as costs for other conditions. No additional, increased or larger deductible can be imposed.

If a health insurance plan excludes benefit payments for pre-existing conditions when the insured's coverage becomes effective, benefits can be denied for medical costs arising from an existing pregnancy.

Employers must provide the same level of health benefits for spouses of male employees as they do for spouses of female employees.

Fringe Benefits

Pregnancy related benefits cannot be limited to married employees. In an all-female workforce or job classification, benefits must be provided for pregnancy related conditions if benefits are provided for other medical conditions.

If an employer provides any benefits to workers on leave, the employer must provide the same benefits for those on leave for pregnancy related conditions.

Employees with pregnancy related disabilities must be treated the same as other temporarily disabled employees for accrual and crediting of seniority, vacation calculation, pay increases and temporary disability benefits.

Filing a Charge

The U.S. Equal Employment Opportunity Commission has issued guidelines, including questions and answers, interpreting the Pregnancy Discrimination Act (29 cfr 1604.10).

Charges of pregnancy discrimination may be filed at any field office of the U.S. Equal Employment Opportunity Commission. Field offices are located in 50 cities throughout the United States and are listed in most local telephone directories under U.S. Government. Information on all EEOC-enforced laws may be obtained by calling toll free on 800-669 EEOC. EEOC's toll free TDD number is 800-800-3302.

November 1992   EEOC-FS/E2

Facts About National Origin Discrimination

Title VII of the Civil Rights Act of 1964 protects individuals against employment discrimination of the basis of national origin as well as race, color, religion and sex.

It is unlawful to discriminate against any employee or applicant because of the individual's national origin. No one can be denied equal employment opportunity because of birthplace, ancestry, culture, or linguistic characteristics common to a specific ethnic group. Equal employment opportunity cannot be denied because of marriage or association with persons of a national origin group; membership or association with specific ethnic promotion groups; attendance or participation in schools, churches, temples or mosques generally associated with a national origin group; or a surname associated with a national origin group.

Special English-Only Rule

A rule requiring employees to speak only English at all times on the job may violate Title VII, unless an employer shows it is necessary for conducting business. If an employer believes the English-only rule is critical for business purposes, employees have to be told when they must speak English and the consequences for violating the rule. Any negative employment decision based on breaking the English-only rule will be considered evidence of discrimination if the employer did *not* tell employees of the rule.

Accent

An employer must show a legitimate nondiscriminatory reason for the denial of employment opportunity because of an individual's accent or manner of speaking. Investigations will focus on the qualifications of the person and whether his or her accent or manner of speaking had a detrimental effect on job performance. Requiring employees or applicants to be fluent in English may violate Title VII if the rule is adopted to exclude individuals of a particular national origin and is not related to job performance.

Harassment

Harassment on the basis of national origin is a violation of Title VII. An ethnic slur or other verbal or physical conduct because of an individual's nationality constitute harassment if they create an intimidating, hostile or offensive working environment, unreasonably interfere with work performance or negatively affect an individual's employment opportunities.

Employers have a responsibility to maintain a workplace free of national origin harassment. Employers may be responsible for any on-the-job harassment by their agents and supervisory employees, regardless of whether the acts were authorized or specifically forbidden by the employer. Under certain circumstances, an employer may be responsible for the acts of non-employees who harass their employees at work.

Immigration-Related Practices Which May Be Discriminatory

The Immigration Reform and Control Act of 1986 (IRCA) requires employers to prove all employees hired after November 6, 1986, are legally authorized to work in the United States. IRCA also prohibits discrimination based on national origin or citizenship. An employer who singles out individuals of a particular national origin or individuals who appear to be foreign to provide employment verification may have violated both IRCA and Title VII. Employers who impose citizenship requirements or give preference to U.S. citizens in hiring or employment opportunities may have violated IRCA, unless these are legal or contractual requirements for particular jobs. Employers also may have violated Title VII if a requirement or preference has the purpose or effect of discriminating against individuals of a particular national origin.

Filing a Charge

If you have been discriminated against on the basis of national origin, you are entitled to a remedy that will place you in the position you would have been in if the discrimination had never occurred. You may be entitled to hiring, promotion, reinstatement, back pay or other remuneration. You may also be entitled to damages to compensate you for future pecuniary losses, mental anguish and inconvenience. Punitive damages may be available as well, if an employer acted with malice or reckless indifference. You may also be entitled to attorney's fees.

Charges of national origin discrimination may be filed at any field office of the U.S. Equal Employment Opportunity Commission. Field offices are located in 50 cities throughout the United States and are listed in most local telephone directories under U.S. Government. Information on all EEOC-enforced laws may be obtained by calling toll free on 800-669-EEOC. EEOC's toll free TDD number is 800-800-3302. This fact sheet is also available in alternate formats, upon request.

For more information about employment rights and responsibilities under the Immigration Reform and Control Act, you may call the Office of Special Counsel for Immigration-Related Unfair Employment Practices on 1-800-255-7688.

January 1994   EEOC-FS/E-1

Facts About Disability-Related Tax Provisions

The Internal Revenue Code has three disability-related provisions of particular interest to business as well as people with disabilities.

Disabled Access Tax Credit
(Title 26, Internal Revenue Code, Section 44)

This new tax credit is available to "eligible small businesses" in the amount of 50 percent of "eligible access expenditures" that exceed $250 but do not exceed $10,250 for a taxable year. A business may take the credit each year that it makes an eligible access expenditure.

Eligible small businesses are those businesses with either:

- $1 million or less in gross receipts for the preceding tax year; or
- 30 or fewer full-time employees during the preceding tax year.

Eligible access expenditures are amounts paid or incurred by an eligible small business for the purpose of enabling the business to comply with the applicable requirements of the Americans with Disabilities Act (ADA). These include amounts paid or incurred to:

- remove architectural, communication, physical, or transportation barriers that prevent a business from being accessible to or usable by individuals with disabilities;
- provide qualified readers, taped texts, and other effective methods of making materials accessible to people with visual impairments;
- provide qualified interpreters or other effective methods of making orally delivered materials available to individuals with hearing impairments;
- acquire or modify equipment or devices for individuals with disabilities; or
- provide other similar services, modifications, materials or equipment.

Expenditures that are not necessary to accomplish the above purposes are not eligible. Expenses in connection with new construction are not eligible. "Disability" has the same meaning as it does in the ADA. To be eligible for the tax credit, barrier removals or the provision of services, modifications, materials or equipment must meet technical standards of the ADA Accessibility Guidelines where applicable. These standards are incorporated in Department of Justice regulations implementing Title III of the ADA (28 CFR Part 36; 56 CFR 35544, July 26, 1991).

Example: Company A purchases equipment to meet its reasonable accommodation obligation under the ADA for $8,000. The amount by which $8,000 exceeds $250 is $7,750. Fifty percent of $7.750 is $3,875. Company A may take a tax credit in the amount of $3,785 on its next tax return.

Example: Company B removes a physical barrier in accordance with its reasonable accommodation obligation under the ADA. The barrier removal meets the ADA Accessibility Guidelines. The company spends $12,000 on this modification. The amount by which $12,000 exceeds $250 but not $10,250 is $10,000. Fifty percent of $10,000 is $5,000. Company B is eligible for a $5,000 tax credit on its next tax return.

Tax Deduction to Remove Architectural and Transportation Barriers to People with Disabilities and Elderly Individuals
(Title 26, Internal Revenue Code, section 190)

The IRS allows a deduction up to $15,000 per year for "qualified architectural and transportation barrier removal expenses." Expenditures to make a facility or public transportation vehicle owned or leased in connection with a trade or business more accessible to, and usable by, individuals who are handicapped or elderly are eligible for the deduction. The definition of a "handicapped individual" is similar to the ADA definition of an "individual with a disability." To be eligible for this deduction, modifications must meet the requirements of standards established by IRS regulations implementing section 190.

Targeted Jobs Tax Credit
(Title 26, Internal Revenue Code, section 51)

Employers are eligible to receive a tax credit up to 40 percent of the first $6,000 of first-year wages of a new employee with a disability who is referred by state or local vocational rehabilitation agencies, a State Commission on the Blind, or the U.S. Department of Veterans Affairs, and certified by a State Employment Service. There is no credit after the first year of employment. For an employer to qualify for the credit, a worker must have been employed for at least 90 days or have completed at least 120 hours of work for the employer. The Tax Extension Act of 1991, Public Law 102-227, extended this tax credit through [1994].

IRS Publication No. 907, providing information on these provisions, may be obtained by calling 1-800-829-3676. For further information, contact the Internal Revenue Service, Office of the Chief Counsel, P.O. Box 7604, Ben Franklin Station, Washington, DC 20044, (202) 566-3292 (voice only).   January 1992 EEOC-FS/E6

Questions and Answers About Sexual Harassment

Identifying Sexual Harassment

What is sexual harassment?
Sexual harassment is a form of sex discrimination which is a violation of Title VII of the Civil Rights Act of 1964. The EEOC's guidelines define two types of sexual harassment: "quid pro quo" and "hostile environment."

What is "quid pro quo" sexual harassment?
Unwelcome sexual advances, requests for sexual favors, and other verbal or physical conduct of a sexual nature constitute "quid pro quo" sexual harassment when (1) submission to such conduct is made either explicitly or implicitly a term or condition of an individual's employment, or (2) submission to or rejection of such conduct by an individual is used as the basis for employment decisions affecting such individual.

What is "hostile environment" sexual harassment?
Unwelcome sexual advances, requests for sexual favors, and other verbal or physical conduct of a sexual nature constitute "hostile environment" sexual harassment when such conduct has the purpose or effect of unreasonably interfering with an individual's work performance or creating an intimidating, hostile or offensive working environment.

What factors determine whether an environment is "hostile?"
The central inquiry is whether the conduct "unreasonable interfered with an individual's work performance" or created "an intimidating, hostile, or offensive working environment." The EEOC will look at the following factors to determine whether an environment is hostile: (1) whether the conduct was verbal or physical or both; (2) how frequently it was repeated; (3) whether the conduct was hostile or patently offensive; (4) whether the alleged harasser was a co-worker or supervisor; (5) whether others joined in perpetrating the harassment; and (6) whether the harassment was directed at more than one individual. No one factor controls; rather, an assessment is made based upon the totality of the circumstances.

What is unwelcome sexual conduct?
Sexual conduct becomes unlawful only when it is unwelcome. The challenged conduct must be unwelcome in the sense that the employee did not solicit or incite it, and in the sense that the employee regarded the conduct as undesirable or offensive.

How will the EEOC determine whether conduct is unwelcome?
When confronted with conflicting evidence as to whether conduct was welcome,

the EEOC will look at the record as a whole and at the totality of the circumstances, evaluating each situation on a case-by-case basis. The investigation should determine whether the victim's conduct was consistent, or inconsistent, with his/her assertion that the sexual conduct was unwelcome.

Who can be a victim of sexual harassment?
The victim may be a woman or a man. The victim does not have to be of the opposite sex. The victim does not have to be the person harassed but could be anyone affected by the offensive conduct.

Who can be a sexual harasser?
The harasser may be a woman or a man. He or she can be the victim's supervisor, an agent of the employer, a supervisor in another area, a co-worker or a non-employee.

Can one incident constitute sexual harassment?
It depends. In "quid pro quo" cases, a single sexual advance may constitute harassment if it is linked to the granting or denial of employment or employment benefits. In contrast, unless the conduct is quite severe, a single incident or isolated incidents of offensive sexual conduct or remarks generally do not create a "hostile environment." A hostile environment claim usually requires a showing of a pattern of offensive conduct. However, a single, unusually severe incident of harassment may be sufficient to constitute a Title VII violation; the more severe the harassment, the less need to show a repetitive seies of incidents. This is particularly true when the harassment is physical. For example, the EEOC will presume that the unwelcome, intentional touching of the charging party's intimate body areas is sufficiently offensive to alter the condition of his/her working environment and constitute a violation of Title VII.

Can verbal remarks constitute sexual harassment?
Yes. The EEOC will evaluate the totality of the circumstances to ascertain the nature, frequency, context, and intended target of the remarks. Relevant factors may include; (1) whether the remarks were hostile and derogatory; (2) whether the alleged harasser singled out the charging party; (3) whether the charging party participated in the exchange; and (4) the relationship between the charging party and the alleged harasser.

What should a sexual harassment victim do?
The victim should directly inform the harasser that the conduct is unwelcome and must stop. It is important for the victim to communicate that the conduct is unwelcome, particularly when the alleged harasser may have some reason to believe that the advance may be welcomed. However, a victim of harassment need not always confront his/her harasser directly, so long as his/her conduct demonstrates that the harasser's behavior is unwelcome.

The victim should also use any employer complaint mechanism or grievance system available. If these methods are ineffective, the victim ehould contact the EEOC as soon as possible (see Filing a Charge, below).

Preventing Sexual Harassment

What specific steps can an employer take to prevent sexual harassment?
Prevention is the best tool to eliminate sexual harassment in the workplace. Employers are encouraged to take all steps necessary to prevent sexual harassment from occurring. An effective preventive program should include an explicit policy against sexual harassment that is clearly and regularly communicated to employees and effectively implemented. The employer should affirmatively raise the subject with all supervisory and non-supervisory employees, express strong disapproval, and explain the sanctions for harassment.

Should an employer have a grievance procedure?
The employer should have a procedure for resolving sexual harassment complaints. The procedure should be designed to encourage victims of harassment to come forward and should not require a victim to complain first to the offending supervisor. They can do so by establishing an effective complaint or grievance process and taking immediate and appropriate action when an employee complains. It should ensure confidentiality as much as possible and provide effective remedies, including protection of victims and witnesses against retaliation.

What if an employer asserts that it has eliminated the harassment?
When an employer asserts it has taken remedial action, the EEOC will investigate to determine whether the action was prompt, appropriate and effective. If the EEOC determines that the harassment has been eliminated, the victims made whole, and preventive measures instituted, the Commission normally will administratively close the charge because of the employers' prompt remedial action.

Filing a Charge

How do I file a charge of discrimination?
Charges of sex discrimination may be filed at any field office of the U.S. Equal Employment Opportunity Commission. Field Offices are located in 50 cities throughout the United States and are listed in most local telephone directories under U.S. Government. To reach the nearest EEOC field office, dial toll free on 800-669-4000. More information on sexual harassment and information on all EEOC-enforced laws may be be obtained by calling toll free on 800-669-EEOC. EEOC's toll free TDD number is 800-800-3302.

What are the time limits for filing a charge of discrimination?
A charge of discrimination on the basis of sex must be filed with EEOC within 180 days of the alleged discriminatory act, or within 300 days, if there is a state or local fair employment practices agency that enforces a law prohibiting the same alleged discriminatory practice. However, to protect legal rights, it is recommended that EEOC be contacted promptly when discrimination is believed to have occurred.

What types of evidence will the EEOC look at to determine whether sexual harassment has occurred?
When investigating allegations of sexual harassment, EEOC will look at the whole record: the circumstances, such as the nature of the sexual advances, and the context in which the alleged incidents occurred. The EEOC recognizes that sexual conduct may be private and unacknowledged, with no eyewitnesses. Corroborative evidence of any nature will be explored.

If I file a discrimination charge, what types of relief are available?
If you have been discriminated against on the basis of sex, you are entitled to a remedy that will place you in the position you would have been in if the discrimination had never occurred. You may also be entitled to hiring, promotion, reinstatement, back pay and other remuneration. You may also be entitled to damages to compensate you for future pecuniary losses, mental anguish and inconvenience. Punitive damages may be available, as well, if an employer acted with malice or reckless indifference. You may also be entitled to attorney's fees.

Can my employer retaliate against me for filing a charge with EEOC?
It is unlawful for an employer or other covered entity to retaliate against someone who files a charge of discrimination, participates in an investigation, or opposed discriminatory practices. Individuals who believe that they have been retaliated against should contact EEOC immediately. Even if an individual has already filed a charge of discrimination, he or she can file a new charge based on retaliation.

What laws does EEOC enforce?"
EEOC enforces Title VII of the Civil Rights Act of 1964, which prohibits employment descrimination based on race, color, religion, sex or national origin; the Age Discrimination in Employment Act; the Equal Pay Act; prohibitions against discrimination affecting individuals with disabilities in the federal government; sections of the Civil Rights Act of 1991; and Title I of the Americans with Disabilities Act, which prohibits discrimination against people with disabilities in the private sector and state and local governments.

THE ABOVE INFORMATION IS INTENDED AS A GENERAL OVERVIEW OF SEXUAL HARASSMENT AND DOES NOT CARRY THE FORCE OF LEGAL OPINION.　　　　December 1992

Sexual Harassment Resources

The U.S. Equal Employment Opportunity Commission (EEOC) Library has compiled this selective list of materials on the topic of sexual harassment for the convenience of business people, their employees, and the general public who wish to familiarize themselves with this issue. The EEOC in no way endorses any of the commercially available videos or books as being official EEOC guidance. A list of sources for the purchase of the books and videos is included. Members of the public can also inquire at their local libraries and bookstores about the availability of these and other materials on sexual harassment.

EEOC Publications

Facts about sexual harassment. A two page overview which briefly defines sexual harassment and gives examples of the circumstances under which it can occur. Tells how to file a charge with the EEOC.

Guidelines on discrimination because of sex. Located in Title 29 of the *Code of Federal Regulations* at part 1604. Part 1604.11 deals specifically with sexual harassment.

Policy guidance on current issues of sexual harassment. EEOC Notice N-915-050, 3/19/90 "...provides guidance on defining sexual harassment and establishing employer liability in light of recent cases." Although written as guidance for EEOC Field Office and Headquarters personnel, this material is also useful for attorneys or other legal staff who are interested in EEOC's official position on the issue of sexual harassment.

Questions and answers about sexual harassment. An informative two-page leaflet giving EEOC's answers to the most commonly asked questions about sexual harassment.

Videos

Costly proposition: sexual harassment at work. BNA Communications Inc., 1986. 31 minutes. Explores the major issues of sexual harassment: hostile work environment, quid pro quo harassment, third party harassment, non-participants' harassment, "gray" areas. Aimed at managers, supervisors, and employees. If the video is viewed by a group, a discussion leader must be present to explain the concepts which are presented using vignettes of workplace scenes.

Handling the sexual harassment complaint (for managers and supervisors). American Media Incorporated, 1990. 15 minutes. Trains managers and supervisors to respond correctly and legally to sexual harassment complaints. Offers specific procedures to follow when receiving, investigating, and taking action on a sexual harassment complaint. Companion to "Sexual Harassment in the Workplace: Identify, Stop, Prevent" video.

Intent vs. impact: recognizing, preventing and resolving sexual harassment. BNA Communications Inc., 1986. Two-tape series. 68 minutes. Shows managers, supervisors, and employees how to recognize the differences between friendly behavior and subtle sexual harassment. Explains the laws and policies that govern sexual harassment and how to resolve such incidents within an organization.

Making advances: what organizations must do about sexual harassment. Coronet/MTI Film & Video, 1988. 30 minutes. Teaches a workable system for recognition, response, and prevention. Trains everyone from top management to line supervisors in how to establish and maintain a harassment-free work environment. Includes interviews with top EEOC officials.

Preventing sexual harassment. BNA Communications, Inc., 1992. 66 minutes. This two-part program, one for managers and the other for employees, is designed to show how to identify and prevent sexual harassment in the workplace. Realistic vignettes depicting workplace and courtroom scenes highlight problems and solutions.

Sexual harassment in the workplace: identify, stop, prevent. American Media Incorporated, 1990. 20 minutes. Designed to be shown to all employees. Explains what sexual harassment is, how to stop it, and how to prevent it. Promotes the concept that sexual harassment of any type is a form of discrimination and does not have to be tolerated by either management or employees. Companion to "Handling the Sexual Harassment Complaint" video.

Sexual harassment: shades of gray. Pacific Resource Development Group, 1989. Five-tape series. 57 minutes. Presented by Susan L. Webb. Segments include: "What are we doing here?" (introductory material); "What is sexual harassment?"; "Why should I worry about it?"; "What does the law say?"; "What am I supposed to do?" Trains all levels of employees in a lecture-style format.

Stopping sexual harassment in the federal workplace. FPMI Communications Inc. A two-tape series which includes 1) "Sexual harassment: not government approved", and 2) "Preventing sexual harassment: some practical answers."

Books

Corporate affairs: nepotism, office romance, & sexual harassment; a BNA special report. Bureau of National Affairs, 1988. Good coverage of case law on sexual harassment (and the other topics mentioned in the title), but only through 1987. Sample company policies are useful, but the bulk of the material will be useful only to attorneys or other human resources staff.

Corporate attractions: an inside account of sexual harassment with the new sexual rules for men and women on the job, by Kathleen Neville. Acropolis Books Ltd., 1990. The major portion of the book is devoted to a retelling of the author's personal experience as a victim of sexual harassment. She also offers advice on how to file a complaint and provides information on EEOC procedures and policies.

Federal manager's guide to preventing sexual harassment, by Dennis K. Reischl and Ralph R. Smith. FPMI Communications, Inc., 1989. Aimed at federal government managers, but useful in the private sector as well. Defines sexual harassment and discusses specific case situations. Tells how to recognize sexual harassment and how to deal with it.

Sexual harassment and the federal employee, by Dennis K. Reischl and Ralph R. Smith. FPMI Communications, Inc., 1990. Easy to read and understand, this 31 page booklet presents basic information about sexual harassment: what it is, how to recognize it, and what to do if you are a victim.

Sexual harassment in employment law, by Barbara Lindemann and David D. Kadue. Bureau of National Affairs, 1991. This recent treatise on sexual harassment law is a major source of information about leading court cases in this subject area. All subjects receive detailed treatment, making this volume the most comprehensive work on sexual harassment law yet published.

Sexual harassment in the federal government: an update. U.S. Merit Systems Protection Board, 1988 (Sold by the U.S. Government Printing Office). Updates a Merit Systems Protection Board study conducted in 1980 in order to determine what changes, if any, had occurred in the federal government relating to incidents of sexual harassment. In 1987, 42% of all women and 14% of all men working for the federal government reported experiencing some form of sexual harassment.

Sexual harassment in the workplace. by Ralph H. Baxter Jr. Executive Enterprises Publications Co. Inc, 1989. Third edition. For managers and supervisors. Offers a comprehensive overview of all major issues in sexual harassment claims.

Sexual harassment on the job. by William Petrocelli and Barbara K. Rapa. Nolo Press, 1992. Nolo Press publications are written for the layperson. This volume describes what sexual harassment is and gives specific strategies to end it, including confronting the harasser, using a company complaint procedure, filing a state or federal sexual harassment claim, and bringing a lawsuit. It also offers guidance to employers who want to create a policy against sexual harassment and procedures for handling complaints.

Step forward: sexual harassment in the workplace, what you need to know, by Susan L. Webb. MasterMedia, 1991. The author, a well-known lecturer and advocate in this field, gives a history of sexual harassment as well as information for both employees and managers in dealing with sexual harassment. The chapter which outlines six, simple steps to stop sexual harassment is very useful.

Sources

Acropolis Books Ltd.
2400 17th St., N.W.
Washington, DC 20009-9964
1-800-451-7771

American Media Incorporated
1454 30th St.
West Des Moines, IA 50265-1390
1-800-262-2557

BNA Communications Inc.
9439 Key West Ave.
Rockville, MD 20850
1-800-233-6067

Bureau of National Affairs
Customer Service Center
9435 Key West Ave.
Rockville, MD 20850
1-800-372-1033

Coronet/MTI Film & Video
Simon & Schuster Supplementary Education Group
108 Wilmot Road
Deerfield, IL 60015
1-800-621-2131

Executive Enterprises Publications Co. Inc.
22 W. 21st St.
New York, NY 10010-6904
1-800-332-1105

FPMI Communications, Inc.
3322 So. Memorial Parkway, Suite 40
Huntsville, AL 35801
205-882-3042

MasterMedia Ltd.
16 E. 72nd, Suite 200
New York, NY 10021
1 800-334-8232

Nolo Press
950 Parker St.
Berkeley, CA 94710
1-800-992-6656

Pacific Resource Development Group
4044 NE 58th
Seattle, WA 98105
206-782-7015

U.S. Equal Employment Opportunity Commission
1801 L St. N.W.
Washington, DC 20507
1-800-669-3362 (Voice)
1-800-800-3302 (TDD)

U.S. Government Printing Office
Superintendent of Documents
Washington, DC 20402
202-783-3238

This publication is available in alternate formats, upon request. To obtain alternate formats, call EEOC's toll free number: 1-800-669-3362 (Voice) or 1-800-800-3302 (TDD)

APPENDIX TWO

THE AMERICANS WITH DISABILITIES ACT: QUESTIONS AND ANSWERS

Employment

What employers are covered by Title I of the ADA, and when is the coverage effective?

The Title I employment provisions apply to private employers, state and local governments, employment agencies, and labor unions. Employers with 25 or more employees were covered as of July 26, 1992. Employers with 15 or more employees were covered two years later, as of July 26, 1994.

What practices and activities are covered by the employment nondiscrimination requirements?

The ADA prohibits discrimination in all employment practices, including job application procedures, hiring, firing, advancement, compensation, training, and other terms, conditions, and privileges of employment. It applies to recruitment, advertising, tenure, layoff, leave, fringe benefits, and all other employment-related activities.

Who is protected from employment discrimination?

Employment discrimination is prohibited against "qualified individuals with disabilities." This includes applicants for employment and employees. An individual is considered to have a "disability" if he or she has a physical or mental impairment that substantially limits one or more major life activities, has a record of such an impairment, or is regarded as having such an impairment. Persons discriminated against because they have a known association or relationship with an individual with a disability also are protected.

The first part of the definition makes clear that the ADA applies to persons who have impairments and that these must substantially limit major life activities such as seeing, hearing, speaking, walking, breathing, performing manual tasks, learning, caring for oneself, and working. An individual with epilepsy, paralysis, HIV infection, AIDS, a substantial hearing or visual impairment, mental retardation, or a specific learning disability is covered, but an individual with a minor, nonchronic condition of short duration, such as a sprain, broken limb, or the flu, generally would not be covered.

The second part of the definition protecting individuals with a record of a disability would cover, for example, a person who has recovered from cancer or mental illness.

The third part of the definition protects individuals who are regarded as having a substantially limiting impairment, even though they may not have such an impairment. For example, this provision would protect a qualified individual with a severe facial disfigurement from being denied employment because an employer feared the "negative reactions" of customers or co-workers.

Who is a "qualified individual with a disability"?

A qualified individual with a disability is a person who meets legitimate skill, experience, education, or other requirements of an employment position that he or she holds or seeks, and who can perform the "essential functions" of the position with or without reasonable accommodation. Requiring the ability to perform "essential functions" assures that an individual with a disability will not be considered unqualified simply because of inability to perform marginal or incidental job functions. If the individual is qualified to perform essential job functions except for limitations caused by a disability, the employer must consider whether the individual could perform these functions with a reasonable accommodation. If a written job description has been prepared in advance of advertising or interviewing applicants for a job, this will be considered as evidence of the essential functions of the job.

Does an employer have to give preference to a qualified applicant with a disability over other applicants?

No. An employer is free to select the most qualified applicant available and to make decisions based on reasons unrelated to a disability. For example, suppose two persons apply for a job as a typist and an essential function of the job is to type 75 words per minute accurately. One applicant, an individual with a disability, who is provided with a reasonable accommodation for a typing test, types 50 words per minute; the other applicant who has no disability accurately types 75 words per minute. The employer can hire the applicant with the higher typing speed, if typing speed is needed for successful performance of the job.

What limitations does the ADA impose on medical examinations and inquiries about disability?

An employer may not ask or require a job applicant to take a medical examination before making a job offer. It cannot make any pre-employment inquiry about a disability or the nature or severity of a disability. An employer may however, ask questions about the ability to perform specific job functions and may, with certain limitations, ask an individual with a disability to describe or demonstrate how he or she would perform these functions.

An employer may condition a job offer on the satisfactory result of a post-offer medical examination or medical inquiry if this is required of all entering employees in the same job category. A post-offer examination or inquiry does not have to be job-related and consistent with business necessity.

However, if an individual is not hired because a post-offer medical examination or inquiry reveals a disability, the reason(s) for not hiring must be job-related and consistent with business necessity. The employer also must show that no reasonable accommodation was available that would enable the individual to perform the essential job functions, or that accommodation world impose an undue hardship. A post-offer medical examination may disqualify an individual if the employer can demonstrate that the individual would pose a "direct threat" in the workplace (i.e., a significant risk of substantial harm to the health or safety of the individual or others) that cannot be eliminated or reduced below the "direct threat" level through reasonable accommodation. Such a disqualification is job-related and consistent with business necessity. A post-offer medical examination may not disqualify an individual with a disability who is currently able to perform essential job functions because of speculation that the disability may cause a risk of future injury.

After a person starts work, a medical examination or inquiry of an employee must be job-related and consistent with business necessity. Employers may conduct employee medical examinations where there is evidence of a job performance or safety problem, examinations required by other federal laws, examinations to determine current "fitness" to perform a particular job, and voluntary examinations that are part of employee health programs.

Information from all medical examinations and inquiries must be kept apart from general personnel files as a separate, confidential medical record, available only under limited conditions.

Tests for illegal use of drugs are not medical examinations under the ADA and are not subject to the restrictions of such examinations.

When can an employer ask an applicant to "self-identify" as having a disability?

Federal contractors and subcontractors who are covered by the affirmative action requirements of Section 503 of the Rehabilitation Act of 1973 may invite individuals with disabilities to identify themselves on a job application form or by other pre-employment inquiry, to satisfy the Section 503 affirmative action requirements. Employers who request such information must observe Section 503 requirements regarding the manner in which such information is requested and used, and the procedures for maintaining such information as a separate, confidential record, apart from regular personnel records.

A pre-employment inquiry about a disability is allowed if required by another federal law or regulation such as those applicable to disabled veterans and veterans of the Vietnam era. Pre-employment inquiries about disabilities may be necessary under such laws to identify applicants or clients with disabilities in order to provide them with required special services.

Does the ADA require employers to develop written job descriptions?

No. The ADA does not require employers to develop or maintain job descriptions. However, a written job description that is prepared before advertising or interviewing applicants for a job will be considered as evidence along with other relevant factors. If an employer uses job descriptions, they should be reviewed to make sure they accurately reflect the actual functions of a job. A job description will be most helpful if it focuses on the results or outcome of a job function, not solely on the way it customarily is performed. A reasonable accommodation may enable a person with a disability to accomplish a job function in a manner that is different from the way an employee who is not disabled may accomplish the same function.

What is "reasonable accommodation"?

Reasonable accommodation is any modification or adjustment to a job or the work environment that will enable a qualified applicant or employee with a disability to participate in the application process or to perform essential job functions. Reasonable accommodation also includes adjustments to assure that a qualified individual with a disability has rights and privileges in employment equal to those of employees without disabilities.

What are some of the accommodations applicants and employees may need?

Examples of reasonable accommodation include making existing facilities used by employees readily accessible to and usable by an individual with a disability; restructuring a job; modifying work schedules; acquiring or modifying equipment; providing qualified readers or interpreters, or appropriately modifying examinations, training, or other programs. Reasonable accommodation also may include reassigning a current employee to a vacant position for which the individual is qualified, if the person is unable to do the original job because of a disability even with an accommodation. However, there is no obligation to find a position for an applicant who is not qualified for the position sought. Employers are not required to lower quality or quantity standards as an accommodation; nor are they obligated to provide personal use items such as glasses or hearing aids.

The decision as to the appropriate accommodation must be based on the particular facts of each case. In selecting the particular type of reasonable accommodation to provide, the principal test is that of effectiveness, i.e., whether the accommodation will provide an opportunity for a person with a disability to achieve the same level of performance and to enjoy benefits equal to those of an average, similarly situated person without a disability. However, the accommodation does not have to ensure equal results or provide exactly the same benefits.

When is an employer required to make a reasonable accommodation?

An employer is only required to accommodate a "known" disability of a qualified applicant or employee. The requirement generally will be triggered by a request from an individual with a disability, who frequently will be able to suggest an appropriate accommodation. Accommodations must be made on an individual basis, because the nature and extent of a disabling condition and the requirements of a job will vary in each case. If the individual does not request an accommodation, the employer is not obligated to provide one except where an individual's known disability impairs his/her ability to know of, or effectively communicate a need for, an accommodation that is obvious to the employer. If a person with a disability requests, but cannot suggest, an appropriate accommodation, the employer and the individual should work together to identify one. There are also many public and private resources that can provide assistance without cost.

What are the limitations on the obligation to make a reasonable accommodation?

The individual with a disability requiring the accommodation must be otherwise qualified, and the disability must be known to the employer. In addition, an employer is not required to make an accommodation if it would impose an "undue hardship" on the operation of the employer's business. "Undue hardship" is defined as an "action requiring significant difficulty or expense" when considered in light of a number of factors. These factors include the nature and cost of the accommodation in relation to the size, resources, nature, and structure of the employer's operation. Undue hardship is determined on a case-by-case basis. Where the facility making the accommodation is part of a larger entity, the structure and overall resources of the larger organization would be considered, as well as the financial and administrative relationship of the facility to the larger organization. In general, a larger employer with greater resources would be expected to make accommodations requiring greater effort or expense than would be required of a smaller employer with fewer resources.

If a particular accommodation would be an undue hardship, the employer must try to identify another accommodation that will not pose such a hardship. Also, if the cost of an accommodation would impose an undue hardship on the employer, the individual with a disability should be given the option of paying that portion of the cost which would constitute an undue hardship or of providing the accommodation.

Must an employer modify existing facilities to make them accessible?

The employer's obligation under Title I is to provide access for an individual applicant to participate in the job application process, and for an individual employee with a disability to perform the essential functions of his/her job, including access to a building, to the work site, to needed equipment, and to all facilities used by employees. For example, if an employee lounge is located in a place inaccessible to an employee using a wheelchair, the lounge might be modified or relocated, or comparable facilities might be provided in a location that would enable the individual to take a break with co-workers. The employer must provide such access unless it would cause an undue hardship.

Under Title I, an employer is not required to make its existing facilities accessible until a particular applicant or employee with a particular disability needs an accommodation, and then the modifications should meet that individual's work needs. However, employers should consider initiating changes that will provide general accessibility, particularly for job applicants, since it is likely that people with disabilities will be applying for jobs. The employer does not have to make changes to provide access in places or facilities that will not be used by that individual for employment-related activities or benefits.

Can an employer be required to reallocate an essential function of a job to another employee as a reasonable accommodation?

No. An employer is not required to reallocate essential functions of a job as a reasonable accommodation.

Can an employer be required to modify, adjust, or make other reasonable accommodations in the way a test is given to a qualified applicant or employee with a disability?

Yes. Accommodations may be needed to assure that tests or examinations measure the actual ability of an individual to perform job functions rather than reflect limitations caused by the disability. Tests should be given to people who have sensory, speaking, or manual impairments in a format that does not require the use of the impaired skill, unless it is a job-related skill that the test is designed to measure.

Can an employer maintain existing production/performance standards for an employee with a disability?

An employer can hold employees with disabilities to the same standards of production/performance as other similarly situated employees without disabilities for performing essential job functions, with or without reasonable accommodation. An employer also can hold employees with disabilities to the same standards of production/performance as other employees regarding marginal functions unless the disability affects the person's ability to perform those marginal functions. If the ability to perform marginal functions is affected by the disability, the employer must provide some type of reasonable accommodation such as job restructuring but may not exclude an individual with a disability who is satisfactorily performing a job's essential functions.

Can an employer establish specific attendance and leave policies?

An employer can establish attendance and leave policies that are uniformly applied to all employees, regardless of disability, but may not refuse leave needed by an employee with a disability if other employees get such leave. An employer also may be required to make adjustments in leave policy as a reasonable accommodation. The employer is not obligated to provide additional paid leave, but accommodations may include leave flexibility and unpaid leave.

A uniformly applied leave policy does not violate the ADA because it has a more severe effect on an individual because of the disability. However, if an individual with a disability requests a modification of such a policy as a reasonable accommodation, an employer may be required to provide it, unless it would impose an undue hardship.

Can an employer consider health and safety when deciding whether to hire an applicant or retain an employee with a disability?

Yes. The ADA permits employers to establish qualification standards that will exclude individuals who pose a direct threat—i.e., a significant risk of substantial harm—to the health or safety of the individual or of others, if that risk cannot be eliminated or reduced below the level of a "direct threat" by reasonable accommodation. However, an employer may not simply assume that a threat exists; the employer must establish through objective, medically supportable methods that there is significant risk that substantial harm could occur in the workplace. By requiring employers to make individualized judgements based on reliable medical or other objective evidence rather than on generalizations, ignorance, fear, patronizing attitudes, or stereotypes, the ADA recognized the need to balance the interests of people with disabilities against the legitimate interests of employers in maintaining a safe workplace.

Are applicants or employees who are currently illegally using drugs covered by the ADA?

No. Individuals who currently engage in the illegal use of drugs are specifically excluded from the definition of a "qualified individual with a disability" protected by the ADA when the employer takes action on the basis of their drug use.

Is testing for the illegal use of drugs permissible under the ADA?

Yes. A test for the illegal use of drugs is

not considered a medical examination under the ADA; therefore, employers may conduct such testing of applicants or employees and make employment decisions based on the results. The ADA does not encourage, prohibit, or authorize drug tests.

If the results of a drug test reveal the presence of a lawfully prescribed drug or other medical information, such information must be treated as a confidential medical record.

Are alcoholics covered by the ADA?

Yes. While a current illegal user of drugs is not protected by the ADA if an employer acts on the basis of such use, a person who currently uses alcohol is not automatically denied protection. An alcoholic is a person with a disability and is protected by the ADA if he or she is qualified to perform the essential functions of the job. An employer may be required to provide an accommodation to an alcoholic. However, an employer can discipline, discharge or deny employment to an alcoholic whose use of alcohol adversely affects job performance or conduct. An employer also may prohibit the use of alcohol in the workplace and can require that employees not be under the influence of alcohol.

Does the ADA override federal and state health and safety laws?

The ADA does not override health and safety requirements established under other federal laws even if a standard adversely affects the employment of an individual with a disability. If a standard is required by another federal law, an employer must comply with it and does not have to show that the standard is job related and consistent with business necessity. For example, employers must conform to health and safety requirements of the U.S. Occupational Safety and Health Administration. However, an employer still has the obligation under the ADA to consider whether there is a reasonable accommodation, consistent with the standards of other federal laws, that will prevent exclusion of qualified individuals with disabilities who can perform jobs without violating the standards of those laws. If an employer can comply with both the ADA and another federal law, then the employer must do so.

The ADA does not override state or local laws designed to protect public health and safety, except where such laws conflict with the ADA requirements. If there is a state or local law that would exclude an individual with a disability from a particular job or profession because of a health or safety risk, the employer still must assess whether a particular individual would pose a "direct threat" to health or safety under the ADA standard. If such a "direct threat" exists, the employer must consider whether it could be eliminated or reduces below the level of a "direct threat" by reasonable accommodation. An employer cannot rely on a state or local law that conflicts with ADA requirements as a defense to a charge of discrimination.

How does the ADA affect workers' compensation programs?

Only injured workers who meet the ADA's definition of an "individual with a disability" will be considered disabled under the ADA, regardless of whether they satisfy criteria for receiving benefits under workers' compensation or other disability laws. A worker also must be "qualified" (with or without reasonable accommodation) to be protected by the ADA. Work-related injuries do not always cause physical or mental impairments severe enough to "substantially limit" a major life activity. Also, many on-the-job injuries cause temporary impairments which heal within a short period of time with little or no long-term or permanent impact. Therefore, many injured workers who qualify for benefits under workers' compensation or other disability benefits laws may not be protected by the ADA. An employer must consider work-related injuries on a case-by-case basis to know if a worker is protected by the ADA.

An employer may not inquire into an applicant's workers' compensation history before making a conditional offer of employment. After making a conditional job offer, an employer may inquire about a person's workers' compensation history in a medical inquiry or examination that is required of all applicants in the same job category. However, even after a conditional offer has been made, an employer cannot require a potential employee to have a medical examination unless a response to a medical inquiry (as opposed to results from a medical examination), shows a previous on-the-job injury, and unless all applicants in the same job category are required to have an examination. Also, an employer may not base an employment decision on the speculation that an applicant may cause increased workers' compensation costs in the future. However, an employer may refuse to hire, or may discharge an individual who is not currently able to perform a job without posing a significant risk of substantial harm to the health or safety of the individual or others, if the risk cannot be eliminated or reduced by reasonable accommodation.

An employer may refuse to hire or may fire a person who knowingly provides a false answer to a lawful post-offer inquiry about his or her condition or worker's compensation history.

An employer also may submit medical information and records concerning employees and applicants (obtained after a conditional job offer) to state workers' compensation offices and "second injury" funds without violating ADA confidentiality requirements.

What is discrimination based on "relationship or association" under the ADA?

The ADA prohibits discrimination based on relationship or association in order to protect individuals from actions based on unfounded assumptions that their relationship to a person with a disability would affect their job performance, and from actions caused by bias or misinformation concerning certain disabilities. For example, this provision would protect a person whose spouse has a disability from being denied employment because of an employer's unfounded assumption that the applicant would use excessive leave to care for the spouse. It also would protect an individual who does volunteer work for people with AIDS from a discriminatory employment action motivated by that relationship or association.

How are the employment provisions enforced?

The employment provisions of the ADA

are enforced under the same procedures now applicable to race, color, sex, national origin, and religious discrimination under Title VII of the Civil Rights Act of 1964, as amended, and the Civil Rights Act of 1991. Complaints regarding actions that occurred on or after July 26, 1992, may be filed with the Equal Employment Opportunity Commission or designated state human rights agencies. Available remedies will include hiring, reinstatement, promotion, back pay, front pay, restored benefits, reasonable accommodation, attorneys' fees, expert witness fees, and court costs. Compensatory and punitive damages also may be available in cases of intentional discrimination or where an employer fails to make a good faith effort to provide a reasonable accommodation.

What financial assistance is available to employers to help them make reasonable accommodations and comply with the ADA?

A special tax credit is available to help smaller employers make accommodations required by the ADA. An eligible small business may take a tax credit of up to $5,000 per year for accommodations made to comply with the ADA. The credit is available for one-half the cost of "eligible access expenditures" that are more than $250 but less than $10,250.

A full tax deduction, up to $15,000 per year, also is available to any business for expenses of removing qualified architectural or transportation barriers. Expenses covered include costs of removing barriers created by steps, narrow doors, inaccessible parking spaces, restroom facilities, and transportation vehicles. Information about the tax credit and the tax deduction can be obtained from a local IRS office, or by contacting the Office of Chief Counsel, Internal Revenue Service.

Tax credits are available under the Targeted Jobs Tax Credit Program (TJTCP) for employers who hire individuals with disabilities referred by state or local vocational rehabilitation agencies, State Commissions on the Blind, or the U.S. Department of Veterans Affairs, and certified by a state employment service. Under the TJTCP, a tax credit may be taken for up to 40 percent of the first $6,000 of first-year wages of a new employee with a disability. This program must be reauthorized each year by Congress. Further information about the TJTCP can be obtained from the state employment services or from state Governors' Committees on the Employment of People with Disabilities.

What are an employer's recordkeeping requirements under the employment provisions of the ADA?

An employer must maintain records such as application forms submitted by applicants and other records related to hiring, requests for reasonable accommodation, promotion, demotion, transfer, lay-off or termination, rates of pay or other terms of compensation, and selection for training or apprenticeship for one year after making the record or taking the action described (whichever occurs later). If a charge of discrimination is filed or an action is brought by EEOC, an employer must save all personnel records related to the charge until final disposition of the charge.

Does the ADA require that an employer post a notice explaining its requirements?

The ADA requires that employers post a notice describing the provisions of the ADA. It must be made accessible, as needed, to individuals with disabilities. A poster is available from EEOC summarizing the requirements of the ADA and other federal legal requirements for nondiscrimination for which EEOC has enforcement responsibility. EEOC also provides guidance on making this information available in accessible formats for people with disabilities.

What resources does the Equal Employment Opportunity Commission have available to help employers and people with disabilities understand and comply with the employment requirements of the ADA?

The Equal Employment Opportunity Commission has developed several resources to help employers and people with disabilities understand and comply with the employment provisions of the ADA.

Resources include:

- A Technical Assistance Manual that provides "how-to" guidance on the employment provisions of the ADA as well as a resource directory to help individuals find specific information.
- A variety of brochures, booklets, and fact sheets.

For information on how to contact the Equal Employment Opportunity Commission, see page 157.

State and Local Governments

Does the ADA apply to state and local governments?

Title II of the ADA prohibits discrimination against qualified individuals with disabilities in all programs, activities, and services of public entities. It applies to all state and local governments, their departments and agencies, and any other instrumentalities or special purpose districts of state or local governments, their departments and agencies, and any other instrumentalities or special purpose districts of state or local governments. It clarifies the requirements of Section 504 of the Rehabilitation Act of 1973 for public transportation systems that receive federal financial assistance, and extends coverage to all public entities that provide public transportation, whether or not they receive federal financial assistance. It establishes detailed standards for the operation of public transit systems, including commuter and intercity rail (AMTRAK).

When do the requirements for state and local governments become effective?

In general, they became effective on January 26, 1992.

How does Title II affect participation in a state or local government's programs, activities, and services?

A state or local government must eliminate any eligibility criteria for participation in programs, activities, and services that screen out or tend to screen out persons with disabilities, unless it can establish that the requirements are necessary for the provision of the service, program, or activity. The state or local government may, however, adopt legitimate safety requirements necessary for safe operation if they are based on real risks, not on stereotypes or generalizations about individuals with disabilities. Finally, a public entity must reasonably modify its policies, practices, or procedures to avoid discrimination. If the public entity can demonstrate that a particular modification would fundamentally alter the nature of its service, program, or activity, it is not required to make that modification.

Does Title II cover a public entity's employment policies and practices?

Yes. Title II prohibits all public entities, regardless of the size of their work force, from discriminating in employment against qualified individuals with disabilities. In addition to Title II's employment coverage, Title I of the ADA and Section 504 of the Rehabilitation Act of 1973 prohibit employment discrimination against qualified individuals with disabilities by certain public entities.

What changes must a public entity make to its existing facilities to make them accessible?

A public entity must ensure that individuals with disabilities are not excluded from services, programs, and activities because existing buildings are inaccessible. A state or local government's programs, when viewed in their entirety, must be readily accessible to and usable by individuals with disabilities. This standard, known as "program accessibility," applies to facilities of a public entity that existed on January 26, 1992. Public entities do not necessarily have to make each of their existing facilities accessible. They may provide program accessibility by a number of methods including alteration of existing facilities, acquisition or construction of additional facilities, relocation of a service or program to an accessible facility, or provision of services at alternate accessible sites.

When must structural changes be made to attain program accessibility?

Structural changes needed for program accessibility must be made as expeditiously as possible, but no later than January 26, 1995. This three-year time period was not a grace period; all alterations should have been accomplished as expeditiously as possible. A public entity that employs 50 or more persons must have developed a transition plan by July 26, 1992, setting forth the steps necessary to complete such changes.

What is a self-evaluation?

A self-evaluation is a public entity's assessment of its current policies and practices. The self-evaluation identifies and corrects those policies and practices that are inconsistent with Title II's requirements. All public entities must have completed a self-evaluation by January 26, 1993. A public entity that employs 50 or more employees must retain its self-evaluation for three years. Other public entities are not required to retain their self-evaluations, but are encouraged to do so because these documents evidence a public entity's good faith efforts to comply with Title II's requirements.

What does Title II require for new construction and alterations?

The ADA requires that all new buildings

constructed by a state or local government be accessible. In addition, when a state or local government undertakes alterations to a building, it must make the altered portions accessible.

How will a state or local government know that a new building is accessible?

A state or local government will be in compliance with the ADA for new construction and alterations if it follows either of two accessibility standards. It can choose either the Uniform Federal Accessibility Standards or the Americans with Disabilities Act Accessibility Guidelines for Buildings and Facilities, which is the standard that must be used for public accommodations and commercial facilities under Title III of the ADA. If the state or local government chooses the ADA Accessibility Guidelines, it is not entitled to the elevator exemption (which permits certain private buildings under three stories or under 3,000 square feet per floor to be constructed without an elevator).

What requirements apply to a public entity's emergency telephone services, such as 911?

State and local agencies that provide emergency telephone services must provide "direct access" to individuals who rely on a TDD or computer modem for telephone communication. Telephone access through a third party or through a relay service does not satisfy the requirement for direct access. Where a public entity provides 911 telephone service, it may not substitute a separate seven-digit telephone line as the sole means for access to 911 services by nonvoice users. A public entity may, however, provide a separate seven-digit line for the exclusive use of nonvoice callers in addition to providing direct access for such calls to its 911 line.

Does Title II require that telephone emergency service systems be compatible with all formats used for nonvoice communications?

No. At present, telephone emergency services must only be compatible with the Baudot format. Until it can be technically proven that communications in another format can operate in a reliable and compatible manner in a given telephone emergency environment, a public entity would not be required to provide direct access to computer modems using formats other than Baudot.

How will the ADA's requirements for state and local governments be enforced?

Private individuals may bring lawsuits to enforce their rights under Title II and may receive the same remedies as those provided under Section 504 of the Rehabilitation Act of 1973, including reasonable attorney's fees. Individuals may also file complaints with eight designated federal agencies, including the Department of Justice and the Department of Transportation.

Public Accommodations

What are public accommodations?

A public accommodation is a private entity that owns, operates, leases, or leases to, a place of public accommodation. Places of public accommodation include a wide range of entities, such as restaurants, hotels, theaters, doctors' offices, pharmacies, retail stores, museums, libraries, parks, private schools, and day care centers. Private clubs and religious organizations are exempt from the ADA's Title III requirements for public accommodations.

Will the ADA have any effect on the eligibility criteria used by public accommodations to determine who may receive services?

Yes. If a criterion screens out or tends to screen out individuals with disabilities, it may only be used if necessary for the provision of the services. For instance, it would be a violation for a retail store to have a rule excluding all deaf persons from entering the premises, or for a movie theater to exclude all individuals with cerebral palsy. More subtle forms of discrimination are also prohibited. For example, requiring presentation of a driver's license as the sole acceptable means of identification for purposes of paying by check could constitute discrimination against individuals with vision impairments. This would be true if such individuals are ineligible to receive licenses and the use of an alternative means of identification is feasible.

Does the ADA allow public accommodations to take safety factors into consideration in providing services to individuals with disabilities?

The ADA expressly provides that a public accommodation may exclude an individual, if that individual poses a direct threat to the health or safety of others that cannot be mitigated by appropriate modifications in the public accommodation's policies or procedures, or by the provision of auxiliary aids. A public accommodation will be permitted to establish objective safety criteria for the operation of its business; however, any safety standard must be based on objective requirements rather than stereotypes or generalizations about the ability of persons with disabilities to participate in an activity.

Are there any limits on the kinds of modifications in policies, practices, and procedures required by the ADA?

Yes. The ADA does not require modifications that would fundamentally alter the nature of the services provided by the public accommodation. For example, it would not be discriminatory for a physician specialist who treats only burn patients to refer a deaf individual to another physician for treatment of a broken limb or respiratory ailment. To require a physician to accept patients outside of his or her speciality would fundamentally alter the nature of the medical practice.

What kinds of auxiliary aids and services are required by the ADA to ensure effective communication with individuals with hearing or vision impairments?

Appropriate auxiliary aids and services may include services and devices such as qualified interpreters, assistive listening devices, notetakers, and written materials for individuals with hearing impairments; and qualified readers, taped texts and brailled or large print materials for individuals with vision impairments.

Are there any limitations on the ADA's auxiliary aids requirements?

Yes. The ADA does not require the provision of any auxiliary aid that would result in an undue burden or in a fundamental alteration in the nature of the goods or services provided by a public accommodation. However, the public accommodation is not relieved from the duty to furnish an alternative auxiliary aid, if available, that would not result in a fundamental alteration or undue burden. Both of these limitations are derived from existing regulations and caselaw under Section 504 of the Rehabilitation Act and are to be determined on a case-by-case basis.

Are restaurants required to have brailled menus?

No, not if waiters or other employees are made available to read the menu to a blind customer.

Is a clothing store required to have brailled price tags?

No, not if sales personnel could provide price information orally upon request.

Is a bookstore required to maintain a sign language interpreter on its staff in order to communicate with deaf customers?

No, not if employees communicate by pen and notepad when necessary.

Are there any limitations on the ADA's barrier removal requirements for existing facilities?

Yes. Barrier removal need be accomplished only when it is "readily achievable" to do so.

What does the term "readily achievable" mean?

It means "easily accomplishable and able to be carried out without much difficulty or expense."

What are examples of the types of modifications that would be readily achievable in most cases?

Examples include the simple ramping of a few steps, the installation of grab bars where only routine reinforcement of the wall is required, the lowering of telephones, and similar modest adjustments.

Do business need to rearrange furniture and display racks?

Possibly. For example, restaurants may need to rearrange tables and department stores may need to adjust their layout of racks and shelves in order to permit access to wheelchair users.

Do businesses need to install elevators?

Businesses are not required to retrofit their facilities to install elevators unless such installation is readily achievable, which is unlikely in most cases.

When barrier removal is not readily achievable, what kinds of alternative steps are required by the ADA?

Alternatives may include such measures as in-store assistance for removing articles from inaccessible shelves, home delivery of groceries, or coming to the door to receive or return dry cleaning.

Must alternative steps be taken without regard to cost?

No, only readily achievable alternative steps must be undertaken.

How is "readily achievable" determined in a multisite business?

In determining whether an action to make a public accommodation accessible would be "readily achievable," the overall size of the parent corporation or entity is only one factor to be considered. The ADA also permits consideration of the financial resources of the particular facility or facilities involved and the administrative or fiscal relationship of the facility or facilities to the parent entity.

Who has responsibility for ADA compliance in leased places of public accommodation, the landlord or the tenant?

The ADA places the legal obligation to remove barriers or provide auxiliary aids and services on both the landlord and the tenant. The landlord and the tenant may decide by lease who will actually make the changes and provide the aids and services, but both remain legally responsible.

What does the ADA require in new construction?

The ADA requires that all new construction of places of public accommodation, as well as of "commercial facilities" such as office buildings, be accessible. Elevators are generally not required in facilities under three stories or with fewer than 3,000 square feet per floor, unless the building is a shopping center or mall; the professional office of a health care provider; a terminal, depot, or other public transit station; or an airport passenger terminal.

Is it expensive to make all newly constructed places of public accommodation and commercial facilities accessible?

The cost of incorporating accessibility features in new construction is less than one percent of construction costs. This is a small price in relation to the economic benefits to be derived from full accessibility in the future, such as increased employment and consumer spending and decreased welfare dependency.

Must every feature of a new facility be accessible?

No, only a specified numbers of elements such as parking spaces and drinking fountains must be made accessible in order for a facility to be "readily accessible." Certain nonoccupiable spaces such as elevator pits, elevator penthouses, and piping or equipment catwalks need not be accessible.

What are the ADA requirements for altering facilities?

All alterations that could affect the usability of a facility must be made in an accessible manner to the maximum extent feasible. For example, if during renovations a doorway is being relocated, the new doorway must be wide enough to meet the new construction standard for accessibility. When alterations are made to a primary function area, such as the lobby of a bank or the dining area of a cafeteria, an accessible path of travel to the altered area must also be provided. The bathrooms, telephones, and drinking fountains serving that area must also be made accessible. These additional accessibility alterations are only required to the extent that the added accessibility costs do not exceed 20% of the cost of the original alteration. Elevators are generally not required in facilities under three stories or with fewer than 3,000 square feet per floor, unless the building is a shopping center or mall; the professional office of a health care provider; a terminal, depot, or other public transit station; or an airport passenger terminal.

Does the ADA permit an individual with a disability to sue a business when that individual believes that discrimination is about to occur, or must the individual wait for the discrimination to occur?

The ADA public accommodations provisions permit an individual to allege discrimination based on a reasonable belief that discrimination is about to occur. This provision, for example, allows a person who uses a wheelchair to challenge the planned construction of a new place of public accommodation, such as a shopping mall, that would not be accessible to individuals who use wheelchairs. The resolution of such challenges prior to the construction of an inaccessible facility would enable any necessary remedial measures to be incorporated in the building at the planning stage, when such changes would be relatively inexpensive.

How does the ADA affect existing state and local building codes?

Existing codes remain in effect. The ADA allows the attorney general to certify that a state law, local building code, or similar ordinance that establishes accessibility requirements meets or exceeds the minimum accessibility requirements for public accommodations and commercial facilities. Any state or local government may apply for certification of its code or ordinance. The attorney general can certify a code or ordinance only after prior notice and a public hearing at which interested people, including individuals with disabilities, are provided an opportunity to testify against the certification.

What is the effect of certification of a state or local code or ordinance?

Certification can be advantageous if an entity has constructed or altered a facility according to a certified code or ordinance. If someone later brings an enforcement proceeding against the entity, the certification is considered "rebuttable evidence" that the state law or local ordinance meets or exceeds the minimum requirements of the ADA. In other words, the entity can argue that the construction or alteration met the requirements of the ADA because it was done in compliance with the state or local code that had been certified.

When are the public accommodations provisions effective?

In general, they became effective on January 26, 1992.

How will the public accommodations provisions be enforced?

Private individuals may bring lawsuits in which they can obtain court orders to stop discrimination. Individuals may also file complaints with the attorney general, who is authorized to bring lawsuits in cases of general public importance or where a "pattern or practice" of discrimination is alleged. In these cases, the attorney general may seek monetary damages and civil penalties. Civil penalties may not exceed $50,000 for a first violation or $100,000 for any subsequent violation.

Miscellaneous

Is the federal government covered by the ADA?

The ADA does not cover the executive branch of the federal government. The executive branch continues to be covered by Title V of the Rehabilitation Act of 1973, which prohibits discrimination in services and employment on the basis of handicap and which is a model for the requirements of the ADA. The ADA, however, does cover Congress and other entities in the legislative branch of the federal government.

Does the ADA cover private apartments and private homes?

The ADA does not cover strictly residential private apartments and homes. If, however, a place of public accommodation, such as a doctor's office or day care center, is located in a private residence, those portions of the residence used for that purpose are subject to the ADA's requirements.

Does the ADA cover air transportation?

Discrimination by air carriers in areas other than employment is not covered by the ADA but rather by the Air Carrier Access Act (49 U.S.C. 1374 (c)).

What are the ADA's requirements for public transit buses?

The Department of Transportation has issued regulations mandating accessible public transit vehicles and facilities. The regulations include requirements that all new fixed-route, public transit buses be accessible and that supplementary paratransit services be provided for those individuals with disabilities who cannot use fixed-route bus service. For information on how to contact the Department of Transportation, see page 156.

How will the ADA make telecommunications accessible?

The ADA requires the establishment of telephone relay services for individuals who use telecommunications devices for deaf persons (TDD's) or similar devices. The Federal Communications Commission has issued regulations specifying standards for the operation of these services.

Are businesses entitled to any tax benefit to help pay for the cost of compliance?

As amended in 1990, the Internal Revenue Code allows a deduction of up to $15,000 per year for expenses associated with the removal of qualified architectural and transportation barriers.

The 1990 amendment also permits eligible small businesses to receive a tax credit for certain costs of compliance with the ADA. An eligible small business is one whose gross receipts do not exceed $1,000,000 or whose workforce does not consist of more than 30 full-time workers. Qualifying businesses may claim a credit of up to 50 percent of eligible access expenditures that exceed $250 but do not exceed $10,250. Examples of eligible access expenditures include the necessary and reasonable costs of removing architectural, physical, communications, and transportation barriers; providing readers, interpreters, and other auxiliary aids; and acquiring or modifying equipment or devices.

Telephone Numbers for ADA Information

This list contains the telephone numbers of federal agencies that are responsible for providing information to the public about the Americans with Disabilities Act and organizations that have been funded by the federal government to provide information through staffed information centers.

The agencies and organizations listed are sources for obtaining information about the law's requirements and informal guidance in understanding and complying with the ADA. They are not, and should not be viewed as, sources for obtaining legal advice or legal opinions about your rights or responsibilities under the ADA.

Architectural and Transportation Barriers Compliance Board
1-800/872-2253 (voice & TDD)

Equal Employment Opportunity Commission
For questions and documents
1-800/669-3362 (voice)
1-800/800-3302 (TDD)

Alternate number for ordering documents (print and other formats)
202/663-4264 (voice)
202/663-7110 (TDD)

Federal Communications Commission
For ADA documents and general information
202/632-7260 (voice)
202/632-6999 (TDD)

Job Accommodation Network
1-800/526-7234 (voice)
1-800/526-7234 (TDD)
Within West Virginia
1-800/526-4698 (voice & TDD)

President's Committee on Employment of People with Disabilities Information Line: ADA Work
1-800/232-9675 (voice & TDD)

U.S. Department of Justice
202/514-0301 (voice)
202/514-03830 (TDD)

U.S. Department of Transportation

Federal Transit Administration
(for ADA documents and information)
202/366-1656 (voice)
202/366-2979 (TDD)

Office of the General Counsel
(for legal questions)
202/366-9306 (voice)
202/755-7687 (TDD)

Federal Aviation Administration
202/376-6406 (voice)

Rural Transit Assistance Program
(for information and assistance on public transportation issues)
1-800/527-8279 (voice & TDD)

Regional Disability and Business Technical Assistance Centers

ADA information, assistance, and copies of ADA documents supplied by the Equal Employment Opportunity Commission and the Department of Justice, which are available in standard print, large print, audio cassette, braille, and computer disk, may be obtained from any of the ten Regional Disability and Business Technical Assistance Centers.

Toll-free for reaching any of the following Centers

1-800/949-4232 (voice & TDD)

Region I (Maine, New Hampshire, Vermont, Massachusetts, Rhode Island, Connecticut)
207/874-6535 (voice & TDD)

Region II (New York, New Jersey, Puerto Rico)
609/392-4004 (voice)
609/392-7004 (TDD)

Region III (Pennsylvania, Delaware, Maryland, District of Columbia, Virginia, West Virginia)
703/525-3268 (voice & TDD)

Region IV (Kentucky, Tennessee, North Carolina, South Carolina, Georgia, Alabama, Mississippi, Florida)
404/888-0022 (voice)
404/888-9098 (TDD)

Region V (Ohio, Indiana, Illinois, Michigan, Wisconsin, Minnesota)
312/403-7756 (voice & TDD)

Region VI (Arkansas, Louisiana, Oklahoma, Texas, New Mexico)
713/520-0232 (voice)
713/520-5136 (TDD)

Region VII (Iowa, Missouri, Nebraska, Kansas)
314/882-3600 (voice & TDD)

Region VIII (North Dakota, South Dakota, Montana, Wyoming, Colorado, Utah)
719/444-0252 (voice & TDD)

Region IX (Arizona, Nevada, California, Hawaii, Pacific Basin)
510/465-7884 (voice)
510/465-3172 (TDD)

Region X (Idaho, Oregon, Washington, Alaska)
206/438-3168 (voice)
206/438-3167 (TDD)

Addresses for ADA Information

U.S. Equal Employment Opportunity Commission
1801 L Street NW
Washington, DC 20507

U.S. Department of Justice
Civil Rights Division
Public Access Section
P.O. Box 66738
Washington, DC 20035-6738

U.S. Department of Transportation
400 Seventh Street SW
Washington, DC 20590

Architectural and Transportation Barriers
Compliance Board
1331 F Street NW
Suite 1000
Washington, DC 20004-1111

Federal Communications Commission
1919 Street NW
Washington, DC 20554

APPENDIX THREE

TAX GUIDE FOR SMALL BUSINESSES

› Appendix 3. Tax Guide for Small Businesses

Part One.

The Business Organization

This Part discusses some of the things you must consider when setting up a business. The first chapter briefly describes the major forms of business organization and discusses how each is taxed. The other chapters discuss recordkeeping, accounting periods, and accounting methods.

1.

Initial Considerations

Introduction

Once you have decided to start a business, you must decide what type of business entity to use. Your decision will depend on legal and tax considerations. The legal considerations are beyond the scope of this publication. However, the tax element is discussed in this chapter. Normally, a business is conducted in the form of either a sole proprietorship, partnership, or corporation.

In the case of a sole proprietorship or a partnership, the business itself does not pay any income taxes. The sole proprietor or the partners include the profits or losses of the business on their personal income tax returns. Profits of a corporation are taxed both to the corporation and to the shareholders when the profits are distributed as dividends. Also, losses sustained by the corporation usually are not available to its stockholders. These two corporate rules do not apply to S corporations. (S corporations are discussed in Chapter 31.)

The tax considerations related to the costs of getting started in a business are discussed under *Going Into Business* in Chapter 5.

Topics
This chapter discusses:
- Sole proprietorships
- Partnerships
- Corporations
- S corporations
- Taxpayer identification numbers

Useful Items
You may want to see:

Publication
- ☐ **1635** Understanding Your EIN

Form (and Instructions)
- ☐ **SS–4** Application for Employer Identification Number
- ☐ **SS–5** Application for a Social Security Card
- ☐ **W–9** Request for Taxpayer Identification Number and Certification
- ☐ **1040** U.S. Individual Income Tax Return
- ☐ **Sch C (Form 1040)** Profit or Loss From Business
- ☐ **Sch C–EZ** Net Profit From Business
- ☐ **1065** U.S. Partnership Return of Income
- ☐ **1120** U.S. Corporation Income Tax Return
- ☐ **1120–A** U.S. Corporation Short-Form Income Tax Return
- ☐ **1120S** U.S. Income Tax Return for an S Corporation

Sole Proprietorships

A sole proprietorship is the simplest form of business organization. This form of business has no existence apart from you, the owner. Its liabilities are your personal liabilities, and your ownership (proprietary) interest ends when you die. You undertake the risks of business to the extent of all your assets, whether used in the business or used personally.

Profit or loss. When you figure your taxable income for the year, you must add in any profit, or subtract any loss, you have from your sole proprietorship. You must report the profit or loss from each of your businesses operated as a sole proprietorship on a separate Schedule C (Form 1040) or Schedule C–EZ (Form 1040). The amount of this business profit or loss is then entered as an item of profit or loss on your individual income tax return Form 1040.

If you are a sole proprietor, you are probably liable for **self-employment tax** (see Chapter 33). Also, ordinarily you will have to make estimated tax payments (see Chapter 28).

Assets. Each asset in your sole proprietorship is treated separately for tax purposes, rather than as part of one overall ownership interest. For example, a sole proprietor selling an entire business as a going concern figures gain or loss separately on each asset. See Chapter 28 for information on the sale of your sole proprietorship.

Rules. Other rules explained in this publication apply to sole proprietorships unless stated otherwise.

Partnerships

A partnership is not a taxable entity. However, it must figure its profit or loss and file a return. A partnership files its return on Form 1065.

A partnership is the relationship existing between two or more persons who join together to carry on a trade or business. Each person contributes money, property, labor, or skill, and expects to share in the profits and losses of the business.

For income tax purposes, the term "partnership" includes a syndicate, group, pool, joint venture, or other unincorporated organization that is carrying on a business and is not classified as a trust, estate, or corporation.

A joint undertaking to share expenses is *not* a partnership. Mere co-ownership of property maintained and leased or rented is *not* a partnership. However, if the co-owners provide services to the tenants, then a partnership exists.

Partnership agreement. The partnership agreement includes the original agreement and any modifications of it agreed to by all the partners or adopted in any other manner provided by the partnership agreement. The agreement or modifications may be oral or written.

The partnership agreement may be modified for a particular tax year after the close of that year, but not later than the date, excluding any extension of time, for filing the partnership return.

Generally, a partner's share of income, gain, loss, deductions, or credits is determined by the partnership agreement.

However, the partnership agreement or any modification of it will be disregarded if the allocation to a partner under the agreement of income, gain, loss, deduction, or credit (or of any item in these categories) does not have substantial economic effect.

In any matter on which the partnership agreement, or any modification of it, is silent, the provisions of local law are treated as part of the agreement.

Partnerships excluded. If all the members agree, some partnerships may choose to be completely or partially excluded from being treated as partnerships, for federal income tax purposes. The exclusion applies only to certain unincorporated investing partnerships and operating agreements where business is not actively conducted. It applies to the joint production, extraction, or use of property, but not for selling services or property produced or extracted. The members of such an organization must be able to figure their income without having to figure partnership taxable income.

For more information on partnerships, see Chapter 29.

Corporations

Corporate profits normally are taxed to the corporation. When the profits are distributed as dividends, the dividends are taxed to the shareholders.

In figuring its taxable income, a corporation generally takes the same deductions as a sole proprietorship. Corporations also are entitled to special deductions that are discussed in Chapter 30.

A corporation, for federal income tax purposes, includes associations, joint stock companies, insurance companies, and trusts and partnerships that actually operate as associations or corporations.

Organizations of professional people. Organizations of doctors, lawyers, and other professional people organized under state professional association acts are generally recognized as corporations for federal income tax purposes. A professional service organization must be both *organized* and *operated* as a corporation to be classified as one. All of the states and the District of Columbia have professional association acts.

Unincorporated organizations. Organizations that are unincorporated and have certain corporate characteristics are classified as associations and are taxed as corporations. These organizations must have associates and must be organized to carry on business and divide any gains from the business. In addition, the organizations must have a *majority* of the following characteristics:

1) Continuity of life,
2) Centralization of management,
3) Limited liability, and
4) Free transferability of interests.

Other factors may also be significant in classifying an organization as an association. An organization will be treated as an association if its characteristics more nearly resemble a corporation than a partnership or trust. The facts in each case determine which characteristics are present.

Income tax return. A corporation must file an income tax return unless it has dissolved.

This applies even if it has ceased doing business and has disposed of all of its assets except for a small sum of cash retained to pay state taxes to keep its corporate charter. A corporation may be required to file a return for any year following the year in which it has been dissolved, if it carries on substantial activities such as the collection of assets or the payment of obligations in connection with the termination of its business affairs.

A corporation with no assets is not required to file an income tax return after it stops doing business and dissolves. This is so even if it is treated as a corporation under state law for limited purposes connected with winding up its affairs, such as suing or being sued. Most corporations file Form 1120 or Form 1120-A.

Formation. Forming a corporation involves a transfer of either money, property, or both, by the prospective shareholders in exchange for capital stock in the corporation.

If money is exchanged for stock, no gain or loss is realized by the shareholder or the corporation. The stock received by the shareholder has a basis equal to the amount of money transferred to the corporation by the shareholder.

If property is exchanged for stock, it may be a nontaxable exchange of property for stock, as discussed in Chapter 22. In other cases, the shareholder who transfers the property to the corporation will realize a taxable gain or loss. Under certain circumstances, as explained under *Sales and Exchanges Between Related Parties* in Chapter 23, any gain recognized which ordinarily would be a capital gain may have to be treated as an ordinary gain, and any loss may be nondeductible.

The gain or loss on a *taxable exchange* is figured by comparing the adjusted basis of the property transferred with its fair market value at the time of the transfer to the corporation. This may be a capital gain or loss. See Chapter 23.

For more information on corporations, see Chapter 30.

S Corporations

A qualifying corporation may choose to be generally exempt from federal income tax. Its shareholders will then include in their income their share of the corporation's separately stated items of income, deduction, loss, and credit and their share of non-separately stated income or loss. A corporation that makes this choice is an S corporation.

Although it generally will not be liable for federal income tax, an S corporation may have to pay a tax on excess net passive investment income, a tax on capital gains, a tax on built-in gains, or the tax from recomputing a prior year's investment credit. An S corporation files its return on Form 1120S.

To make the election to become an S corporation, a corporation, in addition to other requirements, must not have more than 35 shareholders. Also, each shareholder must consent to the election.

For more information on S corporations, see Chapter 31.

Taxpayer Identification Number

You generally use your *social security number* as your taxpayer identification number. You must put this number on each of your individual income tax forms, such as Form 1040 and its schedules.

However, every partnership, corporation (including S corporations), and certain sole proprietors must have an *employer identification number* (EIN) to use as a taxpayer identification number. Sole proprietors must have EINs if they:

1) Pay wages to one or more employees, or
2) Must file any pension or excise tax returns, including those for alcohol, tobacco, or firearms.

If you are required to have an EIN, include it along with your social security number on your Schedule C (Form 1040). If you are not required to have an EIN, only enter your social security number in the appropriate space on the form.

Application for identification number. To apply for a social security number, you should use *Form SS-5*. If you are under 18 years of age, you must furnish evidence, along with this form, of age, identity, and U.S. citizenship. If you are 18 or older, you must appear in person with this evidence at a Social Security office. If you are an alien, you must appear in person and bring your birth certificate and either your alien registration card or your U.S. immigration form.

To apply for an EIN, use Form SS-4. This form is available from IRS and Social Security Administration offices.

Payments to others. If you make payments that require an information return, you must include the payee's taxpayer identification number on the information return. See Chapter 37.

To get the payee's number, use *Form W-9*. This form is available from the IRS. A payee who does not provide you with an identification number may be subject to backup withholding of 31% on the payments you make.

Penalties. A penalty of up to $50 per return applies for each failure to comply by the required due date with certain specified information reporting requirements, up to a maximum of $100,000 for all such failures. Most of these requirements concern furnishing and including taxpayer identification numbers on returns, statements, and other documents. See Chapter 37 for more information on penalties.

Chapter 1 **INITIAL CONSIDERATIONS**

New EIN. You may need to get a new EIN if either the form or the ownership of your business changes.

Change in organization. A new EIN is required for the following changes:

1) A sole proprietorship incorporates;
2) A sole proprietorship takes in partners and operates as a partnership;
3) A partnership incorporates;
4) A partnership is taken over by one of the partners and is operated as a sole proprietorship; or
5) A corporation changes to a partnership or to a sole proprietorship.

A corporation converting to an S corporation does not need a new EIN.

Change in ownership. A new EIN is required for the following changes:

1) You purchase or inherit an existing business that you will operate as a sole proprietorship (You cannot use the EIN of the former owner, even if he or she is your spouse.);
2) You represent an estate that operates a business after the owner's death; or
3) You terminate an old partnership and begin a new one.

2. Books and Records

Topics
This chapter discusses:
- Setting up records
- How to keep records
- Suggestions for effective records
- Requirements for employer records

Useful Items
You may want to see:

Publication

- ☐ **463** Travel, Entertainment, and Gift Expenses
- ☐ **534** Depreciation
- ☐ **583** Taxpayers Starting a Business
- ☐ **917** Business Use of a Car
- ☐ **946** How To Begin Depreciating Your Property

Form (and Instructions)

- ☐ **W-4** Employee's Withholding Allowance Certificate
- ☐ **W-5** Earned Income Credit Advance Payment Certificate
- ☐ **940** Employer's Annual Federal Unemployment (FUTA) Tax Return
- ☐ **940-EZ** Employer's Annual Federal Unemployment (FUTA) Tax Return

---

You must keep records to correctly figure your taxes. Your records must be permanent, accurate, complete, and clearly establish your income, deductions, credits, and employee information. The law does not require you to keep your records in any particular way. However, if you have more than one business, you should keep a complete and separate set of books and records for each business.

Travel expenses. You are required to support your expenses for travel in connection with your business with adequate records or sufficient evidence to prove your own statements. This includes expenses for local travel, gifts, entertainment, and the business use of certain listed property.

Adequate records include account books, diaries, trip sheets, or similar items. Records written at or near the time you have the expenses have more value than oral statements or written records reconstructed much later.

See Publications 463 and 917 for more information.

Listed property. Special rules apply to listed property. Listed property includes:

1) Any automobile, or other property used for transportation,
2) Property used for entertainment, such as photographic and video recording equipment,
3) Cellular telephones or similar equipment, and
4) Computers and related peripheral equipment not used exclusively at a regular business location.

For more information on listed property, see Publication 534 or Publication 946.

Setting Up Your Records

When starting a business, you should set up a system of recordkeeping suitable for your business. Keep in mind the taxes you will have to pay and when you will have to pay them. The *Checklist* near the end of this publication lists the due dates of various taxes that might apply to your business.

Choosing an accounting method and a tax year. You should set up your books using an accounting method that clearly shows your income for the accounting period that is your tax year. See Chapters 3 and 4.

Choosing a bookkeeping system. You must decide whether to use a single- or a double-entry bookkeeping system. The single-entry system is simple and easy to maintain, but it may not be suitable for everyone. You may find the double-entry system better because it has built-in checks and balances to assure accuracy and control.

Single-entry. The single-entry bookkeeping system is based on the income statement (profit or loss statement) and includes only your business income and expense accounts. It can be a simple and very practical system if you are just starting a small business. For tax purposes, this system records the flow of income and expenses through the use of a daily summary of cash receipts and a monthly summary of cash receipts and disbursements. See *Sample Record System* in Publication 583 for an example of single-entry bookkeeping.

Double-entry. The double-entry bookkeeping system uses journals and ledgers and is based on both the income statement and the balance sheet. Transactions are first entered in a journal and then summary totals (usually monthly) of the journal entry transactions are entered in ledger accounts. Ledger accounts include income, expense, asset, liability, and net worth. Income and expense accounts are closed at the end of the annual accounting period. Asset, liability, and net worth accounts are kept on a permanent basis.

The double-entry system is self-balancing. Every journal entry is made up of both debits and credits and the sum of the debits must equal the sum of the credits in each journal entry. After the journal entries are entered in the ledger accounts, the total debits equal the total credits and the accounts are in balance.

At the end of each accounting period, financial statements may be prepared. These statements are generally the income statement and the balance sheet. The income statement reflects the current operations for the year. The balance sheet shows the financial position of the business in terms of assets, liabilities, and net worth on a given date.

Recordkeeping

You should deposit *all business receipts* in a separate bank account. If possible, you should also make all disbursements by check. In this way, both business income and business expenses will be well-documented.

Write checks payable to yourself only when making withdrawals of income from your business for your own use. Avoid writing business checks payable to cash. This will help you identify which disbursements are business and which are personal.

If you must write a check for cash to pay a business expense, include the receipt for the cash payment in your records. If you cannot get a receipt for a cash payment, put a statement in your records at the time of the transaction to explain the payment.

You should establish a petty cash fund for small expenses. All business expenses paid by cash should be clearly supported by documents showing their business purpose.

Support your entries. Sales slips, invoices, canceled checks, paid bills, duplicate deposit slips, and any other documents that explain and support entries made in your books should be filed in an orderly manner and stored in a safe place. Memorandums or sketchy records that approximate income, deductions, or other items affecting your tax liability will not be considered adequate.

Classify your accounts. Classify your accounts by separating them into five groups: income, expenses, assets, liabilities, and equity (net worth). For your assets, you should record the date of acquisition, cost or other basis, depreciation, depletion, and anything else affecting their basis.

Keeping your records. You must keep the books and records of your business available at all times for inspection by the Internal Revenue Service (IRS). The records must be kept as long as they may be needed in the administration of any Internal Revenue law.

Keep records supporting items reported on a tax return until the period of limitations for that tax return runs out. Usually, this is the later of:

Appendix 3. Tax Guide for Small Businesses **165**

1) 3 years after the date your return is due or filed, or
2) 2 years after the date the tax was paid.

However, you should keep some records indefinitely. For example, if you adopt the last-in first-out (LIFO) method of valuing your inventory or change your accounting method, records supporting these decisions may be needed for an indefinite time.

Keep records that support your basis in property for as long as they are needed to figure the correct basis of your original or replacement property (including capital improvements).

Keep copies of your tax returns. They will help you in preparing future tax returns and in making computations if you later file a claim for refund. They may also be helpful to the executor or administrator of your estate or to the IRS if your original return is not available.

Microfilm. Microfilm and microfiche reproductions of general books of accounts, such as cash books, journals, voucher registers, and ledgers, are accepted for recordkeeping purposes if they comply with Revenue Procedure 81–46, in Cumulative Bulletin 1981–2 on page 621. If your micrographic system does not meet the requirements of Revenue Procedure 81–46, you may be subject to penalties.

Computerized systems. If you maintain your records with an automated data processing system, you must be able to produce legible records from the system to provide the information needed to determine your correct tax liability.

You must also keep all machine-sensible records and a complete description of the computerized portion of your accounting system. This documentation must be sufficiently detailed to show the applications being performed; the procedures used in each application, or the controls used to ensure accurate and reliable processing; and controls used to prevent the unauthorized addition, alteration, or deletion of retained records. These records must be retained for as long as they may be material in the administration of any Internal Revenue law.

See Revenue Procedure 91–59, in Cumulative Bulletin 1991–2 on page 841 for more information.

Effective Records

Good records are needed for efficient management, to apply for credit, and to support all items of income and expense reported on your tax return. The following suggestions are provided to help you maintain good records and show you some ways in which they may help you to operate your business.

Identify source of income. The money or property you receive can come from many sources. Your records should identify the source of income so that you can show if an income item is taxable or nontaxable.

Maintain a record of deductible expenses. You may forget expenses when you prepare your tax return unless you record them when they occur. You should also retain the invoice, paid receipt, or canceled check that supports an item of expense in a safe, well-organized file.

Figure depreciation deduction. You should note in a permanent record all business assets you can depreciate. Depreciation allows you to recover the cost of business property by deducting part of it each year on your tax return. You must keep a record of the cost and other information on your assets to figure your depreciation deduction and any gain or loss upon disposition of the asset. If the assets are sold or capital improvements made to them, only a permanent record will show how much of their cost you have recovered. This information is also needed to correctly report a disposition of an asset on your tax return. For more information on capital expenses, see Chapter 5. For information on depreciation, see Chapter 13. For information on sales and dispositions of assets, see Chapter 22.

Figure earnings for self-employment tax purposes. The self-employment tax is part of the system for providing social security coverage for people who work for themselves. The social security benefits you receive when you retire, become disabled, or that will be paid to your family in case of your death, depend on the amount you contributed to your social security account based on your net earnings. Your records should show how much of your earnings are subject to self-employment tax and how much self-employment tax you paid on those earnings. See Chapter 33.

Support items reported on tax returns. If any of your tax returns are examined by the IRS, you may be asked to explain and support the items reported on them. A complete set of records will speed up the examination. Adequate and complete records are always supported by sales slips, invoices, receipts, bank deposit slips, canceled checks, and other documents.

Financial account statements as proof of payment. If you cannot provide a canceled check to prove payment of an expense item, you may be able to prove it with certain financial account statements. This includes account statements prepared by a third party who is under contract to prepare statements for the financial institution. To be acceptable, it must meet the following requirements:

1) An account statement showing a check clearing is accepted as proof if it shows the check number, amount, payee name, and the date the check amount was posted to the account by the financial institution.

2) An account statement prepared by a financial institution showing an electronic funds transfer is accepted as proof if it shows the amount transferred, payee name, and the date the transfer was posted to the account by the financial institution.

3) An account statement prepared by a financial institution showing a credit card charge (an increase to the cardholder's loan balance) is accepted as proof if it shows the amount charged, payee name, and the date charged (transaction date).

These account statements must show a high degree of legibility and readability. For this purpose, legibility is the quality of a letter or number enabling it to be identified positively excluding all other letters and numbers. Readability is the quality of a group of letters or numbers enabling it to be recognized as words or complete numbers. However, this does not mean the information must be typed or printed.

However, proof of payment of an amount alone does not establish that you are entitled to a tax deduction. You should also keep other documents as discussed in *Support items reported on tax returns*, earlier.

Records of Employers

You must keep all your records on employment taxes (income tax withholding, social security, Medicare, and federal unemployment tax) for at least 4 years after the due date of the return or after the date the tax is paid, whichever is later. In addition to the following items required for each specific kind of employment tax, your records should also contain your employer identification number, copies of the returns you have filed, and the dates and amounts of deposits you made.

Income tax withholding. The specific records you must keep for income tax withholding are:

1) Each employee's name, address, and social security number.

2) The total amount and date of each wage payment and the period of time the payment covers.

3) For each wage payment, the amount subject to withholding.

4) The amount of withholding tax collected on each payment and the date it was collected.

5) If the taxable amount is less than the total payment, the reason why it is less.

6) Copies of any statements furnished by employees relating to nonresident alien status, residence in Puerto Rico or the Virgin Islands, or residence or physical presence in a foreign country.

7) The fair market value and date of each payment of noncash compensation

Chapter 2 **BOOKS AND RECORDS**

made to a retail commission salesperson, if no income tax was withheld.

8) For accident or health plans, information about the amount of each payment.

9) The withholding allowance certificates (Form W–4) filed by each employee.

10) Any agreement between you and the employee on Form W-4 for the voluntary withholding of additional amounts of tax.

11) If necessary to figure tax liability, the dates in each calendar quarter on which any employee worked for you, but *not* in the course of your trade or business, and the amount paid for that work.

12) Copies of statements given to you by employees reporting tips received in their work, unless the information shown on the statements appears in another item on this list.

13) Requests by employees to have their withheld tax figured on the basis of their individual cumulative wages, and any notice that the request was revoked.

14) The Forms W–5, *Earned Income Credit Advance Payment Certificate*, and the amounts and dates of the advance payments.

An employee's earnings ledger, which you can buy at most office supply stores, normally has space for the information required in items (1) to (4).

Social security and Medicare taxes. You must also maintain the following information in your records on the social security and Medicare (FICA) taxes of your employees:

1) The amount of each wage payment subject to social security tax.

2) The amount of each wage payment subject to Medicare tax.

3) The amount of social security and Medicare tax collected for each payment and the date collected.

4) If the total wage payment and the taxable amount differ, the reason why they do.

Federal Unemployment Tax Act. For federal unemployment purposes, you must maintain records containing the following information:

1) The total amount paid to your employees during the calendar year.

2) The amount of compensation subject to the unemployment tax, and why it differs from the total compensation if they differ.

3) The amount you paid into the state unemployment fund.

4) Any other information required to be shown on Form 940 (or Form 940–EZ).

For information on the employment taxes you may have to pay, see Chapter 34.

Appendix 3. Tax Guide for Small Businesses 167

3. Accounting Periods

Form (and Instructions)

☐ **1128** Application To Adopt, Change, or Retain a Tax Year

☐ **8716** Election To Have a Tax Year Other Than a Required Tax Year

☐ **8752** Required Payment or Refund Under Section 7519

Introduction

Every taxpayer (business or individual) must figure taxable income and file a tax return on the basis of an annual accounting period. Your "tax year" is the annual accounting period you use for keeping your records and reporting your income and expenses. The accounting periods you can use are:

1) A calendar year, or
2) A fiscal year.

You adopt a tax year when you file your first income tax return. You must adopt your first tax year by the due date (not including extensions) for filing a return for that year.

The due date for individual and partnership returns is the 15th day of the 4th month after the end of the tax year. Individuals include sole proprietors, partners, and S corporation shareholders. The due date for filing returns for corporations and S corporations is the 15th day of the 3rd month after the end of the tax year. If the 15th day of the month falls on a Saturday, Sunday, or legal holiday, the due date is the next day that is not a Saturday, Sunday, or legal holiday.

This chapter discusses: the calendar tax year; the fiscal tax year (including a period of 52 or 53 weeks); the short tax year (including a change in accounting period); improper tax years; accounting period restrictions that apply to partnerships, S corporations, and personal service corporations; and special situations that apply to corporations.

Note. Employment taxes are figured on a calendar year basis. You must use the calendar quarter for withheld income tax and social security and Medicare taxes. You must use the calendar year for federal unemployment tax. Employment taxes are discussed in Chapter 34.

Topics

This chapter discusses:

- Calendar tax years
- Fiscal tax years
- Short tax years

Useful Items

You may want to see:

Publication

☐ **538** Accounting Periods and Methods

Tax Year

Your regular accounting period is either a calendar tax year or a fiscal tax year.

Calendar Tax Year

If you adopt the calendar year for your annual accounting period, you must maintain your books and records and report your income and expenses for the period from January 1 through December 31 of each year.

If you filed your first return using the calendar tax year, and you later begin business as a sole proprietor, or become a partner in a partnership, or become a shareholder in an S corporation, you must continue to use the calendar tax year unless you get permission to change. See *Change in Accounting Period*, later. You must report your income from all sources, including your sole proprietorship, salaries, partnership income, and dividends, using the same tax year.

You must adopt the calendar tax year if:

1) You do not keep adequate records,
2) You have no annual accounting period, or
3) Your present tax year does not qualify as a fiscal year.

Fiscal Tax Year

A regular fiscal tax year is 12 consecutive months ending on the last day of any month except December. A 52–53 week year is a fiscal tax year that varies from 52 to 53 weeks.

If you adopt a fiscal tax year, you must maintain your books and records and report your income and expenses using the same tax year.

52–53 Week Tax Year

You can elect to use a 52–53 week tax year if you keep your books and records and report your income on that basis. If you make this election, your tax year will always be either 52 or 53 weeks long and will always end on the same day of the week. You may choose to have your year always end on either:

1) The date a specified day of the week last occurs in a particular month, or
2) The date that day of the week occurs nearest to the last day of a particular month.

For example, if you elect a tax year that always ends on the last Monday in March, then for the tax year ending in 1995, your tax year will end on March 27, 1995. If you elected a tax year ending on the Monday nearest to the end of January, then for the tax year ending in 1995, your tax year will end on January 30, 1995.

You make the election by filing your tax return for the 52–53 week year and attaching to it a statement showing:

1) The day of the week on which the tax year will always end,
2) Whether it will end on the last such day of the week in the calendar month or on the date such day of the week occurs nearest the end of the month, and
3) The month in which or with reference to which the tax year will end.

Change to a 52–53 week tax year. You may change to a 52–53 week year that ends with reference to the end of the same month with which your present tax year ends, without first getting permission from the IRS. You must attach the statement, just discussed, to the tax return for the year for which the election is made.

Example. If you now use a calendar year and want to change to a 52–53 week year ending on the Friday closest to December 31, prior approval is not needed. You make the election to change by filing the statement described above with your return.

Approval required. If you want to change to a 52–53 week tax year that ends with reference to the end of a month that is not the same month in which your old tax year ended, you must first get approval from the IRS, as explained later in *Change in Accounting Period*.

For example, if you use a calendar year and want to change to a 52–53 week year ending on the Saturday nearest to the end of November, you must first get approval from the IRS.

Change from a 52–53 week tax year. To change from a 52–53 week year to any other tax year, including another 52–53 week year, you must first get approval from the IRS.

Short Tax Year

A short tax year is a tax year of less than 12 months. There are two situations that can result in a short tax year. The first occurs when you (as a taxable entity) are not in existence for an entire tax year. The second occurs when you change your accounting period. Each situation results in a different way of figuring tax for the short tax year.

Not in Existence Entire Year

A tax return is required for the short period during which you were in existence. Requirements for filing the return and paying the tax generally are the same as if the return were for a full tax year of 12 months that ended on the last day of the short tax year.

Example 1. Corporation X came into existence on July 1, 1994. It elected the calendar year as its tax year. Corporation X must file its return by March 15, 1995. The return

Chapter 3 **ACCOUNTING PERIODS**

covers the period July 1, 1994, through December 31, 1994.

Example 2. A calendar year corporation dissolved on July 23, 1995. It must file its final return by October 16, 1995, for the period January 1 through July 23, 1995.

Example 3. Partnership YZ formed on September 4, 1994, and elected to use a fiscal year ending November 30. Partnership YZ is required to file its return by March 15, 1995.

Death of Individual. When an individual dies, a tax return must be filed for the decedent by the 15th day of the 4th month after the close of the individual's regular tax year.

Example. Agnes Jones was a single, calendar year taxpayer. She died on March 6, 1994. Her last tax return for the period January 1 through March 6, 1994, must be filed by April 17, 1995.

Change in Accounting Period

If you change your accounting period, you figure your tax for the short tax year by placing your taxable income for the short period on an annual basis. This computation, and other rules regarding a change in accounting period are explained in Publication 538.

IRS approval. You must, with certain exceptions, get approval from the IRS to change your tax year. To get this approval, you must file a current Form 1128 and enclose a user fee. This form must be filed by the 15th day of the 2nd calendar month after the close of the short tax year. This short tax year begins on the first day after the end of your present tax year and ends on the day before the first day of your new tax year.

Example. You use a calendar tax year and, in 1994, you want to change to a fiscal year ending October 31. You must file Form 1128 by December 15, 1994.

Extension to file. If you file Form 1128 after the due date, it is late and will be considered only if you can show good cause for filing late. However, applications received within 90 days of the date required may qualify for an automatic extension. See *Extension of time to file application,* under *Change in Accounting Method* in Publication 538, and Revenue Procedure 92–85 (C.B. 1992–2, C.B. 490).

Husband and wife. A husband and wife who have different tax years may not file a joint return. If the husband and wife want the same tax year so they can file a joint return, the method of changing a tax year depends on whether they are newly married. See Publication 538 for detailed information.

Improper tax year. If you begin your business on a date other than the first day of a calendar month and end it exactly 12 months from the date it began and this ending date is other than the last day of the month, you have not satisfied the requirements for establishing a calendar year or a fiscal year. Nor does the adoption of an accounting period ending exactly 12 months from the date your business began satisfy the requirements for a 52–53 week tax year. Because you have not satisfied the requirements for either a calendar or a fiscal year, you have adopted an improper tax year. You must either file an amended income tax return on the basis of a calendar year, or, if you want to use a tax year other than the calendar year, you must get approval from the IRS to change your tax year.

Amended return. To file an amended return to correct an improper tax year, you must attach a completed Form 1128 to your amended income tax return that is filed on a calendar year basis. Write "FILED UNDER REV. PROC. 85–15," at the top of your Form 1128. The form and your amended return should be filed with the Internal Revenue Service Center where you filed your original return.

Partnerships, S Corporations, and Personal Service Corporations

Generally, partnerships, S corporations, and personal service corporations must use "required tax years." The required tax year does not have to be used if the partnership, S corporation, or personal service corporation establishes a business purpose for a different period, or makes a *section 444 election,* explained later.

Partnerships

A partnership is required to conform its tax year to its partners' tax years in the following way:

1) If a majority interest (aggregate interest of more than 50%) in partnership capital and profits is held by one partner, or by more than one partner with the same tax year, the partnership must adopt that tax year.

2) If there are no partners who own a majority interest, or if the majority interest partners do not have the same tax year, the partnership is required to change to the tax year of its principal partners. A principal partner is one who has a 5% or more interest in the profits or capital of the partnership.

3) If neither (1) nor (2) applies, the partnership is required to adopt a tax year that results in the least aggregate deferral of income to the partners.

For more information about the required year for partnerships, see Publication 538. For general information on partnerships, see Chapter 29.

S Corporations

A small business corporation can elect to be an S corporation. All S corporations, regardless of when they became S corporations, are required to use a calendar tax year, or any other tax year for which the corporation establishes a business purpose or makes a section 444 election. For general information on S corporations, see Chapter 31.

Personal Service Corporations

Personal service corporations are required to use a calendar tax year unless they can establish a business purpose for a different period, or make a section 444 election. For this purpose, a personal service corporation generally is a corporation in which the principal activity is the performance of personal services that are substantially performed by employee-owners.

Performance of personal services. For this purpose, any activity that involves the performance of services in the fields of health, veterinary services, law, engineering, architecture, accounting, actuarial science, performing arts, or certain consulting services, is considered to be the performance of personal services.

For additional information about a personal service corporation's tax year, see Publication 538.

Section 444 Election

Partnerships, S corporations, and personal service corporations can elect under section 444 to use a tax year that is different from the permitted tax year. Certain restrictions apply to this election. In addition, this election does not apply to any partnership, S corporation, or personal service corporation that establishes a business purpose for a different period.

A partnership, S corporation, or personal service corporation may make a section 444 election if:

1) It is not a member of a tiered structure (see section 1.444–2T of the Income Tax Regulations),

2) It has not previously had a section 444 election in effect, and

3) It elects a year that meets the deferral period requirement.

Deferral period. Generally, a partnership, S corporation, or personal service corporation may make a section 444 election only if the tax year it wants to use results in a deferral period of 3 months or less.

However, an election to change a tax year from its required year will be allowed only if the deferral period of the tax year it wants to use is not longer than the shorter of:

1) Three months, or

2) The deferral period of the tax year being changed.

For a partnership, S corporation, or personal service corporation that wants to **adopt or change** its tax year by making a section 444 election, the deferral period is the number of months between the end of the tax year it wants to use and the close of the required tax year. If the current tax year is the required tax year, the deferral period is zero.

Example 1. BD partnership uses a calendar tax year that is also its required tax year. Because BD's deferral period is zero, BD is not able to make a section 444 election.

Example 2. E, a newly formed partnership, began operations on December 1, 1994. E is owned by calendar year partners. E wants to make a section 444 election to adopt a September 30 tax year. E's deferral period for the tax year beginning December 1, 1994, is 3 months (September 30 to December 31, 1995).

Making the election. You make a section 444 election by filing Form 8716 with the Internal Revenue Service Center where you normally file your returns. Form 8716 must be filed by the earlier of:

1) The due date (without regard to extensions) of the income tax return resulting from the section 444 election, or

2) The 15th day of the 6th month of the tax year for which the election will be effective. For this purpose, count the month in which the tax year begins even if it begins after the first day of that month.

You must attach a copy of Form 8716 to your Form 1065 or appropriate Form 1120 for the first tax year for which the election is made.

Example 1. AB, a partnership, began operations on September 11, 1994, and is qualified to make a section 444 election to use a September 30 tax year for its tax year beginning September 11, 1994. AB must file Form 8716 by January 17, 1995, which is the due date of the partnership's tax return for the period September 11, 1994, to September 30, 1994.

Example 2. The facts are the same as in Example (1) except that AB began operations on October 21, 1994. AB must file Form 8716 by March 15, 1995, the 15th day of the 6th month of the tax year for which the election will first be effective.

Example 3. B is a corporation that first becomes a personal service corporation for its tax year beginning September 1, 1994. B qualifies to make a section 444 election to use a September 30 tax year for its tax year beginning September 1, 1994. B must file Form 8716 by December 15, 1994, the due date of the income tax return for the short period September 1 to September 30, 1994.

Extension of time for filing. You may qualify for an automatic extension of 12 months to make this election. See Revenue Procedure 92–85 for more information.

Effect of election. Partnerships and S corporations that make a section 444 election must make certain required payments.

An electing personal service corporation must make certain distributions. These required payments and distributions are discussed later.

Ending the election. The section 444 election remains in effect until it is terminated. The election ends when the partnership, S corporation, or personal service corporation:

1) Changes to its required tax year,

2) Liquidates,

3) Willfully fails to comply with the required payments or distributions, or

4) Becomes a member of a tiered structure.

The election will also end if an S corporation's S election is terminated, or a personal service corporation ceases to be a personal service corporation. However, if a personal service corporation that has a section 444 election in effect elects to be an S corporation, the S corporation may continue the election of the personal service corporation. Or, if an S corporation terminates its S election and immediately becomes a personal service corporation, the personal service corporation may continue the section 444 election of the S corporation.

If the election is terminated, another section 444 election cannot be made for any tax year.

Required payment for partnerships and S corporations. Partnerships and S corporations must make a "required payment" for any tax year that the section 444 election is in effect and the required payment amount is more than $500. You also must pay if you had a required payment for any prior tax year that was more than $500 and you have a liability of any amount for that applicable year.

Any tax year that a section 444 election is in effect, including the first year, is called an "applicable election year." This required payment represents the value of the tax deferral that the owners receive through the use of a tax year different from the required tax year.

Report the required payment on Form 8752. If the required payment is more than $500 (or the required payment for any prior tax year was more than $500), pay it when Form 8752 is filed. If the required payment is $500 or less, and no payment was required in a prior year, no payment is required, but Form 8752 must be filed showing a zero amount.

When to file. Form 8752 must be filed and the required payment made (or zero amount reported) by May 15 of the calendar year following the calendar year in which the applicable election year begins. For example, if a partnership's applicable election year begins July 1, 1994, Form 8752 must be filed by May 15, 1995.

Required distributions for personal service corporations. If a personal service corporation makes a section 444 election, it must distribute certain amounts to employee-owners by December 31 of each applicable election year. If it fails to make these distributions, it may be required to defer certain deductions for amounts paid to owner-employees. The amount deferred is treated as paid or incurred in the following tax year.

For information on the minimum distribution, see the instructions for Part I of Schedule H (Form 1120), *Section 280H Limitations for a Personal Service Corporation (PSC)*.

Expeditious Approval

A procedure is provided whereby a partnership, S corporation, or personal service corporation may expeditiously obtain approval to change its tax year. For information on this procedure, see Publication 538.

Corporations

A new corporation establishes its tax year when it files its first income tax return. An S corporation or a personal service corporation must use the required tax year rules discussed earlier to establish its tax year. A newly reactivated corporation which has been inactive for a number of years is treated as a new taxpayer for the purpose of adopting a tax year.

Change in Tax Year

A corporation (other than an S corporation or a personal service corporation) generally may change its tax year under section 1.442–1(c) of the Income Tax Regulations without first getting the approval of the IRS if the following conditions are met.

1) It must not have changed its tax year within the 10 calendar years ending with the calendar year in which the short tax year resulting from the change begins,

2) Its short tax year must not be a tax year in which it has a net operating loss,

3) Its taxable income for the short tax year, if figured on an annual basis (annualized), is 80% or more of its taxable income for the tax year before the short tax year, and

4) It must not apply to become an S corporation for the tax year that would immediately follow the short tax year required to effect the change.

For more information, see Publication 538.

4. Accounting Methods

Introduction

An accounting method is a set of rules used to determine when and how income and expenses are reported. Your "accounting method" includes not only the overall method of accounting you use, but also the accounting treatment you use for any material item.

You choose your accounting method when you file your first tax return. After that, if you want to change your accounting method, you must first get consent from the IRS. See *Change in Accounting Method,* later.

No single accounting method is required of all taxpayers. You must use a system that clearly shows your income and expenses and you must maintain records that will enable you to file a correct return. In addition to your permanent books of account, you must keep any other records necessary to support the entries on your books and tax returns.

You must use the same method from year to year. Any accounting method that shows the consistent use of generally accepted accounting principles for your trade or business generally is considered to clearly show income. An accounting method clearly shows income only if all items of gross income and all expenses are treated the same from year to year.

If you do not regularly use an accounting method that clearly shows your income, your income will be figured under the method that, in the opinion of the IRS, clearly shows your income.

Topics
This chapter discusses:

- Allowable methods
- Cash method
- Accrual method
- Change in accounting method

Useful Items
You may want to see:

Publication

☐ **538** Accounting Periods and Methods

Form (and Instructions)

☐ **3115** Application for Change in Accounting Method

Allowable Methods

Generally, you may figure your taxable income under any of the following accounting methods:

1) Cash method,
2) Accrual method,
3) Special methods of accounting for certain items of income and expenses, and
4) Combination (hybrid) method using elements of two or more of the above.

The cash and accrual methods of accounting are explained later.

Special methods. There are special methods of accounting for certain items of income or expense such as:

Depreciation, discussed in Chapter 13,

Amortization and depletion, discussed in Chapter 14,

Deduction for bad debts, discussed in Chapter 15, and

Installment sales, discussed in Chapter 25.

Combination (hybrid) method. Generally, you may use any combination of cash, accrual, and special methods of accounting if the combination clearly shows income and you use it consistently. However, the following restrictions apply:

1) If inventories are necessary to account for your income, you must use an accrual method for purchases and sales. You can use the cash method for all other items of income and expenses. See *Inventories,* in the discussion of expenses under *Accrual Method,* later.

2) If you use the cash method for figuring your income, you must use the cash method for reporting your expenses.

3) If you use an accrual method for reporting your expenses, you must use an accrual method for figuring your income.

Any combination that includes the cash method is treated as the cash method, subject to the limitations applied to that method.

Business and personal items. You may account for business and personal items under different accounting methods. Thus, you may figure the income from your business under an accrual method even though you use the cash method to figure personal items.

Two or more businesses. If you operate more than one business, you generally may use a different accounting method for each separate and distinct business if the method you use for each clearly shows your income. For example, if you operate a personal service business and a manufacturing business, you may use the cash method for the personal service business but you must use an accrual method for the manufacturing business.

No business will be considered separate and distinct if you do not keep a complete and separable set of books and records for that business.

Cash Method

The cash method of accounting is used by most individuals and many small businesses with no inventories. However, if inventories are necessary in accounting for your income, you must use an accrual method for your sales and purchases. If you are not required to keep inventories, you usually will use the cash method. However, see *Limits on Use of Cash Method,* later.

Income

With the cash method, you include in your gross income all items of income you actually or constructively receive during the year. You must include property and services you receive in your income at their fair market value.

Constructive receipt. You have constructive receipt of income when an amount is credited to your account or made available to you without restriction. You do not need to have possession of it. If you authorize someone to be your agent and receive income for you, you are treated as having received it when your agent receives it.

Example 1. You have interest credited to your bank account in December 1994. You must include it in your gross income for 1994 and not for 1995 when you withdraw it or enter it in your passbook.

Example 2. You have interest coupons that mature and are payable in 1994, but you do not cash them until 1995. You must include them in income for 1994. You must include this matured interest in your gross income even though you later exchange the coupons for other property instead of cashing them.

Delaying receipt of income. You cannot hold checks or postpone taking possession of similar property from one tax year to another to avoid paying the tax on the income. You must report the income in the year the property is made available to you without restriction.

Expenses

Usually, you must deduct expenses in the tax year in which you actually pay them. However, expenses you pay in advance can be deducted only in the year to which they apply. In addition, if the uniform capitalization rules apply (see Chapter 8), you may have to capitalize certain costs.

Example. You are a calendar year taxpayer and you pay $1,000 for a business insurance policy that is effective on July 1, 1994, for a one-year period. You may deduct $500 in 1994 and $500 in 1995.

Limits on Use of Cash Method

The cash method, including any combination of methods that includes the cash method, cannot be used by the following entities:

1) Corporations (other than S corporations),
2) Partnerships having a corporation (other than an S corporation) as a partner, and
3) Tax shelters.

Exceptions. An exception allows farming businesses with gross receipts of $25 million or less, qualified personal service corporations, and entities with average annual gross receipts of $5 million or less to continue using the cash method. However, these exceptions do not apply to tax shelters. For more general information, see Publication 538. For more information on the farming exception, see Chapter 3 in Publication 225.

Accrual Method

Under an accrual method of accounting, income generally is reported in the year earned, and expenses are deducted or capitalized in the year incurred. The purpose of an accrual method of accounting is to match your income and your expenses in the correct year.

Income

Generally, all items of income are included in your gross income when you earn them, even though you may receive payment in another tax year. All events that fix your right to receive the income must have happened, and you must be able to figure the amount with reasonable accuracy.

Example. You are a calendar year accrual basis taxpayer. You sold a computer on December 28, 1994. You billed the customer in the first week of January 1995, but you did not receive payment until February 1995. You must include the amount of the sale in your income for 1994 because you earned the income in 1994.

Advance income. Special rules dealing with an accrual method of accounting for advance payments to you are discussed in Chapter 7 under *Prepaid Income*.

Estimating income. When you include an amount in gross income on the basis of a reasonable estimate, and you later determine the exact amount, the difference, if any, is taken into account in the tax year in which the determination is made.

Change in payment schedule for services. If you contract to perform services for a basic rate, you must include the basic rate in your income as it accrues. You must accrue the basic rate even if, as a matter of convenience, you agree to receive payments at a lower rate until you complete your services, at which time you will receive the difference between the basic rate and the amount actually paid to you.

Accounts receivable for services. You may not have to accrue all of your accounts receivable if, based on your experience, you will not collect all of these accounts. This is called the *nonaccrual-experience method*. See section 1.448–2T(b) of the Income Tax Regulations.

Expenses

You deduct or capitalize business expenses when you become liable for them, whether or not you pay them in the same year.

All events test. Before you can deduct or capitalize the expenses, all events that set the amount of the liability must have happened, and you must be able to figure the amount with reasonable accuracy.

Economic performance rule. Generally, you cannot deduct business expenses until economic performance occurs. If your expense is for property or services provided to you, or for use of property by you, economic performance occurs as the property or services are provided or as the property is used. If your expense is for property or services that you provide to others, economic performance occurs as you provide the property or services. An exception allows certain recurring expenses to be treated as incurred during a tax year even though economic performance has not occurred.

Example. You are a calendar year taxpayer and in December 1994 you buy office supplies. You received the supplies and are billed for them in December, but you pay for the supplies in January 1995. You can deduct the expense in 1994 because all events that set the amount of liability and economic performance occurred in that year.

Your office supplies may qualify as a recurring expense. In that case, you may be able to deduct the expense in 1994 even if economic performance (delivery of the supplies to you) did not occur until 1995. See Publication 538 for more information on the economic performance requirement.

Inventories. Inventories are necessary to clearly show income when the production, purchase, or sale of merchandise is an income-producing factor. If inventories are necessary to show income correctly, only an accrual accounting method can be used for purchases and sales. Inventories are discussed in Chapter 8.

Special Rules for Related Persons

You cannot deduct business expenses and interest owed to a related cash basis person *until* you make the payment and the corresponding amount is includible in the gross income of the related person. Determine the relationship, for this rule, as of the end of the tax year for which the expense or interest would otherwise be deductible. If a deduction is denied under this rule, the rule will continue to apply even if your relationship with the person ends before the expenses or interest is includible in the gross income of that person.

Related persons. For the purpose of applying this rule, the following are related persons:

1) Members of the immediate family, including only brothers and sisters (either whole or half), husband and wife, ancestors, and lineal descendants.
2) Two corporations that are members of the same controlled group.
3) The fiduciaries of two different trusts, and the fiduciary and beneficiary of two different trusts if the same person is the grantor of both trusts.
4) Certain educational and charitable organizations and a person (if an individual, including the members of the individual's family) who, directly or indirectly, controls the organization.
5) An individual and a corporation of which more than 50% of the value of the outstanding stock is owned, directly or indirectly, by or for that individual.
6) A trust fiduciary and a corporation of which more than 50% in value of the outstanding stock is owned, directly or indirectly, by or for the trust or by or for the grantor of the trust.
7) The grantor and fiduciary, and the fiduciary and beneficiary, of any trust.
8) Any two S corporations if the same persons own more than 50% in value of the outstanding stock of each corporation.
9) An S corporation and a corporation that is not an S corporation if the same persons own more than 50% in value of the outstanding stock of each corporation.
10) A corporation and a partnership if the same persons own more than 50% in value of the outstanding stock of the corporation and more than 50% of the capital interest or profits or profits interest in the partnership.
11) A personal service corporation and any employee-owner, regardless of the amount of stock owned by the employee-owner.

Indirect ownership of stock. To decide whether an individual directly or indirectly owns any of the outstanding stock of a corporation, the following rules apply:

1) Stock owned, directly or indirectly, by or for a corporation, partnership, estate, or trust is treated as being owned proportionately by or for its shareholders, partners, or beneficiaries.
2) An individual is treated as owning the stock owned, directly or indirectly, by or

Chapter 4 **ACCOUNTING METHODS**

for the individual's family (as defined in item (1) under *Related persons*).

3) Any individual owning (other than by applying rule (2)) any stock in a corporation is treated as owning the stock owned directly or indirectly by that individual's partner, and

4) Stock constructively owned by a person under rule (1), shall, to apply rule (1), (2), or (3), be treated as actually owned by that person. But stock constructively owned by an individual under rule (2) or (3) will not be treated as actually owned by the individual for applying either rule (2) or (3) to make another person the constructive owner of that stock.

Reallocation of income and deductions. Where it is necessary to clearly show income or to prevent evasion of taxes, the IRS may reallocate gross income, deductions, credits, or allowances between two or more organizations, trades, or businesses owned or controlled directly or indirectly by the same interests.

Gains and losses. Gains and losses on sales or exchanges between *related parties* are discussed in Chapter 23. For information on losses from sales or exchanges of property between partners and partnerships, see Chapter 29.

Change in Accounting Method

When you file your first return, you may, without consent from the IRS, choose any permitted accounting method. The method you choose must be used consistently from year to year and clearly show your income.

After your first return is filed, if you want to change your accounting method, you must first get consent from the IRS. This is necessary to notify the IRS that a change is being made and to prevent you from gaining an unlawful tax advantage.

The IRS will consider the need for consistency in the accounting area against your reason for wanting to change your accounting method when the method from which you are changing clearly shows your income.

If you request a change in accounting method (such as from an improper to a proper method), the absence of IRS consent to the change does not prevent the IRS from imposing any penalty or addition to tax, nor diminish the amount of the penalty or the addition to tax.

A change in your accounting method includes a change not only in your overall system of accounting but also in the treatment of any material item. Some examples of changes that *require* consent are:

1) A change from the cash method to an accrual method or vice versa (unless you must change to an accrual method and you make the change automatically),

2) A change in the method or basis used to value inventories, and

3) A change in the method of figuring depreciation (except certain changes to the straight line method as explained in Chapter 13).

Automatic change to accrual method. If you are required to change from the cash method to an accrual method, discussed earlier under *Limits on Use of Cash Method*, you are not required to have prior approval from the IRS to make this change.

Form 3115. Although this change to an overall accrual method is considered automatic, you must complete and file Form 3115 no later than the due date (including extensions) for filing your income tax return. Attach Form 3115 with the applicable user fee to your income tax return. For more information, see Publication 538.

Accounting change information. For information about the procedures to change your accounting method, see Publication 538.

Appendix 3. Tax Guide for Small Businesses

Part Six.

The Business Activity

This Part discusses some of the tax rules that may differ, depending on whether you operate your business as a sole proprietor, a partnership, a corporation, or an S corporation.

28. Sole Proprietorships

Introduction

This chapter explains the filing requirements for a sole proprietor and how a sole proprietor should report the sale or disposition of a business. For information on how to treat the expenses of starting a new business or buying an existing business, see Chapters 5 and 14.

You are a sole proprietor if you are self-employed and are the sole owner of an unincorporated business.

Topics
This chapter discusses:

* Schedule C (Form 1040)
* Schedule C-EZ (Form 1040)
* The sale of a business

Useful Items
You may want to see:

Publication

☐ **505** Tax Withholding and Estimated Tax

☐ **544** Sales and Other Dispositions of Assets

Form (and Instructions)

☐ **Schedule C (Form 1040)** Profit or Loss From Business

☐ **Schedule C-EZ (Form 1040)** Net Profit From Business

☐ **1040-ES** Estimated Tax for Individuals

☐ **2210** Underpayment of Estimated Tax by Individuals, Estates, and Trusts

☐ **4868** Application for Automatic Extension of Time To File U.S. Individual Income Tax Return

Schedule C and Schedule C-EZ

If you are a sole proprietor, you report your income and expenses from your business or profession on Schedule C or Schedule C-EZ (Form 1040) and file it with your Form 1040. Report the amount of net profit (or loss) from Schedule C on line 12 of Form 1040. If you operate more than one business as a sole proprietor, you must prepare a *separate Schedule C or Schedule C-EZ for each business* and attach each of them to your tax return. If you do not prepare a separate Schedule C or Schedule C-EZ for each business, you may have to pay a *penalty* because you did not properly report your income and deductions.

It is important to use the correct business code, since this information will identify market segments of the public for IRS Taxpayer Education programs. This information is also used by the U.S. Census Bureau for their economic census.

Schedule C-EZ (Form 1040). You may be able to use Schedule C-EZ, *Net Profit From Business,* if you had gross receipts from your nonfarm business of $25,000 or less and business expenses of $2,000 or less. Other requirements that must be met are listed on Schedule C-EZ.

Due date. Form 1040 is due, for calendar year 1994, by April 17, 1995. If you use a fiscal year, your return is due by the 15th day of the 4th month after the close of your fiscal year. See the *Checklist* near the end of this publication.

Automatic extension of time to file Form 4868. If you cannot file your return on time, use Form 4868 to request an automatic 4-month extension.

You may not use Form 4868 if:

1) You want the IRS to figure your tax, or
2) You are under a court order to file your return by the regular due date.

You must file Form 4868 by the date your Form 1040 would be due. When you file Form 4868, estimate any tax you will owe and any balance due. Pay as much as you can at this time to limit the interest you will owe. Also, you may be charged the late payment penalty on the unpaid tax from the regular due date of your return.

Withdrawals. If you are a sole proprietor, there is no tax effect if you take money out of your business, or transfer money to or from your business. It is a good idea to set up a drawing account. This will help you identify amounts that are not for business expenses but that are for your own personal use.

Self-employment tax. Generally, if you are a sole proprietor, you will have to pay self-employment tax. See Chapter 33.

Estimated Tax

If you are a sole proprietor, you may have to make estimated tax payments if the total of your estimated income tax and self-employment tax for 1995 will exceed your total withholding and credits by $500 or more.

You use **Form 1040-ES** to estimate your tax. See Publication 505, and the instructions for Form 1040-ES for information on estimated taxes.

Underpayment of tax. If you did not pay enough income tax and self-employment tax for 1994 by withholding or by making estimated tax payments, you may have to pay a penalty on the amount not paid. IRS will figure the penalty for you and send you a bill. Or you can use **Form 2210** to see if you have to pay a penalty and to figure the penalty amount. For more information, see Publication 505.

Sale of a Business

If you are a sole proprietor and sell your business, you are really selling all the individual assets of your business.

Classification of assets. To determine whether the gain or loss on the sale of an asset is capital gain or loss or ordinary gain or loss, you must classify the assets sold into one of the following categories:

1) Capital assets,
2) Real property and depreciable property used in your business and held for more than one year (this includes amortizable section 197 intangibles) (see Chapter 24), and
3) Other property—for example, stock-in-trade, inventory, or property used in your business and held one year or less.

Accounts and notes receivable. Accounts and notes receivable acquired in the ordinary course of your business for services rendered, or from the sale of stock-in-trade,

Chapter 28 **SOLE PROPRIETORSHIPS**

174 APPENDIX 3. TAX GUIDE FOR SMALL BUSINESSES

are not capital assets. They should be classified in category (3).

Installment notes. Installment notes from the sale of stock-in-trade should be classified in category (3). The gain, which is the difference between the basis of the note and the amount realized, is ordinary income.

Merchandise inventories. Merchandise inventories are not capital assets and belong in category (3).

Land and leaseholds. Land and leaseholds used in your business are not capital assets. If you hold them for more than one year, they belong in category (2), and if you hold them one year or less, in category (3).

Buildings, machinery, furniture, and fixtures. Buildings, machinery, furniture, and fixtures that you use in your business are not capital assets. You should put them in category (2) if you hold them for more than one year, and in (3) if you hold them for one year or less.

Patents. Patents that you use in your business should ordinarily be classified in category (2) if you hold them more than one year, and in (3) if you hold them one year or less. But if you are the inventor (or if you are entitled to the same treatment as the inventor, as explained under Patents, in Chapter 23) and you sell all substantial rights to patent property or a patent, or an undivided interest in all such rights, to a person other than a related person, treat the sale as a sale of a long-term capital asset and include it in category (1).

Copyrights. Copyrights that you use in your business should be classified in category (2) if you hold them more than one year, and in (3) if you hold them one year or less. However, if you sell a copyright that you created, or if you sell a copyright that gets its basis from the person who created the property, you should not classify it in category (2). Instead, you should classify it in category (3).

If you acquired patents and copyrights as part of the acquisition of a substantial portion of a business after August 10, 1993 (or after July 25, 1991, if elected), you must amortize their costs over 15 years. If the patent or copyright is not acquired as part of an acquisition of a substantial portion of a business, you must depreciate the cost. For more information, see Chapter 14.

Goodwill. Goodwill is a section 197 intangible. It belongs in category (2). The basis of goodwill is usually its cost if you bought it. When you buy a going business and intend to continue the business, goodwill may be included in the price.

If you acquired a business after August 10, 1993 (or July 25, 1991, if elected), and part of the price included goodwill, you may amortize the cost of the goodwill over 15 years. For more information on section 197 intangibles, see Chapter 14.

Agreement not to compete. An agreement not to compete (also called a covenant not to compete) entered into in connection with the acquisition of an interest in a trade or business is a section 197 intangible and should be classified in category (2). See Chapter 23.

Professional skill or other characteristics of an owner. The amount received from the sale of a professional practice that is for goodwill is determined by the facts in the particular case and not by whether the business is, or is not, dependent solely on the owner's professional skill or other personal characteristics.

If the seller has the right to keep fees collected after the sale for services performed before the sale, or receives payment for giving up all or part of the right to these fees, the amount received is treated as if it were for services performed before the sale rather than for the sale of goodwill, and is ordinary income.

If the seller retains a right to any fees or revenue collected for services performed after the sale, or if the purchaser agrees to pay an amount equal to any part of these fees or revenues, these amounts are ordinary income from the business, not proceeds from the sale of goodwill.

Amounts received by a professional person when admitting partners to that person's practice may be payment for a partial transfer of goodwill (rather than an assignment of anticipated future earnings). In such a case, the goodwill must in fact exist and the consideration allocated to it must actually be a payment for it.

Allocation of selling price. You must allocate the selling price proportionately among all the assets sold. See Chapter 2 in Publication 544 for a discussion of the allocation rules.

Figuring gain or loss. After classifying each asset sold and allocating the selling price, you are ready to figure your gain or loss. You must figure separately the gain or loss for each asset sold, and then treat it according to its classification. The treatment of assets in categories (1) and (2) is discussed in Chapters 22, 23, and 24. Also see Publication 544.

You should treat the gains or losses relating to assets in category (3) as ordinary income or loss.

Transactions between related parties. If there is a direct or indirect sale or exchange of depreciable property between related parties, any gain will be taxed as ordinary income. Losses between related parties are not deductible. See Chapter 23.

Other disposition of a business. You can change the present form of your business without selling your assets. You may do this by joining one or more persons who want to consolidate their individual businesses into a partnership or other form of organization and by transferring your assets to the new form of business. You may change the form of your business by incorporating a sole proprietorship or a partnership. You also may transfer the property of a sole proprietorship or partnership to a previously existing corporation.

29. Partnerships

Important Changes for 1994

Health insurance deduction for the self-employed. The 25% deduction for health insurance costs for self-employed persons expired for tax years beginning after 1993. However, as this publication was being prepared for print, Congress was considering legislation to extend the provision. See Publication 553, *Highlights of 1994 Tax Changes*, for information.

Rental real estate activity. For tax years beginning after 1993, passive activities do not include a rental real estate activity in which the partner materially participates. The partner must meet other conditions. See *Passive activities*, later.

Estimated tax for individuals modified. Generally, the required payment for estimated tax for individuals is the smaller of:

1) 90% of the total expected tax for the current year, or

2) 100% of the total tax shown on the prior year's tax return.

However, for tax years beginning after 1993, individuals with adjusted gross income of more than $150,000 ($75,000 if married and filing a separate return) must substitute 110% in (2) above. This rule does not apply to individuals who receive at least two-thirds of their gross income from farming or fishing. See Publication 505 for more information.

Capital gains exclusion for small business stock. Beginning in 1998, a partner may be able to exclude up to 50% of the gain from the sale or exchange of qualified small business stock that was:

1) Originally issued after August 10, 1993.

2) Held by the partnership for more than 5 years.

See Internal Revenue Code section 1202 for the definition of qualified small business stock and special rules that apply to partners.

Important Reminders

Definition of "substantially appreciated" inventory modified. The definition of substantially appreciated inventory has been modified. If the partnership's inventory is worth more than 120% of its adjusted basis, the inventory is treated as substantially appreciated. The modified definition of substantially appreciated inventory applies to sales, exchanges, and distributions after April 30, 1993. See *Inventory items that have appreciated substantially in value*, later.

Treatment of certain payments to retired or deceased partners. New rules apply to the liquidation of a partner's interest for partners retiring or dying on or after January 5, 1993. They do not apply to any partner retiring on or after that date if a written contract to purchase the partner's interest in the partnership was binding on January 4, 1993, and at all times thereafter. See *Payments in liquidation of retiring or deceased partner's interest*, later.

Discharge of qualified real property business indebtedness. Partners may elect to exclude from gross income certain income from discharge of qualified real property business indebtedness in tax years ending after 1992. See *Discharge of qualified real property business indebtedness* in Publication 541.

Net capital gains treated as investment income. For tax years beginning after 1992, net capital gain from the disposition of property held for investment may be excluded from investment income for purposes of computing the investment interest limitation. For more information, see Publication 550, *Investment Income and Expenses*.

Increased expensing deduction. The amount allowed to be expensed under section 179 of the Code is increased from $10,000 to $17,500 for property placed in service in tax years beginning after 1992. For more information, see Publication 534.

Jobs credit extended. The targeted jobs credit has been extended for employees who begin work for the employer after June 30, 1992, and before January 1, 1995. For an employee who began work after August 9, 1993, the jobs credit is not allowed for any employee who is related to a partner who owns more than 50% of the capital and profits interest of the partnership.

Meal and entertainment expenses. For tax years beginning after 1993, the deductible part of otherwise allowable business meals and entertainment expenses is reduced from 80% to 50%.

Introduction

A partnership is the relationship between two or more persons who join together to carry on a trade or business. Each person contributes money, property, labor, or skill, and each expects to share in the profits and losses. "Person," when used to describe a partner, means an individual, a corporation, a trust, an estate, or another partnership.

Husband-wife partnerships. If spouses carry on a business together and share in the profits and losses, they may be partners whether or not they have a formal partnership agreement. If so, they should report income or loss on Form 1065. They should *not* report the income on a Schedule C (Form 1040) in the name of one spouse as a sole proprietor.

Each spouse should include his or her share of self-employment income shown on Schedule K–1 (Form 1065) on a separate Schedule SE (Form 1040). Usually this will not increase their total tax, but it will give each spouse credit for social security earnings on which retirement benefits are based. See *Family Partnerships*, later.

Topics

This chapter discusses:

- Form 1065
- Partnership income
- Partner's income
- Family partnerships
- Partner's dealings with the partnership
- Contributed property
- Basis of partner's interest
- Optional adjustment to basis of partnership property
- Sales, exchanges, and other transfers
- Unrealized receivables and inventory items

Useful Items

You may want to see:

Publication

- ☐ 541 Tax Information on Partnerships
- ☐ 551 Basis of Assets
- ☐ 556 Examination of Returns, Appeal Rights, and Claims for Refund
- ☐ 925 Passive Activity and At-Risk Rules

Form (and Instructions)

- ☐ Sch SE (Form 1040) Self-Employment Tax
- ☐ Sch K–1 (Form 1065) Partner's Share of Income, Credits, Deductions, Etc.
- ☐ 8082 Notice of Inconsistent Treatment or Amended Return
- ☐ 8736 Application for Automatic Extension of Time To File U.S. Return for a Partnership, REMIC, or for Certain Trusts

Form 1065

Every partnership doing business in or having income from sources within the United States is required to file Form 1065 for its tax year. This is an information return and must be signed by a general partner. If a limited liability company is treated as a partnership and files Form 1065, one of the company members must sign the return. See the instructions for Form 1065 for more information.

Due date. Form 1065 generally must be filed on or before April 15 following the close of the partnership's tax year if its accounting period is the calendar year. A fiscal year partnership generally must file its return by the 15th day of the 4th month following the close of its fiscal year. However, if the date for filing a return or making a tax payment falls on a Saturday, Sunday, or legal holiday, the partnership can file the return on the next day that is not a Saturday, Sunday, or legal holiday.

If a partnership needs more time to file its partnership return, it should file Form 8736 by the regular due date of its Form 1065. The automatic extension is 3 months.

Schedule K-1 due date. The partnership must provide copies of Schedule K-1 (Form 1065) to the partners on or before the date Form 1065 is required to be filed, including extensions.

Penalties. A penalty is assessed against any partnership that must file a partnership return and, unless the failure is due to reasonable cause, it fails to file on time (including extensions), or fails to file a return with all the information required. The penalty is $50 per month (or part of a month) per partner, up to a maximum of 5 months. For more information, see *Penalties* under *Filing Requirements* in Publication 541.

The partnership will also receive a penalty if it fails to provide copies of Schedules K-1 (Form 1065) to the partners, unless the failure is due to reasonable cause and not willful negligence.

Partnership Income

Partnership profits (and other income and gains) are not taxed to the partnership. A partnership determines its income in the same manner as an individual. However, a partnership must state certain items of gain, loss, income, etc. separately and certain deductions are not allowed to the partnership.

Partnership chooses how to compute income. The partnership, not the partners, makes most choices about how to compute income. These include choices for accounting methods (Chapter 4), depreciation methods (Chapter 13), accounting for specific items such as depletion, amortization of certain organization fees, amortization of business start-up costs of the partnership, and reforestation expenditures (Chapter 14), installment sales (Chapter 25), and nonrecognition of gain on involuntary conversions of property (Chapter 26).

However, each partner, not the partnership, decides how to treat foreign and U.S. possessions taxes, certain mining exploration expenses, and income from discharge of indebtedness.

Tax year. Generally, a partnership must use the same tax year as its majority partners. For exceptions to this rule and for more information, see Chapter 3.

Partner's Income

In determining a partner's income tax for the year (on his or her own income tax return), the partner must take into account his or her *distributive share* (whether or not it is distributed) of certain partnership items. These items will be reported to the partner on Schedule K-1 (Form 1065). See the instructions for Form 1065 for more information.

Estimated tax. As a result of partnership distributions, a partner may have to make payments of estimated tax. For more information, see *Estimated tax* under *Partner's Income* in Publication 541.

Treatment of partnership items. Partners must treat partnership items on their individual tax returns as they are treated on the partnership return. If a partner treats an item differently on his or her individual return, the IRS can automatically assess and collect any tax and penalties that result from adjusting the item to make it consistent with the partnership return. However, this does not apply if a partner files Form 8082 with his or her return identifying the different treatment.

Examination procedures. Under current examination procedures, the tax treatment of any partnership item is determined at the partnership level in a unified partnership proceeding rather than at the individual partner's level. After the proper treatment of a partnership item is determined at the partnership level, the IRS can automatically make related adjustments to the tax returns of the partners based on the partners' shares of any adjusted items.

These examination procedures do not apply to small partnerships that have 10 or fewer partners who are individuals (other than nonresident alien individuals) or estates. This rule applies if each partner's share of every partnership item is the same as that partner's share of every other item. However, small partnerships can make an election to have these procedures apply.

For more information on these procedures, see Publication 556.

Distributive Share

Generally, the partnership agreement determines a partner's distributive share of any item or class of items of income, gain, loss, deduction, or credit.

Distributive share determined by interest in partnership. A partner's distributive share of each item is determined by his or her interest in the partnership (taking into account all facts and circumstances) if either of the following applies:

1) The partnership agreement does not provide for the allocation of income, gain, loss, deduction, or credit (or item thereof), or

2) The allocation of income, gain, loss, deduction, or credit (or item thereof) to any partner under the agreement does not have substantial economic effect.

The allocation is done by taking into account the partner's contributions to the partnership, the interests of all partners in profits and losses (if different from interests in taxable income or loss), cash flow, and the rights of the partners to distributions of capital upon liquidation.

Substantial economic effect. An allocation has substantial economic effect if both of the following apply:

1) There is a reasonable possibility that the allocation will substantially affect the dollar amount of the partners' shares of partnership income or loss independently of tax consequences, and

2) The partner to whom an allocation is made actually receives the economic benefit or bears the economic burden corresponding to that allocation.

Character of items. The character of certain items of income, gain, loss, deduction, or credit included in a partner's distributive share is determined as if the partner:

1) Realized the item directly from the same source from which the partnership realized it, or

2) Incurred the item in the same manner as the partnership.

For example, a partner's distributive share of gain from the sale of partnership depreciable property used in a trade or business of the partnership is treated as gain from the sale of depreciable property that the partner used in a trade or business.

Self-employment tax. A partner's distributive share of income from a partnership is usually included in figuring net earnings from self-employment. If an individual partner has net earnings from self-employment of $400 or more for the year, the partner must figure self-employment tax on Schedule SE (Form 1040). See Chapter 33.

Tax preference income. To figure alternative minimum tax, a partner must separately take into account any distributive share of items of income and deductions that enter into the computation of alternative minimum taxable income. For additional information, see the instructions to Form 6251, *Alternative Minimum Tax – Individuals*.

Gross income. When it is necessary to determine the gross income of a partner, the partner's gross income includes his or her distributive share of the partnership's gross income. For example, each partner's share of partnership gross income is used in determining whether an income tax return must be filed by that individual partner.

Certain distributions of property. If a partnership makes a distribution to a partner after June 24, 1992, the partner generally will have a gain equal to the lesser of:

1) The excess of:
   a) The fair market value of any property (other than money) received, over
   b) The adjusted basis of the partner's interest in the partnership immediately before the distribution reduced (but not below zero) by any money received in the distribution, or
2) The net precontribution gain of the partner.

The character of the gain is determined by reference to the proportionate character of the net precontribution gain. This gain is in addition to any gain the partner must recognize if the amount of money distributed is more than his or her basis in the partnership.

Net precontribution gain. This is the net gain that the distributee partner would have recognized if all the partnership property that had been contributed by the partner within 5 years of the distribution, and held by the partnership immediately before the distribution, had been distributed by the partnership to another partner.

Effect on basis. The adjusted basis of the partner's interest in the partnership is increased by any gain recognized by this partner. Other than for purposes of determining the gain, the increase is treated as occurring immediately before the distribution. See *Basis of Partner's Interest*, later.

The partnership must adjust its basis in any property that the partner contributed within 5 years of the distribution to reflect any gain that partner recognizes under this rule.

Exception 1. If any of the distributed property is property which the partner had contributed to the partnership, such property is not taken into account in determining either:

1) The excess of the fair market value of any property received over the adjusted basis of the partner's interest in the partnership, or
2) The partner's net precontribution gain.

If any interest in an entity is distributed, this exception does not apply to the extent that the value of the interest is due to property contributed to the entity after the interest in the entity had been contributed to the partnership.

Exception 2. This rule does not apply to a distribution of either:

1) Unrealized receivables or substantially appreciated inventory items of the partnership, discussed later, in exchange for all or part of a partner's interest in other partnership property, or
2) Other partnership property in exchange for all or part of a partner's interest in unrealized receivables or substantially appreciated inventory items of the partnership.

Losses. A partner's distributive share of partnership loss is allowed only to the extent of the adjusted basis of the partner's interest in the partnership. The adjusted basis is figured at the end of the partnership's tax year in which the loss occurred, before taking the loss into account. Any loss that is more than the partner's adjusted basis is not deductible for that year. However, any loss not allowed for this reason will be allowed as a deduction (up to the partner's basis) at the end of any succeeding year in which the partner increases his or her basis to more than zero. See *Basis of Partner's Interest*, later.

Example. Mike and Joe are equal partners in a partnership. Mike files his individual return on a calendar year basis. The partnership return is also filed on a calendar year basis. The partnership incurred a $10,000 loss last year. Mike's distributive share of the loss is $5,000. The adjusted basis of his partnership interest, before considering his share of last year's loss, was $2,000. He could claim only $2,000 of the loss on last year's individual return. The adjusted basis of his interest at the end of last year was then reduced to zero.

The partnership showed an $8,000 profit for this year. Mike's $4,000 share of the profit increased the adjusted basis of his interest by $4,000 (not taking into account the $3,000 excess loss he could not deduct last year). His return for this year will show his $4,000 distributive share of this year's profits and the $3,000 loss not allowable last year. The adjusted basis of his partnership interest at the end of this year is $1,000.

At-risk limits. At-risk rules apply to most trade or business activities including activities conducted through a partnership, or activities for the production of income. The at-risk rules limit the loss a partner can deduct on the amounts for which that partner is considered at risk in the activity.

A partner is considered at risk for:

1) The amount of money and the adjusted basis of any property he or she contributed to the activity,
2) The income retained by the partnership, and
3) Certain amounts borrowed by the partnership for use in the activity.

However, a partner is generally not considered at risk for amounts borrowed unless that partner is personally liable for repayment, or the amounts borrowed are secured by the partner's property (other than property used in the activity).

A partner is not considered at risk for amounts protected against loss through guarantees, stop-loss agreements, or similar arrangements. Nor is the partner at risk for amounts borrowed if the lender has an interest in the activity (other than as a creditor) or if the lender is related to a person (other than the partner) having such an interest. For more information on determining the amount at risk, see Publication 925.

Passive activities. Generally, Code section 469 limits the amount you can deduct for passive activity losses and credits. The passive activity limits do not apply to the partnership. Instead, they apply to each partner's share of loss or credit from passive activities. Because the treatment of each partner's share of partnership income, loss, or credit depends upon the nature of the activity that generated it, the partnership must report income, loss, or credits separately for each activity.

Generally, passive activities include activities that involve the conduct of a trade or business, if the partner does not materially participate in the activity. The level of each partner's participation in an activity must be determined by the partner.

Rental activities. Passive activities also include rental activities, regardless of the partner's participation. However, for tax years beginning after 1993, passive activities do not include a rental real estate activity in which the partner materially participates. The partner must also meet both of the following conditions for the tax year:

1) More than half of the personal services a partner performs in any trade or business are in a real property trade or business in which the partner materially participates.
2) The partner performs more than 750 hours of service in a real property trade or business in which the partner materially participates.

Limited partners. Limited partners are generally not considered to materially participate in trade or business activities conducted through partnerships.

More Information. For more information on passive activities, see Publication 925 and the instructions to Forms 1065 and 8582.

Family Partnerships

Members of a family can be partners. Members of a family include only spouses, ancestors, and lineal descendants, or any trust for their primary benefit.

Family members as partners. Family members will be recognized as partners only if one of the following requirements is met.

1) If capital is a material income-producing factor, they acquired their capital interest in a bona fide transaction (even if by gift or purchase from another family member), actually own the partnership interest, and actually control the interest, or

Chapter 29 **PARTNERSHIPS**

2) If capital is not a material income-producing factor, they must have joined together in good faith to conduct a business. In addition, they must have agreed that contributions of each entitle them to a share in the profits. Some capital or service must be provided by each partner.

Capital is material. Capital is a material income-producing factor if a substantial part of the gross income of the business comes from the use of capital. Capital is ordinarily an income-producing factor if the operation of the business requires substantial inventories or investments in plant, machinery, or equipment.

Capital is not material. In general, capital is not a material income-producing factor if the income of the business consists principally of fees, commissions, or other compensation for personal services performed by members or employees of the partnership.

Capital interest. A capital interest in a partnership is an interest in its assets that is distributable to the owner of the interest if:

1) He or she withdraws from the partnership, or

2) The partnership liquidates.

The mere right to share in the earnings and profits is not a capital interest in the partnership.

Gift. If a family member receives a gift of a capital interest in a family partnership in which capital is a material income-producing factor, there are limits on the amount that can be allocated to that member (donee) as a distributive share of partnership income. To determine the limits for a donee's share:

1) The partnership income must be reduced by a reasonable compensation for services rendered to the partnership by the donor, and

2) The donee-partner's share of the remaining profits allocated to donated capital must not be proportionately greater than the donor's share attributable to the donor's capital.

Purchase. An interest purchased by one member of a family from another member of the family is considered to be created by gift.

Example. A father sold 50% of his business to his son. The resulting partnership had a profit of $60,000. Capital is a material income-producing factor. The father performed services worth $24,000, which is reasonable compensation, and the son performed no services. The $24,000 must be allocated to the father as compensation. Of the remaining $36,000 of income which is due to capital, at least 50%, or $18,000, must be allocated to the father since he owns a 50% capital interest. The son's share of partnership income cannot be more than $18,000.

Partner's Dealings with the Partnership

For certain transactions between a partner and his or her partnership, the partner is treated as not being a member of the partnership. See Publication 541 for more information on the transactions.

Sales and exchanges. Special rules apply to sales or exchanges of property between certain persons and partnerships.

Losses. Losses will not be allowed from a sale or exchange of property (other than an interest in the partnership) directly or indirectly between a partnership and a person whose direct or indirect interest in the capital or profits of the partnership is more than 50%.

If the sale or exchange is between two partnerships in which the same persons directly or indirectly own more than 50% interest of the capital or profits in each partnership, no deduction of a loss is allowed.

In either case, if the purchaser later sells the property, any gain realized will be taxable only to the extent that it is more than the loss that was not allowed.

Gains. Gains are treated as ordinary income in a sale or exchange of property directly or indirectly between a person and a partnership, or between two partnerships, if both of the following apply:

1) More than 50% of the capital or profits interest in the partnership(s) is directly or indirectly owned by the same person(s), and

2) The property in the hands of the transferee immediately after the transfer is not a capital asset. Property that is not a capital asset includes trade accounts receivable, inventory, stock-in-trade, and depreciable or real property used in a trade or business.

Determining ownership. To determine if there is more than 50% ownership in partnership capital or profits, the following rules apply:

1) An interest directly or indirectly owned by or for a corporation, partnership, estate, or trust is considered to be owned proportionately by or for its shareholders, partners, or beneficiaries.

2) An individual is considered to own the interest that is directly or indirectly owned by or for the individual's family. For this rule, "family" includes only brothers, sisters, half-brothers, half-sisters, spouses, ancestors, and lineal descendants.

3) If a person is considered to own an interest using rule (1), that person (the "constructive owner") is treated as if actually owning that interest when rules (1) and (2) are applied. However, if a person is considered to own an interest using rule (2), that person is not treated as actually owning that interest, thus making another person the constructive owner.

Example. Individuals A and B and Trust T are equal partners in Partnership ABT. A's husband, AH, is the sole beneficiary of Trust T. Trust T's partnership interest will be attributed to AH only for the purpose of further attributing the interest to A. This attribution makes A a more-than-50% partner. This means that any deductions for losses on transactions between her and ABT will not be allowed, and any gains will be treated as ordinary rather than capital gains.

Payments by accrual basis partnership to cash basis partner. A partnership that uses an accrual method of accounting cannot deduct any business expense owed to a cash basis partner until the amounts are paid and the partner includes the payment in income. However, this does not apply to guaranteed payments made to a partner, which are generally deductible when accrued.

Guaranteed payments. A partnership treats guaranteed payments to a partner for services, or for the use of capital, as if they were made to a person who is not a partner. This is true only to the extent the payments are figured without regard to the partnership's income. This treatment is for purposes of determining gross income and deductible business expenses only. For other tax purposes, guaranteed payments are treated as a partner's distributive share of ordinary income. Guaranteed payments are not subject to tax withholding.

The payments are generally deductible by the partnership as a business expense. They are included in Schedules K and K-1 of the partnership return and are reported by the individual partner on Form 1040 as ordinary income, in addition to the appropriate distributive share of the other ordinary income of the partnership.

Guaranteed payments made to partners for organizing the partnership or syndicating interests in the partnership are capital expenditures and are not deductible by the partnership. However, these payments must be included in the partners' individual income tax returns. See *Organizational costs for a partnership* in Chapter 14.

A partner includes the guaranteed payments in income in the partner's tax year in which the partnership's tax year ends.

Example. Under the terms of the partnership agreement, Erica is entitled to a fixed annual payment of $10,000 without regard to the income of the partnership. Her distributive share of the partnership income is 10%. After deducting the guaranteed payment, the partnership has $50,000 of ordinary income. She must include $15,000 as ordinary income on her individual income tax return for her tax year in which the partnership's tax year ends ($10,000 guaranteed payment plus $5,000 ($50,000 × 10%) distributive share).

Minimum payment. If a partner is to receive a minimum payment from the partnership, the guaranteed payment is the amount by which the minimum payment is more than the partner's distributive share of the partnership income **before** taking into account the guaranteed payment.

Example. Under a partnership agreement, Chris is to receive 30% of the partnership income, but not less than $8,000. The partnership has net income of $20,000. Chris's share, without regard to the minimum guarantee, is $6,000 (30% of $20,000). Thus, the amount of the guaranteed payment that may be deducted by the partnership is $2,000 ($8,000 less $6,000). Chris's income from the partnership is $8,000, and the remaining $12,000 will be reported by the other partners in proportion to their shares under the partnership agreement.

If the partnership net income had been $30,000, there would have been no guaranteed payment since his share, without regard to the guarantee, would have been greater than the guarantee.

Payments resulting in loss. If a partnership agreement provides for guaranteed payments to a partner and the payments result in a partnership loss in which the partner shared, the partner must:

1) Report the full amount of the guaranteed payments as ordinary income, and
2) Separately take into account the appropriate distributive share of the partnership loss.

Contributed Property

Usually, neither the partners nor the partnership recognizes a gain or loss when property is contributed to the partnership in exchange for a partnership interest. This applies whether a partnership is being formed or is already operating. The partnership's holding period for the property includes the partner's holding period.

However, a transaction may be treated as an exchange of property on which gain or loss is recognized if a partner contributes property to a partnership and within a short period:

1) Before or after the contribution, other property is distributed to the contributing partner and the contributed property is kept by the partnership, or
2) After the contribution, the contributed property is distributed to another partner.

Special rule for investment companies. Gain is recognized when property is contributed (in exchange for an interest in the partnership) to a partnership that would be treated as an investment company if it were incorporated. A loss realized on a contribution of stock, securities, or other property is not recognized. For more information, see Publication 541.

Interest acquired as compensation. A partner can acquire an interest in partnership capital as compensation for services performed or to be performed. The fair market value of such an interest must generally be included in the partner's gross income in the first tax year in which the partner's interest can be transferred or is not subject to a substantial risk of forfeiture. Such a transfer of partnership interest as compensation for services is subject to the rules discussed under *Payments in restricted property* in Chapter 10.

Partnership's gain or loss on contributed property. For unrealized receivables, inventory items, and certain capital loss property contributed by a partner to a partnership, the character of the partnership's gain or loss on a later disposition is determined by special rules discussed in Publication 541.

Basis of contributed property. If a partner contributes property to a partnership, the partnership's basis for determining depreciation, depletion, gain, or loss on property contributed by a partner is the same as the partner's adjusted basis of the property when it was contributed, increased by any gain recognized by the partner at that time.

The fair market value of property at the time it is contributed may be different from the partner's adjusted basis. The partnership must allocate among the partners any income, deduction, gain, or loss on the property in a manner that will account for all or any part of the difference.

However, the total depreciation, depletion, gain, or loss allocated to partners cannot be more than the depreciation or depletion allowable to the partnership or the gain or loss realized by the partnership. The allocation can apply to all property contributed or only to specific items. This rule also applies to accounts payable and other accrued but unpaid items of a cash basis partner.

Example. Sara and Gail form an equal partnership. Sara contributed $10,000 in cash to a partnership and Gail contributed depreciable property with a fair market value of $10,000 and an adjusted basis of $4,000. The partnership's basis for depreciation is limited to the adjusted basis of the property in Gail's hands, $4,000.

In effect, Sara purchased an undivided one-half interest in the depreciable property with her contribution of $10,000. Assuming that the depreciation rate is 10% a year under the General Depreciation System (GDS), she would have been entitled to a depreciation deduction of $500 per year, based on her interest in the partnership.

However, since the partnership is allowed only $400 per year of depreciation (10% of $4000), no more than $400 can be allocated between the partners.

Basis of Partner's Interest

A partner's basis is determined by using the following rules.

General Basis Rules

The general rules cover the partner's original basis, adjusted basis, and share of partnership liabilities.

Original Basis

The original basis of a partnership interest acquired by a contribution of property, including money, is the money a partner contributed plus the adjusted basis of any property he or she contributed. If the property contribution results in taxable income to the partner, this income will generally be included in the basis of his or her interest. Any increase in a partner's individual liabilities because of an assumption of partnership liabilities is also treated as a contribution of money to the partnership by the partner.

Partner's liabilities assumed by partnership. If the property contributed is subject to indebtedness or if a partner's liabilities are assumed by the partnership, the basis of that partner's interest is reduced by the liability assumed by the other partners. This partner must reduce his or her basis because the assumption of the liability is treated as a distribution of money to that partner. The other partners' assumption of the liability is treated as though they contributed money to the partnership.

Example 1. John acquired a 20% interest in a partnership by contributing property that had an adjusted basis to him of $8,000 and a $4,000 mortgage. The partnership assumed payment of the mortgage. The adjusted basis of John's interest is:

Adjusted basis of contributed property	$8,000
Minus: Part of mortgage assumed by other partners and treated as a distribution (80% of $4,000)	3,200
Basis of John's partnership interest	$4,800

Example 2. If, in the above example, the property John contributed had a $12,000 mortgage, the adjusted basis of his partnership interest would be zero. The difference between the amount of the mortgage assumed by the other partners, $9,600 (80% × $12,000), and his basis of $8,000 would be treated as his gain from the sale or exchange of a capital asset. However, this gain **would not** increase the basis of his partnership interest.

Interest acquired by gift, etc. If a partner acquires an interest in a partnership by gift, inheritance, or under any circumstance other than by a contribution of money or property to the partnership, the partner's basis must be determined using the rules described in Publication 551.

Debt-financed acquisitions. The interest expense on loan proceeds used to purchase an interest in, or make a contribution to, a partnership must be allocated as explained in Chapter 8 of Publication 535.

Adjusted Basis

Increases. The partner's basis of an interest is increased by the partner's:

1) Additional contributions to the partnership.
2) Distributive share of both taxable and nontaxable partnership income.
3) Distributive share of the excess of the deductions for depletion over the basis of the depletable property.

Decreases. The partner's basis is decreased (but never below zero) by:

1) The amount of money and the adjusted basis of property distributed to the partner by the partnership. (See *Partner's Basis of Property Received*, later.)
2) The partner's distributive share of the partnership losses (including capital losses).
3) The partner's distributive share of nondeductible partnership expenses that are not capital expenditures.
4) The amount of the partner's deduction for depletion for any partnership oil and gas wells, up to the proportionate share of the adjusted basis of the wells allocated to the partner.
5) The partner's share of any section 179 expenses, even if the partner cannot deduct the entire amount on his or her individual income tax return.

Book value of partner's interest. The adjusted basis of a partner's interest is determined without considering any amount shown in the partnership books as a capital, equity, or similar account.

Example. Sam contributes to the partnership property that has an adjusted basis of $400 and a value of $1,000. His partner contributes $1,000 cash. While under the partnership agreement each has a capital account in the partnership of $1,000, which will be reflected in the partnership books, the adjusted basis of Sam's interest is only $400 and his partner's basis is $1,000.

Determination of adjusted basis. The adjusted basis of a partner's partnership interest is ordinarily determined at the end of a partnership's tax year. However, if there has been a sale or exchange of all or part of the partner's interest or a liquidation of his or her entire interest in a partnership, the adjusted basis is determined on the date of the sale, exchange, or liquidation.

Partnership liabilities. If a partner's share of partnership liabilities *increases*, or a partner's individual liabilities increase because he or she assumes partnership liabilities, this increase is treated as a contribution of money by the partner to the partnership.

If a partner's share of partnership liabilities *decreases,* or a partner's individual liabilities decrease because the partnership assumes his or her individual liabilities, this decrease is treated as a distribution of money to the partner by the partnership.

For more information on liabilities, see Publication 541.

Alternative Basis Rule

In certain cases, the adjusted basis of a partnership interest can be figured by using the partner's share of the adjusted basis of partnership property that would be distributable to the partner if the partnership terminated.

This alternative rule can be used to determine the adjusted basis of a partner's interest if either of the following applies:

1) The circumstances are such that the partner cannot practicably apply the general basis rules.
2) It is, in the opinion of the IRS, reasonable to conclude that the result produced will not vary substantially from the result under the general basis rules.

Adjustments may be necessary in figuring a partner's adjusted basis of a partnership interest under the alternative rule. For example, adjustments would be required to include in the partner's share of the adjusted basis of partnership property any significant discrepancies that resulted from contributed property, transfers of partnership interests, or distributions of property to the partners.

Partner's Basis of Property Received

Unless there is a complete liquidation of a partner's interest, the basis of property (other than money) distributed to the partner by a partnership is its adjusted basis to the partnership immediately before the distribution. However, the basis of the property to the partner cannot be more than the adjusted basis of his or her interest in the partnership reduced by any money received in the same transaction.

Example 1. The adjusted basis of Betty's partnership interest is $30,000. She receives a distribution of property that has an adjusted basis of $20,000 to the partnership and $4,000 in cash. Her basis for the property is $20,000.

Example 2. The adjusted basis of Mike's partnership interest is $10,000. He receives a distribution of $4,000 cash and property that has an adjusted basis to the partnership of $8,000. His basis for the distributed property is limited to $6,000 ($10,000 minus the $4,000 cash he receives).

Holding period for distributed property. A partner's holding period for property distributed to the partner by the partnership includes the period that the property was held by the partnership. If the property was contributed to the partnership by a partner, then the period it was held by that partner is also included. However, this does not apply for determining the 5-year period for substantially appreciated inventory items (defined later).

Complete liquidation of partner's interest. The basis of property received in complete liquidation of a partner's interest is the adjusted basis of the partner's interest in the partnership reduced by any money distributed to the partner in the same transaction.

Special rule. A partnership distribution is treated as a sale or exchange of property that is not a capital asset if it consists of:

1) Unrealized receivables or substantially appreciated inventory items to a partner in exchange for any part of the partner's interest in other partnership property, including money, or
2) Other property (including money) in exchange for any part of a partner's interest in unrealized receivables or substantially appreciated inventory items.

See *Unrealized Receivables and Inventory Items*, later.

Exceptions. The special rule on certain distributions does not apply in the following situations:

1) A distribution of property to the partner who contributed the property to the partnership, and
2) Certain payments made to a retiring partner or successor in interest of a deceased partner.

Basis divided among properties. Generally, the basis of property received is limited to the adjusted basis of the partner's interest in the partnership, reduced by money received in the same transaction. This basis must be divided among any properties distributed to a partner. The basis must first be allocated to unrealized receivables and inventory items included in the distribution.

The receivables or inventory items generally cannot take a higher basis in the partner's hands than their common adjusted basis to the partnership immediately before the distribution. However, the items could have a higher basis if the distribution is treated as a sale or exchange under the *Special rule,* discussed earlier, or if the partner has a special basis adjustment for the property, discussed later.

Any basis not allocated to unrealized receivables and inventory items must then be divided among any other properties distributed to the partner in the same transaction. The division must be in proportion to their adjusted bases in the hands of the partnership before the distribution.

Example. The adjusted basis of Ted's partnership interest is $30,000. In complete liquidation of his interest, he receives $10,000 in cash, his share of inventory items having a basis to the partnership of $12,000, and two parcels of land having adjusted bases to the partnership of $12,000 and $4,000.

The basis of Ted's partnership interest is reduced to $20,000 by the $10,000 cash. This $20,000 basis is then divided among the properties he receives. The inventory items in his hands now have a basis of $12,000. To divide the balance of $8,000, he adds the bases of the two parcels of land ($12,000 + $4,000) and takes [(12,000 ÷ 16,000) × $8,000] and [(4,000 ÷ 16,000) × $8,000]. The bases of the two parcels of land in his hands are $6,000 and $2,000, respectively.

Partner's interest less than partnership basis. If the partnership's adjusted basis for the unrealized receivables and inventory items distributed to a partner is more than the adjusted basis of the partner's interest, the amount of the partner's basis is allocated among these items in proportion to the partnership's adjusted bases of the items. The partner's basis must be reduced first by any money distributed in the same transaction.

Example. Jenny's basis for her partnership interest is $18,000. In a distribution in liquidation of her entire interest, she receives $12,000 cash, her share of inventory items having an adjusted basis to the partnership of $12,000, and unrealized receivables having a basis to the partnership of $8,000. The basis of her partnership interest is first reduced to $6,000 by the $12,000 cash she receives. This $6,000 basis is then divided proportionately between the inventory items and the unrealized receivables. Jenny's basis for the inventory items is $3,600 [(12,000 ÷ 20,000) × $6,000]. Her basis for the unrealized receivables is $2,400 [(8,000 ÷ 20,000) × $6,000].

Partner's interest more than partnership basis. If the basis of a partner's interest to be divided is more than the partnership's adjusted basis for the unrealized receivables and inventory items distributed, and if no other property is distributed to which the partner can apply the remaining basis, the partner has a capital loss to the extent of the remaining basis of the partnership interest. See Chapter 23 for a discussion of capital losses.

Special adjustment to basis of property received. There is a special rule for figuring the partnership basis of property (other than money) distributed to a partner within 2 years after the partner acquires his or her partnership interest through a sale or exchange or upon the death of a partner. See Publication 541.

Optional Adjustment to Basis of Partnership Property

Generally, a partnership cannot adjust the basis of its property because of a distribution of property to a partner or because of a transfer of interest in the partnership, whether by sale or exchange or because of the death of a partner. The partnership can adjust the basis only if it files an election to make an optional adjustment to the basis of its property upon the transfer. A partnership does not adjust the basis of partnership property for a contribution of property, including money, to the partnership. See *Optional Adjustment to Basis of Partnership Property* in Publication 541 for more information.

Sales, Exchanges, and Other Transfers

The sale or exchange of a partner's interest in a partnership usually results in capital gain or loss. Gain or loss is the difference between the amount realized and the adjusted basis of the partner's interest in the partnership. If the selling partner is relieved of any partnership liabilities, the selling partner must include the amount of liability relief as part of the amount realized for his or her interest.

Example 1. Fred became a limited partner in the ABC Partnership by contributing $10,000 in cash on the formation of the partnership. The adjusted basis of his partnership interest at the end of the current year is $20,000, which includes his share of partnership liabilities of $15,000. The partnership has no other liabilities and no unrealized receivables or substantially appreciated inventory items. Fred sells his interest in the partnership for $10,000 in cash. He had been paid his share of the partnership income for the tax year.

The amount realized by Fred from the sale of his partnership interest is $25,000, consisting of the $10,000 cash payment and his share of partnership liabilities of which he is relieved, $15,000. Since the adjusted basis of his interest in the partnership is $20,000, he realizes a gain of $5,000, which he reports as a capital gain

Example 2. The facts are the same as in Example 1, except that instead of selling his interest for $10,000, Fred withdraws from the partnership when the adjusted basis of his interest in the partnership is zero. In this situation he is considered to have received a distribution of money from the partnership of $15,000, the amount of liabilities of which he is relieved. Since the partnership has no unrealized receivables or substantially appreciated inventory items, he reports a capital gain of $15,000.

Exchange of partnership interests. Exchanges of partnership interests generally do not qualify as nontaxable exchanges of like-kind property. However, under some circumstances, certain exchanges may be treated as a tax-free contribution of property to a partnership. See Publication 541.

An interest in a partnership that has a valid election in effect under section 761(a) of the Internal Revenue Code to be excluded from all the partnership rules of the Code is treated as an interest in each of the partnership assets and not as a partnership interest.

Liquidation of Partner's Interest

Payments made by the partnership to a retiring partner or successor in interest of a deceased partner in return for the partner's entire interest in the partnership may have to be allocated. The allocation is made between payments in liquidation and other payments.

For income tax purposes, a retiring partner or a successor in interest to a deceased partner is treated as a partner until his or her interest in the partnership has been completely liquidated.

Payments in liquidation of retiring or deceased partner's interest. Payments in liquidation of the interest of a retiring or deceased partner in exchange for his or her interest in partnership property are considered a distribution, not a distributive share or guaranteed payment that could give rise to a deduction (or its equivalent) for the partnership.

Special rule. Payments in exchange for an interest in partnership property do not include amounts paid for:

1) Unrealized receivables of the partnership, or

2) Goodwill of the partnership, except to the extent that the partnership agreement provides for a payment for goodwill.

This rule applies only if:

1) Capital is not a material income-producing factor for the partnership, and

2) The retiring or deceased partner was a general partner in the partnership.

Thus, if the retiring partner was not a general partner or if capital is a material income-producing factor, the partnership will not receive a deduction or its equivalent (distributive share) for the payments to the retired partner.

Capital is not a material income-producing factor if substantially all the gross income of the business consists of fees, commissions, or other compensation for personal services performed by a partner. The practice of his or her profession by a physician, dentist, lawyer, architect, or accountant is not treated as a trade or business in which capital is a material income-producing factor, even though the practitioner may have a substantial capital investment in the professional equipment or physical plant of the practice, so long as the capital investment is merely incidental to the professional practice.

This rule applies to partners retiring or dying on or after January 5, 1993. It does not apply to any partner retiring on or after that date if a written contract to purchase the partner's interest in the partnership was binding on January 4, 1993, and at all times thereafter.

Partner's valuation. Generally, the partners' valuation of a partner's interest in partnership property in an arm's-length agreement will be treated as correct. If the valuation reflects only the partner's net interest in the property (total assets less liabilities), it must be adjusted so that both the value of and the basis for the partner's interest include the partner's share of partnership liabilities.

Remaining partners' distributive shares. The remaining partners' distributive shares are reduced by payments in exchange for a retired or deceased partner's interest when those payments are treated as distributive shares of partnership income or guaranteed payments.

Other payments. Payments in liquidation of a general partnership interest in a partnership where capital is not a material income-producing factor are treated as distributive shares of partnership income or guaranteed payments if they are **not** made in exchange for an interest in partnership property. This rule applies regardless of the time over which the payments are to be made. It includes payments made for the partner's share of unrealized receivables and goodwill not treated as a distribution.

If the amount is based on partnership income, the payments are taxable as distributive shares of partnership income. These payments, reported by the recipient, retain the same character they would have had if they had been reported by the partnership. If the amount is not based on partnership income, it is treated as a guaranteed payment. The recipient reports guaranteed payments as ordinary income.

These payments are included in income by the recipient for his or her tax year that includes the end of the partnership tax year for which the payments are a distributive share or in which the partnership is entitled to deduct them as guaranteed payments.

Former partners who continue to make guaranteed periodic payments to satisfy the partnership's liability to a retired partner after the partnership is terminated can deduct the payments as a business expense in the year paid.

Partner's taxable income. If a partner disposes of his or her **entire interest** in a partnership, the partner must include his or her distributive share of partnership items in taxable income for the tax year in which membership in the partnership ends. To compute the distributive share of these items, the partnership's tax year is considered ended on the date the partner disposed of the interest. To avoid an interim closing of the partnership books, the partners can agree that the distributive share can be estimated by taking a prorated amount of the items the partner would have included in income if he or she remained a partner for the entire partnership tax year.

A partner who sells or exchanges only **part of an interest** in a partnership, or whose interest is reduced (whether by entry of a new partner, partial liquidation of a partner's interest, gift, or otherwise), reports his or her distributive share of partnership items by taking into account his or her varying interests during the partnership year.

Deceased partner. If a partner dies, the partner's estate or other successor in interest reports on its return the decedent's distributive share of the partnership items for the partnership tax year ending after the death occurred.

For example, if the partnership and the partners all use a calendar year as their tax year and one of the partners dies on June 10, none of the income of the partnership for that year will be reported in the final return of the deceased partner. All of it will be included in the return of the partner's estate or other successor in interest.

However, if the partnership terminates with the death of the partner, the partnership year closes for all partners. The deceased partner's share of income for that year will be included in the deceased partner's final return. If the decedent's tax year is different from the partnership's, the decedent's final return will include his or her share of partnership items for both the partnership year ending with the decedent's death and any partnership year ending earlier in the decedent's last tax year. See Publication 541 for more information.

Unrealized Receivables and Inventory Items

If a partner receives money or property in exchange for any part of a partnership interest, the amount that is due to his or her share of the partnership's unrealized receivables or substantially appreciated inventory items results in ordinary income or loss. Any such amount received is treated as if it were received for the sale or exchange of property that is not a capital asset.

Unrealized receivables. Unrealized receivables are any rights to payments not already included in income for:

1) Goods delivered or to be delivered, to the extent that the payment would be treated as received for property other than a capital asset, or

2) Services rendered or to be rendered.

These rights must have arisen under contracts or agreements that existed at the time of sale or distribution, even though the partnership may not be able to enforce payment until a later date. For example, unrealized receivables include trade accounts receivable of a cash method partnership and rights to payment for work or goods begun but incomplete at the time of the sale or distribution of the partnership share.

The basis for any unrealized receivables includes all costs or expenses for the receivables that were paid or accrued but not previously taken into account under the partnership's method of accounting.

Items included as unrealized receivables. When either of the following partnership transactions occur, unrealized receivables include the section 1245 gain that would be treated as ordinary income (depreciation recapture) if the partnership had sold certain depreciable property at its fair market value.

1) A distribution by a partnership to a partner, or

2) A sale or exchange of an interest in a partnership by a partner.

Unrealized receivables also include the amount of potential gain that would be ordinary income from:

1) Mining property.

2) Stock in an Interest Charge Domestic International Sales Corporation (IC-DISC).

3) Certain farmland for which expenses for soil and water conservation or land clearing were deducted.

4) Franchises, trademarks, or trade names.

5) Oil, gas, or geothermal property.

6) Stock of certain controlled foreign corporations.

7) Market discount bonds and short-term obligations.

8) Recapture of deductions under sections 1245 (discussed earlier), 1250, 1253, etc.

See Publication 541 for more information.

Inventory items that have appreciated substantially in value. Before May 1, 1993, inventory items of the partnership were considered to have appreciated substantially in value if, at the time of the sale or distribution, their total fair market value is more than:

1) 120% of the partnership's adjusted basis for the property, and

2) 10% of the fair market value of all partnership property other than money.

However, if a principal purpose for acquiring inventory property was to avoid ordinary income treatment by reducing the appreciation to less than 120%, that property is excluded.

Modified definition. For sales, exchanges, and distributions made after April 30, 1993, the definition of substantially appreciated inventory has been modified to eliminate the requirement that the partnership's inventory exceed 10% of the value of all partnership property, other than money, in order to be substantially appreciated. If the partnership's inventory is worth more than 120% of its adjusted basis, the inventory is treated as substantially appreciated.

Items included as inventory. Inventory items are not just stock-in-trade of the partnership. They include any property that is part of inventory on hand at the end of the tax year or that is held primarily for sale to customers in the normal course of business. They include any asset which, if sold or exchanged by the partnership, would not be a capital asset or treated as a capital asset. They also include any other property held by the partnership that would be considered inventory items if held by the selling or distributee partner. Inventory also includes trade or accounts receivable acquired for services or from the sale of inventory.

See Publication 541 for more information.

30. Corporations

Introduction

This chapter explains the application of various tax provisions to corporations. Certain areas of corporation taxation are not covered in this publication. For a more complete discussion of corporation taxation, please get Publication 542.

Topics
This chapter discusses:

- Special provisions for corporations
- Figuring tax
- Estimated tax
- Filing requirements
- Capital contributions and retained earnings
- Distributions

Useful Items
You may want to see:

Publication

☐ **542** Tax Information on Corporations

Form (and Instructions)

☐ **1120** U.S. Corporation Income Tax Return

☐ **1120–A** U.S. Corporation Short–Form Income Tax Return

☐ **1120–W** (WORKSHEET) Estimated Tax for Corporations

☐ **1120X** Amended U.S. Corporation Income Tax Return

☐ **2220** Underpayment of Estimated Tax by Corporations

☐ **7004** Application for Automatic Extension of Time To File Corporation Income Tax Return

☐ **8109** Federal Tax Deposit Coupon

Special Provisions

Rules on income and deductions that apply to individuals also apply, for the most part, to corporations. However, a corporation can take certain *special deductions* in figuring its taxable income.

Dividends-Received Deduction

A corporation can deduct a percentage of certain dividends received during its tax year.

Dividends from domestic corporations. A corporation can deduct, with certain limits, 70% of the dividends received if the corporation receiving the dividend owns less than 20% of the distributing corporation.

20%-or-more owners allowed 80% deduction. A corporation can deduct, with certain limits, 80% of the dividends received or accrued if it owns 20% or more of the paying domestic corporation. This corporation is a *20%-owned corporation.*

Ownership. Determine ownership, for these rules, by the amount of voting power and value of stock (other than certain preferred stock) the corporation owns.

Small business investment companies. Small business investment companies can deduct 100% of the dividends received from a taxable domestic corporation.

Affiliated corporations. Members of an affiliated group of corporations can deduct 100% of the dividends received from a member of the same affiliated group if they meet certain conditions. See section 243 of the Internal Revenue Code for the definition of an affiliated group of corporations.

Dividends from regulated investment company. Regulated investment company dividends received are subject to certain limits. Capital gain dividends do not qualify for this deduction. For more information, see section 854 of the Internal Revenue Code.

Dividends on preferred stock of public utilities. For tax years beginning after 1992, corporations can deduct 42% of the dividends it receives on certain preferred stock (issued before October 1942) of a less-than-20%-owned taxable public utility. For tax years beginning after 1992, a 20%-or-more owned taxable public utility can deduct 48%. For more information, see section 244 of the Internal Revenue Code.

Dividends from foreign corporations. A corporation can deduct a percentage of the dividends it receives from 10%-owned foreign corporations. For more information, see section 245 of the Internal Revenue Code.

Dividends on debt-financed portfolio stock. For dividends received on debt-financed portfolio stock of domestic corporations, reduce the 70%, or 80%, dividend-received deduction. Reduce the deduction by a percentage related to the amount of debt incurred to purchase the stock. This applies to stock whose holding period begins after July 18, 1984. For more information, see section 246A of the Internal Revenue Code.

Dividends in property. When a corporation receives a dividend from a domestic corporation in the form of property other than cash, it includes the dividend in income. The amount included is the lesser of the property's fair market value (FMV), or the adjusted basis of the property in the hands of the distributing corporation increased by any gain recognized by the distributing corporation on the distribution.

No deduction is allowed for certain dividends. Corporations cannot take a deduction for dividends received from:

A real estate investment trust,

A corporation exempt from tax either for the tax year of the distribution or the preceding tax year,

A corporation whose stock has been held by your corporation for 45 days or less,

A corporation whose stock has been held by your corporation for 90 days or less if the stock has preference as to dividends and the dividends received on it are attributable to a period or periods totaling more than 366 days, or

Any corporation, if your corporation is under an obligation (pursuant to a short sale or otherwise) to make related payments for positions in substantially similar or related property.

Dividends on deposits. So-called dividends on deposits or withdrawable accounts in domestic building and loan associations, mutual savings banks, cooperative banks, and similar organizations are interest. They do not qualify for this deduction.

Limit on deduction for dividends. The total deduction for dividends received or accrued is generally limited (in the following order) to:

1) 80% of the difference between taxable income and the 100% deduction allowed for dividends received from affiliated corporations, or by a small business investment company, for dividends received or accrued from 20%-owned corporations, and

2) 70% of the difference between taxable income and the 100% deduction allowed for dividends received from affiliated corporations, or by a small business investment company, for dividends received or accrued from less than 20%-owned corporations (reducing taxable income by the total dividends received from 20%-owned corporations).

Figuring limit. In figuring this limit, determine taxable income without:

1) The net operating loss deduction,
2) The deduction for dividends received,
3) Any adjustment due to the part of an extraordinary dividend that is not taxable (see *Reduction in Basis of Stock),* later,
4) The deduction for contributions to a Capital Construction Fund (CCF), and
5) Any capital loss carryback to the tax year.

Effect of net operating loss. If your corporation has a net operating loss (defined in Chapter 21) for a tax year, the limit of 80% (or 70%) of taxable income does not apply. To determine whether a corporation has a net operating loss, figure the dividends-received deduction without the 80% (or 70%) of taxable income limit.

Example 1. A corporation loses $25,000 from operations. It receives $100,000 in dividends from a 20%-owned corporation. Its taxable income is $75,000 before the deduction for dividends received. If it claims the full dividends-received deduction of $80,000 ($100,000 × 80%) and combines it with the operations loss of $25,000, it will have a net operating loss of $5,000. Therefore, the 80% of taxable income limit does not apply. The corporation can deduct $80,000.

Example 2. Assume the same facts as in Example 1 except that the corporation loses $15,000 from operations. Its taxable income is $85,000 before the deduction for dividends received. However, after claiming the dividends-received deduction of $80,000 ($100,000 × 80%), its taxable income is $5,000. But because the corporation will not have a net operating loss after a full dividends-received deduction, its allowable dividends-received deduction is limited to 80% of its taxable income, or $68,000 ($85,000 × 80%).

Reduction in Basis of Stock

If a corporation receives an extraordinary dividend on stock held 2 years or less before the dividend announcement date, it reduces its basis in the stock by the nontaxed part of the dividend. Do not reduce the basis of the stock below zero. The total nontaxed part of dividends on stock that did not reduce the basis of the stock, due to the limit on reducing basis below zero, is treated as gain from the sale or exchange of the stock for the tax year you sell or exchange the stock.

An *extraordinary dividend* is any dividend on stock that equals or exceeds:

- 5% for stock that is preferred as to dividends, or
- 10% for other stock

of the corporation's adjusted basis in the stock. Treat all dividends received that have ex-dividend dates within an 85-consecutive-day period as one dividend. Treat all dividends received that have ex-dividend dates within a 365-consecutive-day period as extraordinary dividends if the total of the dividends exceeds 20% of the corporation's adjusted basis in the stock. Do not include qualifying dividends, discussed earlier under *Affiliated corporations,* in the definition of extraordinary dividends.

The corporation can elect to determine whether the dividend is extraordinary by using the FMV of the stock rather than its adjusted basis. To make this election the corporation must establish, to the satisfaction of the IRS, the FMV of the stock as of the day before the ex-dividend date. (See Revenue Procedure 87–33 in the 1987 Cumulative Bulletin, Volume 2, on page 402.)

The **nontaxed part** is any dividends-received deduction allowable for the dividends.

The **dividend announcement date** is the date the corporation declares, announces, or agrees to either the amount or the payment of the dividend, whichever is earliest.

Disqualified preferred stock. The rules apply to an extraordinary dividend on disqualified preferred stock regardless of the period the corporation held the stock.

Disqualified preferred stock is any stock preferred as to dividends if:

1) The stock when issued has a dividend rate that declines (or can reasonably be expected to decline) in the future,

2) The issue price of the stock exceeds its liquidation rights or stated redemption price, or

3) The stock is otherwise structured to avoid the rules for extraordinary dividends and to enable corporate shareholders to reduce tax through a combination of dividends-received deductions and loss on the disposition of the stock.

These rules apply to stock issued after July 10, 1989, unless issued under a written binding contract in effect on that date and thereafter before the issuance of the stock.

Charitable Contributions

A corporation can claim a limited deduction for any charitable contributions made in cash or other property. The contribution is deductible if made to or for the use of community chests, funds, foundations, corporations, or trusts, organized and operated exclusively for religious, charitable, scientific, literary, or educational purposes. The contribution can also be made to foster national or international amateur sports competition, or for the prevention of cruelty to children or animals.

You cannot take a deduction if any of the net earnings of an organization receiving contributions benefit any private shareholder or individual.

The organization to which you make a contribution should be able to tell you if the contribution is deductible.

Cash method corporation. A corporation using the cash method of accounting can deduct contributions only in the tax year paid.

Accrual method corporation. A corporation using an accrual method of accounting can choose to deduct unpaid contributions for the tax year the board of directors authorizes them if it pays them within 2½ months after the close of that tax year. Make the choice by reporting the contribution on the corporation return for the tax year. A copy of the resolution authorizing the contribution and a declaration stating the board of directors adopted the resolution during the tax year must accompany the return. The president or other principal officer must sign the declaration.

Limit. A corporation cannot deduct contributions that total more than 10% of its taxable income. Figure taxable income for this purpose without the following:

Deduction for contributions,

Deduction for dividends received and dividends paid,

Deduction for contributions to a Capital Construction Fund (CCF),

Any net operating loss carryback to the tax year, and

Any capital loss carryback to the tax year.

Carryover of excess contributions. You can carry over (with certain limits) any charitable contributions made during the year that are more than the 10% limit to each of the following 5 years. You lose any excess not used within that period. For example, if a corporation has a carryover of excess contributions paid in 1993 and it does not use all the excess on its return for 1994, it can carry the remainder over to 1995, 1996, 1997, and 1998. Do not deduct a carryover of excess contributions in the carryover year until after you deduct contributions made in that year, subject to the 10% limit. You cannot deduct a carryover of excess contributions to the extent that it increases a net operating loss carryover in a succeeding tax year.

Related Taxpayers

The related-party rules apply to transactions between an individual and a corporation the individual controls. They apply to sales or exchanges of property and the deduction of certain unpaid business expenses and interest. Under certain conditions, the IRS can reallocate income and deductions between two or more businesses directly or indirectly controlled by the same interests. These rules are discussed in Chapters 4 and 23.

Complete liquidations. The disallowance of losses from the sale or exchange of property between related parties does not apply to liquidating distributions. It does not apply to any loss of either the distributing corporation or a distributee for a distribution in complete liquidation.

Interest paid to related parties. A corporation's deduction for interest expense may be limited if it is paid (or accrued) interest to related parties *not subject to tax on the interest* received. The deduction for this interest is disallowed for any tax year that the corporation has:

- Excess interest expense, and
- A debt to equity ratio greater than 1.5 to 1 at the end of that tax year.

Chapter 30 **CORPORATIONS**

However, the deduction is disallowed only to the extent of the corporation's excess interest expense. The corporation can carry the disallowed interest to later years.

"Not subject to tax on the interest" means that the related party is not subject to U.S. income tax on the interest income. For example, the related party may be a foreign parent corporation not subject to U.S. tax.

Excess interest expense. Excess interest expense is the excess of the corporation's net interest expense over the sum of 50% of its adjusted taxable income plus any *excess limit* carryforward.

Excess limit. Excess limit means the excess of 50% of the corporation's adjusted taxable income over its net interest expense.

If a corporation has an excess limit for a tax year, that amount becomes an excess limit carryforward to the next tax year. When the corporation does not use it up in the next tax year, it can carry it forward only to the following 2 tax years.

More information. For more information, including the definition of "adjusted taxable income," see section 163(j) of the Internal Revenue Code.

Figuring Tax

Beginning January 1, 1993, corporate taxable income is subject to the tax rate system shown in Table 1.

Controlled group of corporations. A controlled group of corporations gets only one apportionable $50,000, $25,000, and $9,925,000 (in that order) amount for each taxable income bracket. For more information, see the instructions for Schedule J of Form 1120.

Personal service corporations. The tax rate for qualified personal service corporations for tax years that began on or after January 1, 1993, is 35% of taxable income. These corporations cannot use the graduated tax rates that apply to other corporations.

A corporation is a *qualified personal service corporation* if:

At least 95% of the value of its stock is held by employees, or their estates or beneficiaries, and

Its employees perform services at least 95% of the time in any of the following fields:
- Health
- Law
- Engineering
- Architecture
- Accounting
- Actuarial science
- Veterinary services
- Performing arts
- Consulting

Credits

A corporation *decreases* its tax liability by credits, such as:

1) Credit for fuels used for certain purposes (see Publication 378),
2) Foreign tax credit (use Form 1118),
3) General business credit (see Chapter 32),
4) Orphan drug credit (use Form 6765),
5) Possessions tax credit (use Form 5735),
6) Credit for fuel produced from a nonconventional source, and
7) The qualified electric vehicle credit (see Form 8834).

Other Taxes

A corporation *increases* its tax liability by:

1) Personal holding company tax (attach Schedule PH (Form 1120)),
2) Investment credit recapture (see Chapter 32),
3) Low-income housing credit recapture (Form 8611),
4) Alternative minimum tax (see Chapter 35), and
5) Environmental tax.

Environmental tax. A corporation is liable for the tax if its modified alternative minimum taxable income is over $2 million.

Modified alternative minimum taxable income. This is alternative minimum taxable income (defined in Chapter 35) without the:

1) Alternative tax net operating loss deduction,
2) Alternative tax energy preference deduction, and
3) Deduction for the environmental tax.

Estimated Tax

Every corporation that expects its tax to be $500 or more must make estimated tax payments. A corporation's estimated tax is its expected tax liability (including alternative minimum tax (AMT) and environmental tax) less its allowable tax credits.

Time and amount of deposits. If a corporation's estimated tax is $500 or more, it deposits its estimated tax with an authorized financial institution or a Federal Reserve Bank. Use Form 8109 to make deposits. Follow the instructions in the coupon book.

Deposit a corporation's estimated tax in installments by the 15th day of the following months of the corporation's tax year.

Required Installment	Month Due
1st	4th month
2nd	6th month
3rd	9th month
4th	12th month

Generally, each installment payment must equal 25% of the required annual estimated tax.

Example 1. The Penn Corporation, a calendar year taxpayer, estimates its tax will be $40,000. The corporation deposits the estimated tax in four $10,000 installments: on April 15, June 15, September 15, and December 15.

Example 2. The Jones Company has a fiscal year beginning April 1 and ending March 31. Its estimated tax is $12,000. It deposits $3,000 of its estimated tax on July 15, September 15, December 15, and March 15.

Amended estimated tax. If, after depositing estimated tax, a corporation determines its tax will be substantially larger or smaller than estimated, it refigures the tax before the next installment to determine the amount of its remaining deposits.

Example. A calendar year corporation estimates its tax will be $20,000. The corporation deposits the first two installments on April 15 and June 15 in the amount of $5,000 each (25% of $20,000). On July 1, the corporation estimates its tax will be $40,000. The installments payable on September 15 and

Table 1. **Tax Rate Schedule**
If taxable income (line 30, Form 1120, or line 26, Form 1120-A) on page 1 is:

Over—	But not over—	Tax is:	Of the amount over—
$0	$50,000	15%	$0
50,000	75,000	$7,500 + 25%	50,000
75,000	100,000	13,750 + 34%	75,000
100,000	335,000	22,250 + 39%	100,000
335,000	10,000,000	113,900 + 34%	335,000
10,000,000	15,000,000	3,400,000 + 35%	10,000,000
15,000,000	18,333,333	5,150,000 + 38%	15,000,000
18,333,333	-----	35%	0

December 15 will be $15,000 each, figured as follows:

Refigured estimated tax	$40,000
Less: Deposited tax	10,000
Unpaid balance	$30,000
Installments due September 15, and December 15 (Unpaid balance ($30,000) divided by 2 remaining installments)	$15,000

Penalty

A corporation that fails to pay a correct installment of estimated tax in full by the due date may be subject to a penalty. The penalty rate applies to the period of underpayment for any installment. Figure the penalty at a rate of interest published quarterly by the IRS.

Figuring the underpayment. The underpayment of any installment is the payment required minus the amount paid by the due date.

For tax years beginning after December 31, 1993, the estimated tax payment required in installments is the lesser of:

1) 100% of the tax shown on the return for the preceding year, or

2) 100% of the tax shown for the current year (the current year tax may be determined on the basis of actual income or annualized income).

However, a large corporation can use (1) or (2), whichever applies, only for determining the amount of its first installment in any tax year. If the installment determined under (1) is greater than that determined and paid under (2), add the difference to the next required installment. A large corporation is one with at least $1 million of taxable income in any of the last 3 years.

For tax years that begin after June 30, 1992, and before January 1, 1994, the payment required in installments is the lesser of:

1) 97% of the tax shown on the return for the tax year (or if no return filed, 97% of the tax for the year), or

2) 100% of the tax on the return for the preceding year, if that year was a 12-month tax year and a return filed for that year showed a tax liability.

Order of crediting payments. Credit an estimated tax payment against unpaid installments in the required order of payment.

Annualizing. If you base an installment on 100% of the current year's tax that you would owe if you annualized income, *no penalty* applies. You can estimate total income for the tax year by annualizing income. You annualize income by treating income received over a specified period in the tax year as if received at the same rate over the full 12-month year. Add any reduction in a required installment from using the annualization exception to the next required installments if not taken into account in earlier installments.

For tax years beginning after December 31, 1993, you now have three sets of periods over which income may be annualized. The tax law specifies a particular set of periods for annualizing income unless you elect one of two alternative sets of periods by making an election on Form 8842. Once made, the election cannot be revoked. See the instructions for Form 8842 for more information.

Recurring seasonal income. When figuring the penalty for an underdeposit of an installment of estimated tax, there is a special rule for a corporation with recurring seasonal income. The rule applies to corporations whose taxable income for any period of 6 consecutive months has averaged 70% or more of its taxable income for the year during each of the past 3 tax years.

No penalty applies to an installment of estimated tax if the total deposits made by the installment date equals or exceeds 100% of the amount, figured as follows:

1) Take the taxable income for all months in the tax year before the month the installment is due,

2) Divide the amount in (1) by the base period percentage, defined next, for those months,

3) Figure the tax on the amount figured in (2), and

4) Multiply the tax figured in (3) by the base period percentage for the filing month and all months during the tax year before the filing month.

The *base period percentage* for any period of months is the average percentage that the taxable income for the same period of months in each of the 3 preceding tax years bears to the taxable income for those 3 tax years.

Form 1120–W. As an aid in determining the estimated tax and required installments, a calendar year corporation should get Form 1120–W. Keep the form. Do not file it.

For tax years beginning after December 31, 1993, fiscal year corporations use the 1994 revision of Form 1120–W to determine the estimated tax payments for the 1994 fiscal year.

Form 2220. Use Form 2220 to determine any underpayment of estimated tax. If it appears from your Form 1120 or 1120–A that you underpaid your estimated tax, use Form 2220 to compute any penalty.

Quick Refund of Overpayments

A corporation that overpays its estimated tax can apply on Form 4466 for a quick refund of any overpayment. File the form after the close of the corporation's tax year but before:

1) The 16th day of the 3rd month after the close of the tax year, and

2) The day the corporation files its return for that tax year.

The overpayment must be:

1) At least 10% of the amount estimated by the corporation on its application as its income tax liability for the tax year, and

2) At least $500.

The IRS will credit or refund the overpayment within 45 days after you file the application.

Filing Requirements

Each corporation, unless it is specifically exempt or has dissolved, must file a tax return even if it had no taxable income for the year and regardless of its gross income for the tax year. The income tax return for ordinary corporations is Form 1120. Certain small corporations can file Form 1120–A. Corporations that normally file Form 1120 may save time if they can use Form 1120–A.

Who Can File Form 1120-A

A corporation can use Form 1120–A to report its taxable income if it meets the following requirements:

- Its gross receipts must be under $500,000,
- Its total income must be under $500,000,
- Its total assets must be under $500,000,
- It does not have ownership in a foreign corporation,
- It does not have foreign shareholders who own, directly or indirectly, 50% or more of its stock,
- It is not a member of a controlled group,
- It is not a personal holding company,
- It is not a consolidated corporate return filer,
- It is not a corporation undergoing a dissolution or liquidation,
- It is not filing its final tax return,
- Its only dividend income is from domestic corporations, and those dividends qualify for the 70% deduction,
- It has no nonrefundable tax credits other than the general business credit and the credit for prior-year minimum tax,
- It is not subject to environmental tax,
- It has no liability for interest relating to certain installment sales of timeshares and residential lots, or interest on deferred tax liability or installment payments of tax,
- It has no liability for interest due under the look-back method on completion of a long-term contract,

- It is not required to file Form 8621,
- It has no liability for tax on a nonqualified withdrawal from a capital construction fund,
- It is not making an election to forgo the carryback period of an NOL,
- It is not electing to pay tax on the sale of an intangible as described in section 197(f)(9)(B)(ii) of the Internal Revenue Code, and
- It is not an organization such as an S corporation, life or mutual insurance company, political organization, etc., required to file a specialized form such as Form 1120S, 1120-L, 1120-POL, etc.

For more information, see *Instructions for Forms 1120 and 1120-A*.

Amending Return

If, after filing Form 1120 or 1120-A, you have to correct an error on the return, use **Form 1120X**. File this form if you understated or overstated income, or failed to claim deductions or credits.

Due Date of Return

If a corporation files its income tax return on a calendar year basis, file it by March 15 following the close of the tax year. If a corporation uses a fiscal year, file its return by the 15th day of the 3rd month following the close of its fiscal year. See the checklist at the end of this publication.

Extension of time to file. A corporation will receive an automatic 6-month extension of time for filing its return by submitting an application for an extension on Form 7004. File this form with the Internal Revenue Service Center where the corporation will file its income tax return. The IRS can terminate this extension at any time by mailing a notice of termination to the corporation. File Form 7004 by the due date of the corporation's income tax return.

Any automatic extension of time for filing a corporation income tax return will not extend the time for paying the tax due on the return. Deposit the amount of tax shown on line 6 of Form 7004 using Form 8109.

Interest. If the tax reported on Form 7004 is less than the actual tax due, interest is charged on the difference.

Where To File

A corporation files its income tax return with the Internal Revenue Service Center serving the area for the location of the principal office for keeping its books and records. The instructions to the forms have the Service Center locations.

The separate income tax returns of a group of corporations located in several Service Center regions can be filed with the Service Center for the area in which the principal office of the managing corporation (that keeps all the books and records) is located.

Payment of Tax

Deposit the balance of any income tax due, after estimated tax installments, by the due date of the return.

Make income tax deposits to either an authorized financial institution or a Federal Reserve Bank. Make all deposits with Form 8109 according to the instructions in the coupon book.

Penalties

There are several penalties that can apply to a corporation. Some of them are discussed next.

Failure to pay tax. Payments made after the due date are subject to an interest charge, even if filing extensions were granted. Payments of tax, other than estimated tax, made after the due date may also be subject to a penalty of 0.5% a month or part of a month up to a maximum of 25%. In certain situations, the penalty will increase to 1% a month or part of a month up to a maximum of 25%.

Failure to deposit taxes. If a corporation deposits taxes after the due date or does not deposit the required tax, it can be charged a penalty. Deposits of tax after the due date are subject to a penalty on the underpayment. The underpayment is the excess of the required tax deposit over the tax deposited by the due date.

Figuring the penalty. The amount of the penalty is figured by multiplying the underpayment by one of the following percentages:

1) 2% if deposited by the 5th day after the deposit due date,
2) 5% if deposited after the 5th day but by the 15th day after the deposit due date, or
3) 10% if deposited after the 15th day after the deposit due date.

The percentage is 15% if the tax is not deposited by the earlier of:

1) The day that is 10 days after the date of the first delinquency notice to the corporation, or
2) The day on which notice and demand for immediate payment is given.

This penalty does not apply to estimated taxes when the penalty discussed earlier under *Estimated Tax* applies.

Failure to file. If a corporation does not file its income tax return by the due date (including extensions), and it cannot show reasonable cause, a delinquency penalty of 5% of the tax due will apply if the delinquency is for one month or less. An additional 5% is imposed for each additional month or part of a month that the delinquency continues, not exceeding a total of 25%. The tax due is the tax liability that would be shown on a return less credits and any tax payments before the due date. Reduce the delinquency penalty by an amount equal to that imposed under the failure-to-pay-tax penalty, discussed earlier.

If the return is not filed within 60 days of the due date (including extensions), the penalty for failure to file will be at least $100 or the balance of tax due, whichever is less, unless reasonable cause is shown.

Reasonable cause. A corporation that wishes to avoid a penalty for failure to either file a tax return, pay tax on time, or deposit taxes must show reasonable cause. This is done by filing, with the Director of the Service Center where the corporation must file the return, a statement of the facts establishing reasonable cause for the corporation's failure to file a return or deposit the tax on time. In addition, the statement must contain a declaration that it was made under the penalties of perjury.

Capital Contributions and Retained Earnings

Contributions to the capital of a corporation, whether or not by shareholders, are **paid-in capital**. These contributions are not taxable to the corporation.

Basis. For the basis of property contributed by a shareholder, see *Issuance of Stock* under *Forming a Corporation* in Publication 542.

The basis of property contributed to capital, by a person other than a shareholder, is zero.

If a corporation receives a cash contribution from a person other than a shareholder, reduce the basis of property acquired with the money during the 12-month period beginning on the day it received the cash contribution by the amount of the contribution. If the amount contributed is more than the cost of the property acquired, then reduce, but not below zero, the basis of the other properties held by the corporation on the last day of the 12-month period in the following order:

1) Depreciable property,
2) Amortizable property,
3) Property subject to cost depletion but not to percentage depletion, and
4) All other remaining properties.

Reduce the basis of property in one category to zero before going to the next category. There may be more than one piece of property in each category.

Accumulation of retained earnings. A corporation can accumulate its earnings for a possible expansion or other bona fide business reasons. However, for tax years beginning on or after January 1, 1993, if a corporation allows earnings to accumulate beyond the reasonable needs of the business, it can be subject to an accumulated earnings tax of 39.6%. If the accumulated earnings tax applies, interest applies to the underpayments

Chapter 30 **CORPORATIONS**

of the tax from the date the corporate return was originally due, without extensions. This tax applies regardless of the number of shareholders.

Treat an accumulation of $250,000 or less generally as within the reasonable needs of a business. However, treat an accumulation of $150,000 or less within the reasonable needs of a business whose principal function is performing services in the fields of:

- Health,
- Law,
- Engineering,
- Architecture,
- Accounting,
- Actuarial science,
- Veterinary services,
- Performing arts, or
- Consulting.

In determining if the corporation has accumulated earnings and profits beyond its reasonable needs, value the listed and readily marketable securities owned by the corporation and purchased with its earnings and profits at net liquidation value, not at cost.

The reasonable needs of a business include:

- Specific, definite, and feasible plans for the use of the accumulation in the business, and
- The amount necessary to redeem the corporation's stock included in a deceased shareholder's gross estate, if the amount does not exceed the reasonably anticipated total estate and inheritance taxes, and funeral and administration expenses incurred by the shareholder's estate.

If a corporation with accumulated earnings of more than $250,000 does not make regular distributions to its stockholders, it should be prepared to show a bona fide business reason for not doing so.

For a corporation to avoid liability for accumulated earnings tax, it must show that tax avoidance by its shareholders is not one of the purposes of the accumulation. The simple existence of a tax avoidance purpose is sufficient for imposing the accumulated earnings tax.

Earnings and Profits Computations

In determining the taxable status of corporate distributions to stockholders, it is necessary to know the corporation's earnings and profits.

Taxable distributions come first from current earnings and profits and then from accumulated earnings and profits. Accumulated earnings and profits means earnings and profits accumulated since February 28, 1913. To the extent that the distributions are more than both the current and accumulated earnings and profits, the distributions may be partly or completely nontaxable.

If the distributions are either partly or completely nontaxable because they exceed current and accumulated earnings and profits, the corporation attaches Form 5452 to its income tax return. See the instructions to Form 5452 for more information.

Distributions

Any distribution to shareholders from earnings and profits is generally a *dividend*. However, a distribution is not a taxable dividend if it is a return of capital to the stockholder. Most distributions are in money, but they may also be in stock or other property. For information on stockholder reporting of dividends and other distributions, see Publication 550, *Investment Income and Expenses*.

File a Form 1099–DIV with the IRS for each stockholder to whom a corporation pays dividends of $10 or more during a calendar year. The corporation files Form 1096 to summarize and transmit its Forms 1099–DIV. File Form 5452 if the corporation pays dividends that are not taxable. For a discussion of Forms 1096 and 1099, see *Instructions for Forms 1099, 1098, 5498, and W-2G*.

Withholding on dividends. Backup withholding may require a corporation to withhold tax equal to 31% of the dividends paid to certain shareholders. See Publication 505 for more information on backup withholding.

Amount of distribution. The amount of a distribution received by any stockholder is the money received plus the FMV of other property received by the shareholder. Reduce (but not below zero) the amount of the distribution by liabilities of the corporation assumed by the shareholder and by liabilities to which the property is subject.

The basis of property received by the shareholder is its FMV.

The part of a distribution from either current or accumulated earnings and profits is a dividend. First, the part of the distribution that is more than the earnings and profits reduces the adjusted basis of the stock in the hands of the stockholder. Second, any amount that exceeds the adjusted basis of that stock is treated by the stockholder as a gain from the sale or exchange of property (usually a capital gain).

Property. Property means any property including money, securities, and indebtedness to the corporation except stock of the distributing corporation or rights to acquire such stock.

Transfers of property to shareholders for less than fair market value. A sale or exchange of property between a corporation and shareholder may be a dividend to the shareholder.

If the FMV of the property on the date of distribution exceeds the price paid by the shareholder, the excess is a property distribution.

Corporation canceling shareholder's debt. If a corporation cancels a shareholder's debt, without repayment by the shareholder, treat the amount canceled as a distribution to the shareholder.

Nontaxable dividends. Nontaxable dividends are distributions to stockholders on their stock in the ordinary course of business. They are not taxable as dividends because the amount of the distributions is greater than the corporation's earnings and profits. Attach Form 5452 to the corporate return if nontaxable dividends are paid to stockholders. Tax-free stock dividends and distributions in exchange for stock in liquidations or redemptions are not nontaxable dividends.

Adjustment to earnings and profits. For a cash distribution, decrease the current earnings and profits by the amount distributed, but not below zero.

For a distribution of an obligation of the distributing corporation, decrease the earnings and profits by the principal amount of that obligation, but not below zero.

For the distribution of an original issue discount obligation, decrease earnings and profits by the total issue price of the obligation.

For a distribution of other property, decrease the earnings and profits by the adjusted basis of that property, but not below zero.

Constructive dividends—insurance premiums. If a corporation pays part or all of the premiums on insurance issued on the lives of certain stockholders, and both the corporation and stockholders derive benefits from it, part or all of the premiums paid by the corporation will be a constructive dividend. This is especially true in a closely held corporation. See Chapter 18 for a discussion of insurance.

Distribution of stock and stock rights. A shareholder does not include a distribution of stock or rights to acquire stock in your corporation in his or her gross income unless it is one of the following:

- A distribution instead of money,
- A disproportionate distribution,
- A distribution on preferred stock,
- A distribution of convertible preferred stock, unless your corporation can establish to the satisfaction of the IRS that the distribution will not result in a disproportionate distribution, described later, or
- A distribution of common and preferred stock resulting in the receipt of preferred stock by some common shareholders and receipt of common stock by other common shareholders.

Even if the distribution falls into one of these five categories, there must be sufficient earnings and profits for the distribution to be a dividend. If the distribution does not fall into one of these categories, the corporation does not adjust its earnings and profits.

A *distribution is instead of money* if any shareholders have an election to get either stock, rights to acquire stock, or property. This applies regardless of whether:

1) The distribution is actually made in whole or in part in stock or in stock rights,

2) The election or option is exercised or exercisable before or after the declaration of the distribution,

3) The declaration of the distribution provides that it will be made in one type unless the shareholder specifically requests payment in the other,

4) The election governing the nature of the distribution is provided for in the declaration of the distribution, corporate charter, or arises from the circumstances of the distribution, or

5) All or part of the shareholders have the election.

If the common shareholders receive a pro rata distribution of preferred stock with an option to immediately redeem it for money, the distribution is instead of money. They must include the distribution in gross income.

A *distribution is disproportionate* if some shareholders receive cash or other property and other shareholders receive increased proportionate interests in the assets or earnings and profits of the corporation. However, it is not required that shareholders receive the cash or property by means of a distribution or series of distributions as long as the result is that they did receive it in their capacity as shareholders and that such distribution is one which would be subject to the rules that apply to the taxing of dividends.

In order for a distribution of stock to be considered as one of a series of distributions, it is not necessary that it be pursuant to a plan to distribute cash or property to some shareholders and to increase the proportionate interests of other shareholders. It is sufficient if there is either an actual or deemed distribution of stock and as a result of it, some shareholders receive cash or property and other shareholders increase their proportionate interests.

Example. Your corporation has two classes of common stock outstanding. If it pays regular cash dividends on one class and stock dividends on the other (whether in common stock or preferred stock), there is a disproportionate distribution. The stock dividends are distributions of property that may be ordinary dividends.

If there is more than one class of stock outstanding, you must consider each class of stock separately for determining whether a shareholder has increased his or her proportionate interest in the assets or earnings and profits of a corporation.

In determining whether a distribution or series of distributions has the result of a disproportionate distribution, treat any security convertible into stock (whether or not convertible during the tax year) or a right to acquire stock (whether or not exercisable during the tax year) as outstanding stock.

You cannot deduct the expenses of issuing a stock dividend. These include printing, postage, cost of advice sheets, fees paid to transfer agents, and fees for listing on stock exchanges. Capitalize these costs.

31.
S Corporations

Important Reminders for 1994

Discharge of real property business indebtedness. S corporations may elect to exclude from gross income certain income from the discharge of qualified real property business indebtedness. This applies to discharges after December 31, 1992, in tax years ending after that date. For more information, see Chapter 7.

Increase in corporate estimated tax percentage. An S corporation that bases its estimated tax on its current year's tax must pay estimated tax equal to 100% of the tax shown on the current year's return. For more information, see Publication 589.

Increase in corporate tax rates. The highest corporate rate of tax is 35% for tax years beginning on or after January 1, 1993.

Introduction

An eligible domestic corporation can avoid double taxation (once to the corporation and again to the shareholders) by electing to be treated as an S corporation under the rules of Subchapter S of the Internal Revenue Code. In this way, the S corporation passes its items of income, loss, deduction, and credits through to its shareholders to be included on their separate returns. Individual shareholders may benefit from a reduction in their taxable income during the first years of the corporation's existence when it may be operating at a loss.

This chapter discusses how to become an S corporation and how to terminate an S corporation. For a complete discussion of S corporations, see Publication 589.

Topics
This chapter discusses:
- Becoming an S corporation
- Terminating S corporation status

Useful Items
You may want to see:

Publication
- ☐ 589 Tax Information on S Corporations

Form (and Instructions)
- ☐ 1120S U.S. Income Tax Return for an S Corporation
- ☐ 1128 Application To Adopt, Change, or Retain a Tax Year
- ☐ 2553 Election by a Small Business Corporation
- ☐ 6251 Alternative Minimum Tax—Individuals
- ☐ 8716 Election To Have a Tax Year Other Than a Required Tax Year
- ☐ 8752 Required Payment or Refund Under Section 7519

Becoming an S Corporation

A corporation can become an S corporation if:

1) It meets the requirements of S corporation status,
2) All its shareholders consent to S corporation status,
3) It uses a permitted tax year, or elects to use a tax year other than a permitted tax year, explained later, and
4) It files Form 2553 to indicate it chooses S corporation status.

Requirements of an S Corporation

To qualify for S corporation status, a corporation must meet *all* the following requirements:

1) It must be a domestic corporation. It must be a corporation that is either organized in the United States or organized under federal or state law. The term "corporation" includes joint-stock companies, insurance companies, and associations.
2) It must have only one class of stock. See *One class of stock*, later.
3) It must have no more than 35 shareholders. See *Counting shareholders*, later.
4) It must have as shareholders only individuals, estates (including estates of individuals in bankruptcy), and certain trusts. See *Trusts*, later. Partnerships and corporations cannot be shareholders in an S corporation.
5) All of its shareholders must be citizens or residents of the United States.

Certain Domestic Corporations Ineligible

Certain domestic corporations are ineligible to elect S corporation status. They are:

1) A member of an affiliated group of corporations. Generally, an affiliated group means one or more chains of corporations connected through stock ownership with a common parent corporation that is also part of the group. The common parent must directly own stock that possesses at least 80% of the total voting power of the stock of at least one of the corporations. In addition, the stock the common parent owns must have a value equal to at least 80% of the total value of the stock of that same corporation. Stock does not include certain preferred stock. A corporation is a member of an affiliated group if it directly owns at least 80% of the total combined voting power of stock entitled to vote and at least 80% of the total value of all stock, except preferred stock, of another corporation. See *Subsidiaries*, later, for exceptions to this rule.

2) A DISC (Domestic International Sales Corporation) or former DISC.

3) A corporation that takes the Puerto Rico and possessions tax credit for doing business in a United States possession.

4) A financial institution that is a bank, including mutual savings banks, cooperative banks, and domestic building and loan associations.

5) An insurance company taxed under Subchapter L of the Internal Revenue Code.

One Class of Stock

For tax years beginning before May 28, 1992, an S corporation had more than one class of stock if the rights in the profits and assets of the corporation were not identical for all holders of the outstanding stock. Differences in voting rights were allowed.

The new one-class-of-stock rules, discussed here, apply to corporate tax years beginning after May 27, 1992. However, an S corporation and its shareholders may apply these new rules to prior years. For more information, see *Effective date*, later in this discussion.

A corporation that has more than one class of stock does not qualify as an S corporation. A corporation is treated as having only one class of stock if all outstanding shares of stock of the corporation confer identical rights to distribution and liquidation proceeds. Stock may have differences in voting rights and still be considered one class of stock. For example, a corporation may have voting and nonvoting common stock, a class of stock that may vote only on certain issues, irrevocable proxy agreements, or groups of shares that differ with respect to rights to elect members of the board of directors.

Identical rights to distribution and liquidation proceeds. Generally, the determination of whether stock has identical rights to distribution and liquidation proceeds is made based on the governing provisions of the corporate charter, articles of incorporation, bylaws, applicable state law, and binding agreements relating to distribution and liquidation proceeds.

A commercial contractual agreement, such as a lease or loan agreement, is not a binding agreement relating to distribution and liquidation proceeds, and is not a governing provision unless a principal purpose of the agreement is to get around this one-class-of-stock provision. Although a corporation is not treated as having more than one class of stock as long as its governing provisions provide for identical distribution and liquidation rights, the tax effect of any distribution that differs in timing or amount will depend on the facts and circumstances.

State laws may require a corporation to pay or withhold state income taxes on behalf of some or all of the corporation's shareholders. These laws are disregarded in finding whether all outstanding shares have identical rights to distribution and liquidation proceeds if, when the constructive distributions resulting from the payment or withholding of taxes by the corporation are taken into account, the shares have identical rights. A difference in timing between the constructive distributions and the actual distributions to the other shareholders does not cause the corporation to be treated as having more than one class of stock.

Buy-sell and redemption agreements. Bona fide agreements to redeem or purchase stock at the time of death, divorce, disability, or termination of employment are disregarded for the one-class-of-stock rules. Also disregarded are buy-sell agreements, redemption agreements, and agreements restricting the transferability of stock unless:

1) A principal purpose of the agreement is to get around the one-class-of-stock rules, and

2) The agreement establishes a purchase price that, at the time of the agreement, is significantly above or below the fair market value of the stock.

Treatment of straight debt. An instrument or obligation that is straight debt is generally not treated as a second class of stock. The term "straight debt" means any written unconditional promise to pay a fixed amount on demand or on a specified date if:

1) The interest rate and interest payment dates are not contingent on profits, the borrower's discretion, or similar factors,

2) The debt cannot be converted into stock, or any other equity interest of the S corporation, and

3) The creditor is an individual (other than a nonresident alien), an estate, or a trust eligible to hold stock in an S corporation.

Subordination. An obligation that is subordinated (placed in a lower position) to other debt of the corporation does not prevent the obligation from qualifying as straight debt.

Straight debt modified or transferred. An obligation that originally qualifies as straight debt ceases to qualify if:

1) The obligation is materially modified so that it no longer satisfies the definition of straight debt, or

2) It is transferred to a third party who is not an eligible shareholder in the S corporation.

Second class of stock. Instruments, obligations, or other arrangements issued by a corporation may be treated as a second class of stock in the following two situations:

1) They are treated as equity.

2) They are call options or warrants.

Treated as equity. An instrument, obligation, or other arrangement, regardless of whether it is called a debt, is treated as a second class of stock if:

1) It constitutes equity or otherwise results in the holder being the owner of stock under federal tax law principles, and

2) A principal purpose of the transaction is to get around the one-class-of-stock rules or the limitations on eligible shareholders listed earlier under *Requirements of an S Corporation.*

See *Treatment of straight debt,* earlier and section 1.1361–1(l) of the Income Tax Regulations for certain exceptions.

Call options and warrants. A call option, warrant, or similar instrument is treated as a second class of stock if, taking into account all facts and circumstances:

1) It is substantially certain to be exercised, and

2) It has a strike price substantially below the fair market value of the underlying stock on the date the call option is issued.

See section 1.1361–1(l) of the regulations for exceptions and more information.

Not treated as outstanding stock. The general requirement for having only one class of stock is that all outstanding shares of stock have identical rights to distribution and liquidation proceeds. Exceptions to the requirement that all outstanding shares of stock are taken into account apply to:

1) Restricted stock, and

2) Deferred compensation plans.

Restricted stock. Stock that is issued in connection with the performance of services, and that is substantially nonvested, is generally not treated as outstanding stock. The holder of that stock is not treated as a shareholder unless he or she makes an election to include in income the fair market value of the stock at the time of the transfer minus the amount paid for the stock. Whether that nonvested stock is treated as a second class of stock depends on the facts and circumstances.

Deferred compensation plans. An instrument, obligation, or arrangement is not treated as outstanding stock if:

1) It does not convey the right to vote,

2) It is an unfunded and unsecured promise to pay money or property in the future,

3) It is issued to an employee or independent contractor in connection with the performance of services for the corporation, and

4) It is issued pursuant to a plan under which the employee or independent contractor is not taxed currently on income.

Unissued stock. Authorized but unissued stock and treasury stock are not considered in determining if a corporation has more than one class of stock. Nor is special stock issued to the Federal Housing Administration considered when making this determination. The existence of outstanding options, warrants to acquire stock, or convertible debentures will not, by itself, be considered a second class of stock.

Effective date. The rules for one class of stock generally apply to tax years beginning after May 27, 1992. However, they do not apply to an instrument, obligation, or arrangement issued before May 28, 1992, and not materially modified after that date. Nor do they apply to a buy-sell agreement, redemption agreement, or agreement restricting transferability entered into before May 28, 1992, or a call option or similar instrument issued before that date. In addition, an S corporation and its shareholders may apply these rules to prior tax years.

Counting Shareholders

An S corporation cannot have more than 35 shareholders. When counting shareholders, the following rules apply:

1) Count the individual, estate, or other person who is considered the shareholder if the stock is actually held by a trust. See *Trusts,* later. Do not count the trust itself as a shareholder.

2) Count a husband and wife, and their estates, as one shareholder, even if they own stock separately.

3) Otherwise, count everyone who owns any stock, even if the stock is owned jointly with someone else.

Trusts

The following trusts, other than foreign trusts, can be shareholders of an S corporation:

1) A trust that is treated as entirely owned by an individual who is a United States citizen or resident. The individual, not the trust is treated as the shareholder.

2) A trust that qualified under (1) immediately before the owner's death, and continues to exist after the owner's death, may continue to be an S corporation shareholder for stock held by the trust when the owner died. This is valid

only for a period of 60 days, beginning on the date of the owner's death. However, if the entire corpus of the trust is included in the owner's gross estate, the 60-day period becomes a 2-year period. The owner's estate is treated as the shareholder.

3) A trust created primarily to exercise the voting power of stock transferred to it. Each beneficiary of the trust is treated as a shareholder.

4) Any trust the stock is transferred to under the terms of a will, but only for 60 days, beginning with the day the stock was transferred to the trust. The estate of the person leaving the will is treated as the shareholder.

A trust that qualifies as an IRA cannot be a shareholder in an S corporation.

Qualified subchapter S trusts. The beneficiaries of certain other trusts can choose to have their trusts qualify as a trust described in (1), above. These trusts are known as "qualified subchapter S trusts (QSST)." See Publication 589 for the definition of a QSST and how to elect to qualify a QSST as a shareholder.

Subsidiaries
Generally, an S corporation cannot have a subsidiary that would cause it to be a member of an affiliated group of corporations. However, this rule may not apply if the subsidiary is inactive, a former DISC, or a foreign corporation.

Inactive subsidiary. An inactive subsidiary is one that, during any period in a tax year:

1) Has not begun business at any time by the close of that period, and
2) Does not have gross income for that period.

Former DISC or foreign corporation as a subsidiary. A corporation that holds a foreign corporation or former DISC as a subsidiary is not eligible to be an S corporation, unless it qualified under the "grandfather rules" of the Subchapter S Revision Act of 1982.

Shareholder Consents
The corporation's election of S corporation status is valid only if all shareholders consent to the election. A shareholder's consent is binding and may not be withdrawn after a valid election is made by the corporation.

Form of consent. Shareholders may consent by providing the required information on Form 2553 and signing in the appropriate space.

Each person who is a shareholder at the time Form 2553 is filed must consent. If the consent is filed before the 16th day of the 3rd month of the year for which it is to be effective, all shareholders in the corporation who held stock on any day in the tax year before the date Form 2553 is filed must also consent.

An election made before the 16th day of the 3rd month of the tax year is considered made for the following tax year if one or more of the persons who held stock in the corporation during the tax year and before the election was made did not consent to the election.

An election made after the 15th day of the 3rd month but before the end of the tax year will also be considered as made for the following tax year.

The shareholder may also consent by signing a separate written consent statement, under penalties of perjury, which should be attached to Form 2553. The separate consent should provide the following information:

1) The name, address, and taxpayer identification number of the corporation,
2) The name, address, and taxpayer identification number of the shareholder,
3) The number of shares of stock owned by the shareholder and the date or dates acquired,
4) The day and month of the end of the shareholder's tax year, and
5) A statement that the shareholder consents to the election of S corporation status.

The consents of all shareholders may be included in one statement. The corporation's election of S corporation status is invalid if any consent is not filed on time. However, if the corporation's election would be valid except for the failure of a shareholder to file a consent on time, an extension of time to file the consent can be requested. The request for an extension of time to file should be sent to the Internal Revenue Service Center where Form 2553 was filed.

The time for filing a consent may be extended, if:

1) It is shown to IRS's satisfaction that there was reasonable cause for the failure to file the consent and that the government's interest will not be jeopardized by treating the election of S corporation status as valid, and
2) The request for the extension is made within a reasonable period of time under the circumstances.

Consents must be filed within the extended period by all persons:

1) Who were shareholders at any time beginning with the date of the invalid election and ending on the date the extension of time is granted, and
2) Who have not previously consented to the election.

Who must consent. Generally, each person who is a shareholder at the time the election is made must consent. If the election is made during the corporation's first tax year in which S corporation status is effective, each person who was a shareholder at any time during the part of the tax year before the election is made must also consent to S corporation status for the corporation.

Co-owners. Each co-owner, tenant by the entirety, tenant in common, and joint tenant must consent. If stock is owned as community property, or if income from the stock is community property, both husband and wife must consent.

Minors. The consent of a minor must be made by the minor or his or her legal representative (or a natural or adoptive parent of the minor if no legal representative has been appointed).

Estates. The consent of an estate holding stock in an S corporation must be made by the executor or administrator of the estate.

Trusts. The consent of a qualified trust holding stock in a newly electing S corporation must be made by the person who is treated as a shareholder to determine whether the corporation meets the S corporation requirements. If a husband and wife have a community interest in the trust, both must consent. See *Trusts*, earlier, under *Requirements of an S Corporation*.

Tax Year
The term "tax year" is the annual accounting period that is used for keeping records and reporting income and expenses. It is either a calendar year or a fiscal year.

Permitted tax year. A permitted tax year is a calendar year or any other accounting period for which the corporation establishes a substantial business purpose to the satisfaction of the IRS. In addition, an S corporation may elect under section 444 to have a tax year other than the permitted tax year.

For more information on substantial business purpose, see Publication 589.

A corporation electing S corporation status does not need the approval of the IRS to choose a calendar year as its tax year. An electing S corporation should use Form 2553, discussed later, to request a tax year other than a calendar year or to make the section 444 election.

Change of tax year. An S corporation should file Form 1128 to apply for permission to change its tax year to a year other than a year ending December 31. This form should be filed by the 15th day of the 2nd calendar month after the close of the short tax year. This short tax year begins on the first day after the end of the corporation's present tax year and ends on the day before the opening date of its new tax year.

User fee. The corporation must submit a user fee with Form 1128. Form 1128 and the user fee should be filed with:

The Commissioner of Internal Revenue
Attention: CC:CORP:T
P.O. Box 7604
Benjamin Franklin Station
Washington, DC 20044

Washington, DC 20044

The package should be marked "Ruling Request Submission."

The application should contain all the requested information. It should show that there is a business purpose for the change. The deferral of income to shareholders generally will not be treated as a business purpose.

Note. Form 1128 should not be used to request a tax year for or during the first year the corporation elects to be an S corporation.

User fees are charged by the Internal Revenue Service for requests for changes in accounting periods and methods, and for certain tax rulings and determination letters. For more information and a schedule of fees, see Publication 1380, *User Fees.*

Section 444 election. S corporations may elect to use a tax year that is different from the permitted tax year. Certain restrictions apply to this election.

For more information on the section 444 election, see Chapter 3.

Making the election. Unless you are a corporation electing S corporation status, make the section 444 election by filing **Form 8716** with the Internal Revenue Service Center where you normally file your returns. Form 8716 must be filed by the earlier of:

1) The 15th day of the 6th month of the tax year for which the election will first be effective, or

2) The due date, without extensions, of the income tax return resulting from the section 444 election.

In addition, you must attach a copy of Form 8716 to your Form 1120S for the first tax year for which the election is made.

Required payment for S corporations. S corporations generally must make a required payment for any tax year that:

1) The section 444 election is in effect, and

2) The required payment amount is more than $500 for the tax year or any previous tax year.

Form 8752. Form 8752 is used to figure the required payment or refund.

For more information on the required payment, see the instructions for Form 8752.

Ending the election. The section 444 election remains in effect until it is terminated. The election ends when the S corporation:

1) Changes to its required tax year,

2) Liquidates,

3) Willfully fails to comply with the required payments or distributions, or

4) Becomes a member of a tiered structure.

The election will also end if an S corporation's S election is terminated. If an S corporation terminates its S election and immediately becomes a personal service corporation, the personal service corporation may continue the section 444 election of the S corporation.

If an S corporation with a tax year other than the required tax year decides to terminate its section 444 election, the entity must file a "short-period" return for the required tax year by its due date (including extensions) to effect a valid termination. When filing the short-period return or extension request, type or print legibly at the top of the first page of Form 1120S or the extension request, **SECTION 444 ELECTION TERMINATED.**

If the election is terminated, another section 444 election cannot be made for any tax year.

Form 2553—Electing S Corporation Status

To be treated as an S corporation, a corporation must file Form 2553 to indicate its election of S corporation status. The corporation must qualify as an S corporation when it files its Form 2553. Form 2553 should also be used to file shareholder consents and to select a tax year.

Form 2553 should be filed with the Internal Revenue Service Center shown in the instructions to the form.

When to file Form 2553. In general, the election of S corporation status is effective for a tax year if Form 2553 is filed:

1) Any time during the previous tax year, or

2) By the 15th day of the 3rd month of the tax year to which the election is to apply.

For detailed information on filing Form 2553, see the instructions for Form 2553.

Terminating S Corporation Status

The corporation's status as an S corporation may be terminated in any of the following ways:

1) By revoking the election.

2) By ceasing to qualify as an S corporation.

3) By violating the passive investment income restrictions on S corporations with pre-S corporation earnings and profits for three consecutive tax years.

Five-year waiting period. If a corporation's status as an S corporation has been terminated, it generally must wait 5 tax years before it can again become an S corporation. If it gets the permission of the IRS, the waiting period may be less than 5 years.

Revoking S Corporation Status

An S corporation election may be revoked by the corporation for any tax year. The S corporation status can be revoked only if shareholders who collectively own more than 50% of the outstanding shares in the S corporation's stock (including any nonvoting stock) consent to the revocation. The consenting shareholders must own their stock in the S corporation at the time the revocation is made.

How to revoke. The revocation must be made by the corporation in the form of a statement. The statement must provide:

1) That the corporation is revoking its election to be treated as an S corporation under section 1362(a) of the Internal Revenue Code,

2) The name, address, and taxpayer identification number of the corporation,

3) The number of shares of stock (including nonvoting stock) outstanding at the time the revocation is made, and

4) The date on which the revocation is to be effective for revocations that specify a prospective revocation date.

This statement must be signed by any person authorized to sign the S corporation's return. It must be sent to the Service Center where the corporation filed its election to be an S corporation.

To this statement of revocation, the corporation should attach a statement of consent, which must be signed by each shareholder, under penalties of perjury, who consents to the revocation. It must also provide the name, address, and taxpayer identification number of each shareholder, the number of shares of outstanding stock (including nonvoting stock) each consenting shareholder holds at the time the revocation is made, the date or dates the stock was acquired, the date the shareholder's tax year ends, the name and taxpayer identification number of the S corporation, and the election to which the shareholder consents.

Effective date of revocation. The revocation is effective:

1) On the first day of the tax year if the revocation is made by the 15th day of the 3rd month of the same tax year.

2) On the first day of the following tax year if the revocation is made after the 15th day of the 3rd month of a tax year.

3) On the date specified if the revocation specifies a date on or after the day the revocation is made.

A corporation that specifies a prospective date for revocation that is other than the first day of the tax year will create an S termination year.

See *S Termination Year,* later, for information on filing returns for the S termination year.

Ceasing To Qualify

A corporation's status as an S corporation will be terminated if at any time the corporation ceases to qualify as an S corporation. If the corporation inadvertently ceases to qualify, see the discussion of *Inadvertent termination.*

Certain events can cause the corporation to cease qualifying as an S corporation. Some of these include:

1) Having more than 35 shareholders,

2) Transferring stock in the S corporation to:

   • A corporation,

   • A partnership,

   • An ineligible trust, or

   • A nonresident alien,

3) Creating a second class of stock, and

4) Acquiring a subsidiary, other than certain nonoperating subsidiaries.

Effective date of termination. A termination of S corporation status will be effective as of the date the terminating event occurred.

A corporation that ceases to be an S corporation on a date other than the first day of the tax year will create an S termination year. For more information on filing tax returns for the S termination year, see *S Termination Year,* later.

Violating the Passive Income Restriction

A corporation's status as an S corporation will be terminated if both of the following conditions occur for 3 consecutive tax years:

1) It has pre-S corporation earnings and profits at the end of each tax year, and

2) Its passive investment income for each tax year is more than 25% of gross receipts.

See Publication 589 for a discussion of passive investment income.

Effective date of termination. A termination of S corporation status because of a violation of the passive income restriction will be effective on and after the first day of the tax year that follows the third consecutive tax year referred to above. See also *Inadvertent termination,* discussed later.

S Termination Year

Any termination described previously in *Revoking S Corporation Status* and *Ceasing To Qualify* that is effective during the tax year on a date other than the first day of that tax year will create an S termination year. The part of the S termination year ending on the date before the effective date of the termination is an 1120S (S corporation) short tax year. The part of the S termination year beginning on the first day on which the termination is effective is an 1120 (C corporation) short tax year.

After the S termination year is divided into an 1120S short year and an 1120 short year, the separately stated items of income, loss, credit, and deduction, and the amount of the nonseparately stated income or loss must be divided between the periods. There are two methods that can be used to make this division. They are:

1) A pro rata allocation, or

2) An allocation based on normal tax accounting rules.

After the separately stated items and the nonseparately stated income or loss are divided, one set of amounts is used for the 1120S short year and the other set of amounts is used for the 1120 short year.

The corporation will have to file two returns to cover the S termination year. One covers the 1120S short year and one covers the 1120 short year. The S termination year will count only as one year for figuring carrybacks and carryovers, even though two returns are filed for the year.

For more information, see Publication 589.

Inadvertent Termination

If the corporation is terminated because it ceased to qualify as an S corporation, or it violated the restriction on passive investment income, the IRS may waive the termination. The termination may be waived if the IRS determines that the termination was inadvertent, the corporation takes steps to correct the terminating event within a reasonable period of time, after discovering it, and the corporation and its shareholders agree to any adjustments the IRS may require.

For more information on inadvertent terminations, see Publication 589.

GLOSSARY

Business Law Terms

acceleration clause A clause in a lease, mortgage, financial instrument, or other legal document that gives someone lending money or otherwise extending credit the right to declare that all the money lent must be repaid immediately. Normally, the right to invoke the acceleration clause is limited to situations where the debtor is in default, such as when a tenant has failed to pay the rent on time.

acceptance Generally, the act of taking something in order to signify agreement or consent. In contract law, there must be an offer, acceptance of the offer, and consideration in order to have a valid contract. Acceptance of a contractual offer is typically indicated expressly, such as by signing a written agreement.

account A record of the amounts due and owing from a debtor to a creditor. For example, a store ledger indicating items purchased, amounts paid, and any balance due and owing is a type of account.

actual damages The dollar amount that represents a person's or entity's actual losses from the wrongful acts of another; the amount necessary to compensate or make whole a party that has been wronged by another party. Actual damages are distinct from **punitive damages.**

adhesion contract A standardized, preprinted form of contract typically used between large companies and consumers on a take-it-or-leave-it basis, meaning that the consumer cannot negotiate over the terms but must either accept or refuse the preprinted offered terms. Adhesion contracts are not necessarily invalid, but in legal proceedings the court may look at the effect of the consumer's lack of bargaining power.

agency A legal relationship in which one person has the power and authority to act for another person, either with respect to certain very specific and narrow matters (such as with a real estate agent) or with respect to many broad matters (such as under a power of attorney). "Agency" is the legal description of such a relationship, "agent" is the noun used to describe a person entrusted with such powers, and "principal" is the noun used to describe a person conveying such powers.

agreement A meeting of the minds; a concurrence between two or more parties on the terms of a particular proposed transaction, offer, plan of action, etc.; uniting in pursuing a common purpose. The word *agreement* is often used interchangeably with *contract,* but *agreement* is in fact broader and covers any type of written or oral concurrence.

anticipatory breach of contract In certain situations one party to a contract may sue the other party to a contract before the other party has committed any breach or default—but the other party must have positively and unequivocally stated that he, she, or it will not or cannot do what is required under the contract by the specified due date.

antitrust A generic term for those federal and state laws that in general make it illegal to form business monopolies and in particular forbid activities such as price-fixing between major corporations.

apparent authority A term in the law of **agency** where a principal through some sort of action or inaction permits an agent to acquire the appearance of having certain powers. In certain situations, a principal (such as an employer) may be bound by or liable for the actions of an agent (perhaps an employee) with apparent authority, despite the original or intended principal-agent (or employer-employee) legal relationship. See **express authority** and **implied authority.**

arbitration The resolution of legal disputes outside of a court of law before a third party who is not a judge. There are many types of arbitration: Some are binding and some are nonbinding, some are informal and some are as formal as regular court proceedings.

articles of incorporation A document filed with state authorities that creates a corporation and formally gives that corporation the status of a legal entity. Sometimes called the certificate of incorporation or referred to informally as the corporate charter. The content requirements of the articles of incorporation are set forth in each state's corporate statutes and may include the corporate name, the name(s) of the director(s), the corporation's principal place of business, the nature of the corporation's business, and the amount of stock that the corporation is authorized to issue. If the state does not accept the articles of incorporation for filing, no corporation is created.

artificial persons A term used to describe legal entities such as corporations that exist, own property, conduct business, and can sue or be sued independently of the actual human beings who comprise them.

assignment The act of transferring legal obligations from one person or entity to another person or entity. Most legal agreements, including contracts, leases, and financial instruments, can be assigned if 1) all of the parties to the original agreement consent and 2) the party or parties to whom obligations are being assigned consent. Generally, either the law and/or the terms of the agreement require that assignments be in writing and signed by the parties in order to be valid. A person or entity making an assignment is called the "assignor," and the person or entity receiving an assignment is called the "assignee."

bad faith The opposite of good faith, namely, taking wrongful, fraudulent, or deceitful actions consciously and deliberately in the course of performing one's legal duties, carrying out legal obligations, or entering into legal agreements. Carrying on one's legal and business obligations with no intention of acting honestly and above-board, but with the intention of pursuing one's own dishonest objectives regardless of ethics and/or the requirements of the law.

bankrupt Being unable to meet one's financial obligations; having more financial liabilities that must be paid than can be met with one's assets and available financial resources. No one who is bankrupt is entitled to the protection of federal bankruptcy laws until the proper proceedings are begun in the federal bankruptcy court for the appropriate federal judicial district.

blue sky laws A commonly used term for those state laws and regulations concerning securities offerings and related transactions. The term does not include federal securities laws and regulations. Both the federal government and the state governments have the right and power to legislate with respect to securities.

board of directors The individuals who are elected by the stockholders of a corporation to oversee the corporation's affairs, including appointing corporate officers, declaring dividends, approving transactions outside the ordinary course of business, and so forth.

bond A type of security that can take many forms but that in general is a written certificate promising to pay money with interest to the owner of the bond.

breach of contract When someone cannot or will not perform the obligations placed upon them by a contract, and there is no legal excuse for this failure, then they have breached the contract. See **anticipatory breach of contract.**

breach of duty A term used to describe the violation of, or failure to perform, legal obligations imposed by law rather than by contract (see **breach of contract**). For example, a partner in a partnership, or a director in a corporation, who takes business funds for his or her own use may be liable for breach of the fiduciary duty imposed on such individuals by law.

business judgment rule This term refers to the legal principle that a corporation's management is generally immune from individual liability for actions taken in connection with the corporation's business activities, so long as those actions were reasonable, within the scope of their authority, and not illegal.

bylaws In business law, this term typically means the internal rules and regulations of a corporation, which set forth the duties of corporate officers, procedures for calling stockholder meetings and board of directors meetings, and other matters relating to the corporation's legal mechanics.

caveat emptor Latin for "let the buyer beware." Until modern times, this phrase succinctly described the fact that a purchaser was on his or her own to guard against fraud, deceit, and misrepresentation in buying goods. State and federal legislation and court decisions have largely made caveat emptor an obsolete term, although the principle still has some validity in the area of "as is" sales and judicial auctions.

claim A legal term, not limited to business law, meaning the right, or basis of asserting a right, to compensation in the judicial system.

collateral In commercial law, property that secures a debt or other obligation. Sometimes collateral is held by the creditor. For example, a pawnshop holds collateral until the debt is repaid, and the shop has the right to sell the property if the debt is not repaid. Other times, the collateral is held by the debtor but the creditor has a right to possession if the debt is not repaid. This is the case with a homeowner with a mortgage; the homeowner continues to live in his or her house, but if the mortgage is not paid, the lender may be able to seize the house, the collateral, and sell it to pay off the debt.

commercial law A generic term used to describe those laws and legal principles governing business transactions. Includes the **Uniform Commercial Code.**

company A common term for two or more persons who are engaged in business. Can be used to describe both corporations and partnerships. The term *company* has no legal significance by itself, and a company is not a legal entity unless it is organized as a corporation, partnership, or other creation of the law.

consideration One of the three elements necessary to form a valid contract, namely, an **offer, acceptance** of the offer, and consideration. Unlike the straightforward concepts of offer and acceptance, consideration is an indefinite and often confusing notion that is badly defined by the law. Generally, any relevant cost incurred, payment, financial exchange, or obligation accepted will be adequate consideration for a valid contract under the law. There are many exceptions, however.

contract An agreement between two or more people to do specified things in exchange for other specified things. To form a valid contract, the basic requirements are an **offer, acceptance** of the offer, and **consideration.** Contracts are normally written, but they can be oral. There are many types of contracts and many laws that affect their enforceability.

conveyance A generic term for the transfer of land, goods, money or other property from one party or parties to another party or parties.

copyright The legally protected right of ownership to various forms of original literary and creative property. Includes books, other written items, pictorial and artistic works, musical compositions, movies, sculptures, recordings, computer software, etc.

corporate book A popular term for the binder, folder, file, or other container of a corporation's minutes, stockholder ledger, and other important documents.

corporation A legal entity created for the purpose of permitting individuals to conduct business through the entity, with personal risk and liability being limited to the corporation's assets and the money invested in the corporation.

covenant A generic term for legally binding obligations, which can include contracts, the clauses of a real estate deed, the clauses of a lease, other written agreements, and generally any form of binding promise.

creditor Any person or entity that has a claim for money and/or property against another person or entity.

debtor The opposite of a creditor. Any person or entity that owes money and/or property to another person or entity.

deed A legal document that conveys property, normally real estate, from one person or entity to another person or entity. State law typically dictates the form of the deed and how the deed must be written in order to be effective, and it provides for the recording of deeds in the official public records.

directors The individuals who comprise a corporation's **board of directors.**

dissolution In business law, the ending of the legal existence of a corporation or partnership. The process of dissolution involves winding up business affairs, paying off creditors, collecting debts, firing employees, selling property, completing legal obligations, and distributing money and/or property to the business's owners.

dividend A payment by a corporation to its shareholders that represents a distribution of the corporate profits to the owners of the business. The size of the dividend, if any is to be paid, is determined by the **board of directors.** The amount of dividends received by shareholders (see **stockholder**) depends on the amount of stock owned. For example, if the board of directors declares a dividend of $1 a share, then a shareholder with one share will receive $1, and a shareholder with 10,000 shares will receive $10,000.

domestic corporation Every corporation is a domestic corporation in the state in which it was incorporated, but nowhere else. A corporation incorporated in Florida is a domestic corporation in Florida, but not in any other state. See **foreign corporation.**

employee A person employed by another person or by an entity. Often synonymous with "servant" under the law. An employee is subject to the orders and control of the employer and typically must report to work at a fixed place for a fixed period of time in exchange for his or her compensation. Whether a person is an employee or not has important consequences under federal and state tax laws (such as payroll tax laws), determines whether a person is entitled to various benefits, and determines whether or not the employer is liable for the wrongful acts of the employee.

employment agreement A contract specifying the terms of employment between an employer and an employee. Terms that may be present include salary, commissions, bonuses, benefits, an obligation to keep employer secrets confidential, and severance pay. Employment agreements are usually reserved for upper-level employees.

environmental impact statement Paperwork concerning certain projects, such as industrial development, that may have a significant impact on the environment. Environmental impact statements are reviewed by the Environmental Protection Agency and state environmental protection authorities as well.

ERISA Employee Retirement Income Security Act. The act contains a series of federal statutes concerning pension plans and their control, administration, financing, and the right to benefits from them. ERISA's provisions have created a massive amount of litigation in the federal courts.

express authority A direct and unequivocal grant of authority by one person to another person to act as his or her agent with respect to some specific matter. Between an employer and an employee, instructions to "do this" or "take care of that" are everyday examples of the delegation of express authority in the workplace. See **agency, apparent authority,** and **implied authority.**

fiduciary duty A duty to act like a trustee and take good care of certain assets, financial interests, and/or monies of another. Regardless of the terms or lack of terms in written documents, the law frequently imposes a fiduciary duty on people in business relationships. For example, the officers and directors of a corporation have a fiduciary duty to the corporation, and partners in a partnership have a fiduciary duty to each other. If a person breaches or ignores a fiduciary duty, the other person or persons affected may sue for damages.

financial institutions A generic term for businesses engaged in investing and lending money, buying and selling securities, and holding money for others on deposit. This term includes banks, savings and loans, credit unions, trust companies, brokerage houses, and to a certain degree insurance companies.

financing statement A term in commercial law, specifically Article Nine in the **Uniform Commercial Code,** covering secured transactions, which refers to a document filed in public records to give public notice that there is a security interest in someone's property, which secures a debt. The creditor usually files the financing statement, not the debtor, because the financing statement protects the creditor's security interest and protects the creditor's right to collect the debt.

foreign corporation Every corporation is a foreign corporation in every state, except the one in which it was incorporated. A corporation incorporated in Florida is a foreign corporation in every state but Florida, where it is a domestic corporation. The significance of being a "foreign corporation" is that in order to transact business in states outside the state of incorporation, a corporation usually must register and obtain a certificate of authority or similarly named document to transact business in the other state or states. Thus, a Florida corporation that does business in Florida and Virginia needs a certificate of authority to transact business in Virginia, but not in Florida. See also **domestic corporation.**

fraudulent conveyance In general, a transfer or sale of property with the primary purpose or intent of putting that property outside the reach of creditors. If a person about to declare bankruptcy sells his house to a friend for $1, that sale might be attacked as a fraudulent conveyance, especially if there is evidence to suggest that the bankrupt person will get the house back once bankruptcy proceedings are over.

fungible goods A commercial law term that means goods that are collectively identical to each other, such as ordinary wheat. If a good is fungible, it can usually be obtained from other sources. Thus, if the seller fails to deliver fungible goods, the purchaser may not be able to claim the same sort of damages it might be able to claim if the seller failed to deliver nonfungible goods, such as specialty items.

general partner A partner who has unlimited personal liability for the debts of the partnership. In a general partnership, all the partners are general partners. In a limited partnership, at least one of the partners must be a general partner. See **limited partner.**

good faith A rather vague term, but one that is important and frequently used in the law. In general, to act in "good faith" means to act honestly, above-board, without deceit, without fraud, without misrepresentation; to disclose and/or not conceal the facts; to act in compliance with applicable laws; to act ethically, reasonably, and in accordance with local business customs, etc. See also **bad faith.**

goods A generic term that, if not specifically defined in a business transaction, simply refers to practically every form of personal property involved in commerce. For example, television sets can be goods, and beer cans can be goods.

guaranty A legal undertaking to assume the debts or obligations of another if that other person or entity defaults in his, her, or its debts or obligations.

implied authority The implied power to perform certain acts that a principal gives an agent or that an employer gives an employee. Even if certain powers and/or responsibilities are not directly or openly stated and given, the law may decide that there is implied authority if such authority is "necessary, usual and proper" to what has been expressly authorized. See **agency, apparent author-**

ity, and express authority.

implied warranty of fitness for a particular purpose A term in commercial law, specifically Article Two of the **Uniform Commercial Code,** which governs sales. Generally, if a seller of goods at the time of the contract knows that the buyer is purchasing the goods for a particular purpose and that the buyer is relying on the seller's advice or expertise in selecting particular goods, there may be an implied warranty of fitness for a particular purpose.

incorporate, incorporation The act of formally establishing a corporation under state law.

incorporator The person or persons who sign **articles of incorporation** and have those articles filed under state law in order to incorporate a corporation.

indemnify To reimburse another for certain costs and expenses. For example, if a corporate director is sued for matters relating to corporate activities, the corporation may be able to indemnify the director by paying for the legal bills and other expenses of the lawsuit.

independent contractor A person who agrees to perform some work or service for another, but who is not an **employee** because the employer has contracted only for the final product or result. In other words, the employer is not significantly concerned about where, when, or how the independent contractor works, but only cares about getting the end result. Whether a person is an independent contractor or not has important consequences under federal and state tax laws (such as payroll tax laws), determines whether a person is entitled to various benefits, and determines whether or not the employer is liable for the wrongful acts of the independent contractor.

indorsement A signature on a financial instrument, such as on the back of a check, that enables the financial instrument to be transferred to someone else.

insider information/insider trading *Insider information* is a term that typically refers to information not released to the public that may affect the value of a corporation's stocks or bonds on the securities markets. Under the securities laws, upper-level corporate management and other corporate insiders are severely restricted from using such insider information to make a profit by buying and/or selling the corporation's stocks or bonds. Such illegal transactions are called *insider trading.*

joint venture Similar to a partnership, but refers to an association of two or more persons or business entities in order to pursue a particular business activity or profitable project. Unlike a partnership, in a joint venture there is no intent between the parties to enter into a close, binding, personal business relationship that encompasses a potentially wide spectrum of business activities.

lease A generic term for agreements in which a person or entity that owns something agrees to let another person or entity use that thing for a certain period of time in exchange for monthly or other periodic payments. Leases can take literally thousands of forms, given the wide variety of property that can be leased and the equally wide variety of terms that can be included in a lease. The most basic types of leases are 1) real estate leases, in which a landlord leases real estate (such as an office building) to a tenant (such as a business) and 2) personal property leases, in which the owner of property leases something (such as a copier or other item of machinery) to someone else (again, such as a business).

lien A claim against property and/or assets, which may or may not ever be enforced but which can be legally present for years as a form of security for the holder of the lien. For example, when someone buys a house and finances it with a 30-year mortgage from a bank, the bank has a type of lien against the house for 30 years unless the mortgage is paid off earlier.

limited partner A partner in a limited partnership whose personal liability is limited to the amount invested in the limited partnership and/or paid for that limited partnership ownership interest.

limited partnership A type of partnership in which there are one or more **limited partners** and at least one **general partner.**

mechanic's lien A type of **lien** recognized under state law for people and/or entities who provide services and/or materials relating to constructing or repairing buildings.

minimum wage The minimum hourly wage for workers under state and federal law.

minutes In corporate law, a term for the written representation of the events at a board of directors' meeting or a stockholders' meeting. Minutes are supposed to be kept in a **corporate book** for safekeeping.

negotiable instrument A term in commercial law, specifically in Article Three of the **Uniform Commercial Code,** that in general means a financial instrument that can be routinely transferred in the commercial financial markets.

nonprofit corporation A special type of corporation that has been created for a charitable, educational, religious, social, cultural, or some other not-for-profit reason. Nonprofit corporations must be created under state nonprofit corporation statutes, and then be recognized by the Internal Revenue Service as an "exempt organization."

offer In contract law, one of the three basic requirements for the formation of a valid **contract;** the other two requirements are **acceptance** of the offer and **consideration.** Essentially, an offer is a proposal to enter into a transaction, contract, business relationship, or other type of activity.

officer In corporate law, a person elected by a corporation's **board of directors** to take care of certain duties. The four basic types of corporate officers generally recognized by state law are the **president, vice president, treasurer,** and **secretary.** State law also generally permits assistant vice presidents, assistant treasurers, and assistant secretaries. Finally, state law also generally permits, but gives no special legal status to, other corporate officer designations such as chief executive officer and chief operating officer.

ordinary course of business The normal, customary, and reasonable conduct of business. Buying and selling, transacting business, making a profit, and so forth with no extraordinary, suspicious, or unusual actions. Actions outside the ordinary course of business, or actions without the necessary approval, may expose the persons involved to individual legal liability.

partnership A legal relationship between two or more people who agree to go into business together and split the profits or losses from that business.

partnership agreement The written document that contains the mutually agreed-upon terms and conditions of a partnership between all of the partners.

patent A legal right, protected by federal law, to the exclusive use and ownership of a new machine, device, or technological principle.

performance A generic term for completing an obligation or legal duty.

personal liability Being financially responsible for legal matters out of one's own personal financial assets, including personal bank accounts, savings, real estate, retirement plans, insurance policies, etc.

president In corporate law, the top executive officer in charge of a corporation's affairs.

punitive damages A dollar amount imposed by a court or jury on a party to a lawsuit as punishment for particularly wrongful conduct. Normally, punitive damages cannot be imposed in contract lawsuits, but there are exceptions. Finally, punitive damages are usually separate and distinct from **actual damages,** because they are designed primarily to punish wrongful conduct. A small amount of actual damages might not prevent the imposition of a large amount of punitive damages, and conversely, the presence of a large amount of actual damages might not prevent the imposition of little or no punitive damages.

respondeat superior Latin for "let the master answer." A legal principle meaning that an employer may be liable for the wrongful acts of an employee committed in the course of the employee's employment, and a principal may be liable for the wrongful acts of an agent committed within the scope of the agent's authority.

Rule 10b-5 Probably the broadest securities investor protection regulation issued by the Securities and Exchange Commission. In connection with the purchase or sale of a security, 10b-5 prohibits 1) any untrue statement of a material fact or 2) failing to state a material fact necessary in order to make the statements made, in light of the circumstances under which they were made, not misleading.

secretary In corporate law, the officer in charge of keeping documents, recording minutes, witnessing signatures, holding the corporate seal, and other administrative tasks.

secured transaction A financial transaction, such as lending money, that is secured by giving the lender or creditor a legal interest in property of the debtor. This legal interest is recorded in public records (see financing statement) and gives the lender or creditor the right to seize that property and sell it in order to pay off the debt. Article Nine of the **Uniform Commercial Code** covers secured transactions.

security A generic term for many types of investments, including stocks, bonds, and mutual funds. The Supreme Court has stated that under the federal securities laws, a security is "an investment of money, in a common enterprise, with the expectation of profits, solely from the efforts of others." For example, certain types of real estate investments may qualify as securities.

servicemark The legally protected right to use a particular name, symbol, drawing, design, or other marking in advertising or promoting a service business. A servicemark protects the exclusive right of an individual or entity to use that valuable name, symbol, drawing, design, or other marking in commerce. See **trademark.**

Statute of Frauds A popular term for those statutes, enacted in one form or another in virtually every state, that state that certain types of contracts and other transactions must be in writing or they cannot be enforced in courts of law.

stock certificate The piece of paper that evidences in writing that a particular person owns a certain number of shares of stock in a corporation.

stockholder A person or entity who owns one or more shares of stock in a corporation. Basically synonymous with shareholder.

Subchapter S corporation Under Subchapter S of the Internal Revenue Code, certain small corporations organized under state law may be given the advantage of being treated as partnerships for federal tax purposes without losing their state law limited liability privileges as corporations.

trademark The legally protected right to use a particular name, symbol, drawing, design, or other marking in advertising or in promoting a business that sells goods and products. A trademark protects the exclusive right of an individual or entity to use that valuable name, symbol, drawing, design, or other marking in commerce. See **servicemark.**

treasurer In corporate law, the officer in charge of supervising the corporation's finances and maintaining the appropriate documentation.

unconscionable A term in contract law that may be used as the basis for holding that some or all of a contract is unenforceable. The term is badly defined by the courts, but in general means a contract or terms in a contract that are so unfair or oppressive that a court in good conscience will not enforce it.

Uniform Commercial Code (UCC) A legal organization called The National Conference of Commissioners on Uniform State Laws wrote the UCC as an example of model state commercial law legislation. The UCC is now the standard for state commercial law legislation and business transactions throughout the country.

vicarious liability An expression for indirect legal liability, such as if an employer is held liable for the wrongful acts of an employee.

vice president In corporate law, the secondary executive officer in the corporate hierarchy. He or she may take over the duties of the **president** if the president dies, becomes incapacitated, or resigns. Otherwise, the vice president (or vice presidents) may have such powers and responsibilities as the president decides to give them.

workers' compensation State laws that give workers financial compensation for work-related injuries.

RESOURCES

For Further Information

The following are some helpful reference sources on business law. If there is a law school law library near you, or a bar association law library near you, the librarians may be able to provide you with additional suggested reference works.

Brown, Gordon W. *Understanding Business and Personal Law.* 8th ed. New York: McGraw-Hill, 1987.

Brown, Gordon W., and others. *Business Law With Uniform Commercial Code Applications.* 7th ed. New York: McGraw-Hill, 1989.

Bruce, Jon W. *Real Estate Finance in a Nutshell.* St. Paul, MN: West Publishing Co., 1985.

Christianson, Stephen G. *100 Ways to Avoid Common Legal Pitfalls Without a Lawyer.* New York: Carol Publishing Group, 1992.

Gross, Jerome S. *Encyclopedia of Real Estate Leases.* Englewood Cliffs, NJ: Prentice-Hall, Inc., 1980.

Hancock, William A. *The Small Business Legal Advisor.* New York: McGraw-Hill, 1986.

Hoffman, Alan M. *Israels (sic) on Corporate Practice.* New York: Practising Law Institute, 1983.

Jenkins, Michael D., and the Entrepreneurial Services Group of Ernst & Young. Starting and Operating a Business series. The series includes *Starting and Operating a Business in Virginia, Starting and Operating a Business in Maryland,* etc. Grants Pass, OR: The Oasis Press.

Lovett, William A. *Banking and Financial Institutions Law in a Nutshell.* St. Paul, MN: West Publishing Co., 1984.

Reader's Digest Legal Problem Solver. Editors. Pleasantville, NY: The Reader's Digest Association, Inc., 1994.

Resolving Disputes Without Litigation. Editors. Washington, DC: Bureau of National Affairs, 1985.

Rhodes, Lisa. *Understanding Personal Bankruptcy.* Stamford, CT: Longmeadow Press, 1993.

Roberson, Cliff. *The Businessperson's Legal Advisor.* Summit, PA: TAB Books, 1986.

Sardell, William, Reviser. *Encyclopedia of Corporate Meetings, Minutes and Resolutions.* 2 volumes. Englewood Cliffs, NJ: Prentice-Hall, Inc., 1978.

Uniform Commercial Code and Related Procedures. Editors. Anoka, MN: Registre. Published annually. You may have a hard time finding this in a bookstore. The book currently costs $15.95, and it can be ordered directly from the publisher by calling (612) 421-1713.

In addition, there are two major legal encyclopedias that discuss all types of legal subjects, including business law matters. They are sort of a lawyer's version of the *World Book Encyclopedia,* but you can only find them in law libraries.

American Jurisprudence 2d. Editors. Rochester, NY: Lawyers Cooperative Publishing Company. Revised and updated annually.

Corpus Juris Secundum. Editors. St. Paul, MN: West Publishing Co. Revised and updated annually.

Index

B

Bankruptcy Law 113-118
  Bankruptcy
    Alternatives to
      State Law Alternatives 114
      Workouts 114
    Automatic Stay 115
    Bankruptcy Estate 115
    Chapter 7 Bankruptcy 115-116
    Chapter 11 Bankruptcy 117-118
      Classes of creditors 117-118
      Reorganization plan 117-118
    Chapter 13 Bankruptcy 118
  Bankruptcy Act of 1978 113
  Bankruptcy Code 113
    Exemptions 115-116
    Nondischargeable debts 116
  Bankruptcy Court 113
Business Liability 39
  Acts of employees 39-42
    Four requirements for business liability 39
    Personal liability in business 40
      Directors 41
      Officers 40
      Piercing the corporate veil 41
    Potential personal liability of general expectancy 42
      General partners 42
      Limited Partners 42
    Potential personal liability of officers, directors, and shareholders 40-42
    Plaintiff 39
    Scope of employment 40

C

Contracts 45-51
  Breach of Contract 48-49
    Liability for 48-49
      Actual damages 49
        Expectancy 49
        Restitution 49
      Anticipatory breach of contract 48
      Punitive damages 49
  Definition of 45
  Elements of 46-48
    Acceptance 46
      Verbal and written 46
      Meeting of the minds 46
    Consideration 47
    Offer 46
      Conditional offers 46
  Enforcing a contract 49
    Federal Trade Commission, address of 51
    Fraudulent contracts 50
    Illegal contracts 50
    Lack of capacity 50
    Statute of frauds 50
    Statute of limitations 50
    Unconscionable contract 50
      Adhesion contract 50
    Violation of Consumer Protection Laws 50
Corporation(s) 11-22
  Advantages, disadvantages 15-16
  Annual meeting 13
  Bylaws 17
  Definition of 11-12
  Directors 13-15
  Dissolution, liquidation 16
  Incorporation process 16-18
  Articles of incorporation 17
    addresses of agencies by state 18-22
  Legal requirements 16
  Limited liability 12, 16
    Articles of organization 37
    IRS Revenue Ruling 88-76 38
    States allowing Limited Liability status 38
  Minutes 13, 14
  Officers 12-15
    Chief executive officer 14
    Chief operation officer 14
    President 14
    Required by states 15
    Secretary 14
      Responsible for 14
        Corporate seal 14
        Corporate records 14
        Minutes 14
    Treasurer 14
    Vice president 14
  Organizational meeting 17
  Partnership 11
  Perpetual existence 12
  Registered agent 12
  Shareholders, stockholders 12
  Sole proprietorship 11
  Stock 12
  Stockholders (see shareholders)
  Subchapter S corporation(s) 31-37
    Application for Subchapter S corporation status 37
    Articles of organization 37
    Basic requirements 31, 32
    IRS Form 2553 37
    Limited liability company 37
    Managers 38
    Restrictions to Subchapter S corporation status 32-37
      Affiliated groups 32
      Insurance corporations 32
      Financial institutions 32
      Puerto Rican and U.S. possession corporations 32-37

D

Delaware, incorporating in 17
Double taxation of income 16, 23, 27, 31
Department of Labor, address of 85
  Occupational Safety and Health Administration (OSHA), address of 85
  Department of Labor, state level, addresses of 85-89

E

Employee vs. Independent contractor 79-80
Employer identification number (EIN) 18
Employer, obligations of
  Federal Labor Laws 80-85
    Age Discrimination in Employment Act 85
    Americans with Disabilities Act 80
    Civil Rights Act of 1964 80
    Comprehensive Omnibus Budget Reconciliation Act (COBRA) 85
    Employee Polygraph Act 80
    Employee Retirement Income Security Act (ERISA) 80
    Equal Pay Act 80
    Fair Credit Reporting Act 85
    Fair Labor Standards Act 80
    Family Medical Leave Act 85
    Immigration Reform and Control Act 85
    Labor-management Relations Act 80
    Occupational Safety and Health Administration (OSHA) 80

208 INDEX

Worker Adjustment and Retraining Notification Act 85
Withholdings 77-80
   Federal, state and local income taxes 77-79
   Social Security taxes 78
   Self-employment tax 78
   Court imposed mandatory deductions 78
     Garnishments 78
     Child custody/support payments 78
Worker's Compensation 78
Unemployment Compensation 78-79

G
Goodwill 25

H
Hiring and Firing 67-75
   Discrimination 67
   Employment agreements 70
   Employment at will doctrine, limitations of 70-75
   Hiring procedures 67-69
     Antidiscrimination laws and regulations 67-69
Americans with Disabilities Act 69-70

I
Independent Contractor vs. Employee 79-80
Intellectual Property 59-63
   Copyrights 62-63
     definition of 62
     Copyright Office, address of 63
   Definition of 59
   Patents 59-60
     Design patents 59
     Patent infringement 60
     Plant patent 59
     U.S. Patent and Trademark Office (PTO), address of 60
     Utility patents 59
   Trademarks and Servicemarks 60-62
     Servicemark, definition of 60
     Trademark, definition of 60
     Secondary meaning of descriptive phrases 61

L
Limited liability companies 27-30

P
Partners, partnerships 11, 23-30
   Advantages, disadvantages 26
   General partners, partnerships 23-26
     Action for an accounting 25
     Contributions 25
     Fidiciary duties 24-25
     Rights 24-25
     Uniform Partnership Act 24-25
     Unlimited personal liability 24
   Limited partners, partnerships 27-30
     Distributions 27
     Legal requirements 24
     Limited liability 27
   Partnership agreement 26

R
Revised Uniform Limited Partnership Act (RULPA) 29
Risk, corporations vs. partnerships, proprietorships 11-12

S
Secutities Laws and Regulations, state and federal levels 103-112
   Blue Sky Laws 106
     Antifraud provisions 106
     Requirements of 106
   Effects of Federal Secutities Laws 105-110

Investment Advisors Act of 1940 103
Investment Company Act of 1940 103
Public Utility Holding Company Act of 1935 103
Securities Act 103
Securities and Exchange Commission, addresses of
   federal 107
   states 107-112
Securities Exchange Act 103
Securities Investor Protection Act of 1970 103
Security, definition of 104
Trust Indenture Act of 1939 103
U.S. Securities and Exchange Commission SEC 104
Uniform Securities Act 107
Sole proprietor, proprietorship 11, 31

U
Uniform Partnership Act 24-25
Uniform Commercial Code (UCC) 53-57
   Articles of 53-54
     Acceptance and exclusion by U.S. states and territories 53
     Provisions of 53-54
   Definition of 53
   Sale of Goods 54-56
     Buyer's rights 56
       Specific performance 56
     Risk of loss 55-56
     Seller's rights 56
     Warranties 54
       Affirmation of fact 54
       Express warranty 54
       Implied warranties 55
         ...of fitness for a particular purpose 55
         ...of merchantability 55
       Warranty against infringement 54
       Warranty of title 54
   Secured Transactions 56-57
     Security interest 57
       Basic types 57
       financing statement 57
         UCC-1 57
         UCC-3 57

Z
Zoning 93-102
   Comprehensive plan 93
   Environmental Law, federal 95-96
     Clean Air Act 96
     Comprehensive Environmental Response, Compensation, and Liability Act (CERCLA) 96
     Council on Environmental Quality 95
     Environmental impact statements 95-96
     Environmental Protection Agency (EPA) 95
       addresses of
         federal 97
         states 97-102
     Lead Contamination Control Act, The 96
     Marine Protection, Research, and SanctuariesAct, The 96
     National Environmental Policy Act (NEPA) 95
     Oil Pollution Act 96
     Resource and Recovery Act 95-96
     Safe Drinking Water Act 96
     Water Pollution Control Act 96
   Environmental Laws, state and local 96-97
     Garbage dumps and other landfills 97
     Mandatory recycling 97
     Waste disposal requirements 97
   Nonconforming use 94
     Grandfather clause 94
   Variance 95